H. DE BALZAC

COMÉDIE HUMAINE

Edited by

GEORGE SAINTSBURY

Honoré

H. DE BALZAC

A PRINCESS'S SECRETS

(*Les Secrets de la Princesse de Cadignan*)

Translated by

ELLEN MARRIAGE

with a Preface by

GEORGE SAINTSBURY

LONDON

J. M. DENT AND CO.

NEW YORK: THE MACMILLAN COMPANY

MDCCCXCVIII

Edinburgh: T. and A. CONSTABLE, Printers to Her Majesty

CONTENTS

		PAGE
PREFACE	.	ix
A PRINCESS'S SECRETS	.	I
BUREAUCRACY	.	70

LIST OF ETCHINGS

THEN SHE STOPPED D'ARTHEZ (p. 31) . . . *Frontispiece*

PAGE

ONE OF THE MINISTER'S CARRIAGES USED TO COME FOR
DES LUPEAULX AT HALF-PAST FOUR, JUST AS HE
HIMSELF WAS OPENING HIS UMBRELLA . . 142

'A WORD OR TWO WITH YOU, MY LORD!' . . 253

Drawn and Etched by J. Ayton Symington.

PREFACE

As is the wont of Balzac's collections of mixed stories (with the possible exception of the wonderful volume which opens with *La Recherche de l'Absolu*), and as is naturally very often the case with collections of short stories in general, the volume which originally began with *La Maison Nucingen* [1] is a little unequal. One of its contents, *Sarrasine*, though powerful in its way, is tarred with the same brush of morbidness which stains *Une Passion dans le Désert* and *La Fille aux Yeux d'Or*; so that it will not, at any rate for the present, be given—an exclusion which still leaves the volume rather longer than the average.

The other contents are a little miscellaneous, and were very variously grouped in Balzac's successive rearrangements of the Comedy. Indeed, in the so-called *édition définitive*, the minor stories are separated from *La Maison Nucingen*, while an earlier arrangement still was different again.

The long piece entitled *Les Employés*, which fills more than half the entire volume, and nearly two-thirds of it without *Sarrasine*, has rather dubious claims to be called a novel or a story at all. Balzac, either from the fact of his father having been employed in the civil

---

[1] Included in the volume *The Unconscious Mummers* in this edition.

b

department of the army, or because he had been destined himself by kind family friends to the *rond-de-cuir* (the office-stool), or because he was a typical Frenchman— for while half the French nation sits on these stools, the other half divides its time between laughing at them and envying them—was always exceedingly intent on the ways and manners of government offices. One of the least immature scenes of his *Œuvres de Jeunesse*, the opening passage of *Argow le Pirate*, concerns the subject. The collection of his *Œuvres Diverses*, only of late years opened to the explorer who has less than libraries at his command, contains repeated returns to it, of which the *Physiologie de L'Employé* was the best known and most popular; and the novels proper are full of dealings with it. In this particular piece, indeed, Balzac has actually incorporated something from his earlier *Physiologie*, and has thus made it even less of a story than it was when it first appeared under the title of *La Femme Supérieure*. In that condition it was divided into three parts—*Entre deux Femmes*, *Les Bureaux*, and *A qui la place*. The later shape, with the additions just referred to, tended to overweight the middle part still more at the expense of the two ends; and as it stands, it is little more than a criticism, partly in argument, partly in dialogue, of administration and administrative methods, with a certain slight personal interest at both ends.

Le Secret de la Princesse de Cadignan, on the other hand, is, or rather is part of, one of Balzac's most remarkable fictitious creations—the history of Diane de Maufrigneuse. This lady, who pervades at least a dozen of the stories, shorter and longer, is the subject of dispute between those who say that Balzac's *grandes dames* are rather creatures of the stage and of the inner consciousness than of life, and those who, as the saying is, take them for gospel. The latter do not seem to bring forward any argument except Balzac's greatness and a certain fascination about the personage. The former, besides dwelling on the obvious touches of exaggeration in the portrait, ask what opportunity Balzac had of really acquainting himself with the ways and manners of the Faubourg Saint-Germain? They admit the competence of the Duchesse de Castries, but point out that he did not know her very long; that he was to all appearance in the position, dangerous for a faithful portrait-painter, of having been taken up and dropped by her; and that she was, so far as is known, his only intimate or much-frequented acquaintance of the kind. It is not necessary to argue this question at length. The piece, however, has the special interest of having been at first dedicated to Theophile Gautier. It was written at Les Jardies in June 1839, and first appeared two months afterwards in the *Presse*, under the title of *La Princesse Parisienne*. This it kept when it appeared next year in volume form, published by Souverain, but forming part of a collection entitled *Le Foyer de l'Opéra*. In both these forms it was divided into eight chapters, with titles in the newspaper, without them in the book. In 1844, when it entered the *Comédie* as a *Scène de la Vie Parisienne*, it lost its old divisions and took its present title. *Les Employés* was a slightly older book, being originally dated July 1836. It also appeared in the *Presse* just a year after its composition, but was then called *La Femme Supérieure*, which name it kept on its publication by Werdet as a book in

1838. It was here enlarged, and had *La Torpille* (the first title of *Esther* or *Comment aiment les Filles*) and *La Maison Nucingen* for companions. There were, as usual, chapter divisions and titles. At its first appearance in the *Comédie* the actual title and *La Femme Supérieure* were given as alternatives, but later *Les Employés* displaced the other.   G. S.

A PRINCESS'S SECRETS

To Théophile Gautier

AFTER the disasters of the Revolution of July 1830 had wrecked the fortunes of many a noble family dependent upon the Court, Mme. la Princesse de Cadignan had the address to blame political events for the total ruin due in reality to her own extravagance. The Prince had left France with the Royal Family, but the Princess stayed on in Paris, the very fact of her husband's absence securing her from arrest. He, and he alone, was responsible for a burden of debt which could not be discharged by the sale of all his available property. The creditors had taken over the revenues of the entail, and the affairs of the great family were, in short, in as bad a way as the fortunes of the elder branch of the Bourbons. Things being thus, the Princesse de Cadignan (the lady so celebrated in her day as the Duchesse de Maufrigneuse) made up her mind to live in complete retirement, and tried to make the world forget her. And in the dizzy current of events which swept Paris away, Mme. de Maufrigneuse was soon lost to sight in the Princesse de Cadignan, an became almost a stranger to society; the new actors brought upon the stage by the Revolution of July knew nothing of the metamorphosis.

In France the title of duke takes precedence over all others, even over the title of prince; albeit it is laid down unequivocally in heraldry that titles signify absolutely nothing, and that all the nobly born are

A

perfectly equal. This admirable theory was conscientiously put in practice in former times by the royal house of France ; indeed, it is still carried out in the letter at any rate, for kings of France are careful to give their sons the simple title of count. By virtue of the same system Francis I. signed himself ' Francis, Lord of Vanves,' thereby eclipsing the splendid array of titles assumed by that pompous monarch, Charles V. Louis XI. had even gone further when he gave his daughter to Pierre de Beaujeu, a simple gentleman. The feudal system was so thoroughly broken up by Louis XIV. that the title of duke in his reign became the supreme and most coveted honour.

Nevertheless, there are two or three families in France, in which the principality consists of great territorial possessions, handed down from former times, and in these it ranks above the duchy. The House of Cadignan is one of these exceptions, the eldest son is the Duc de Maufrigneuse, and the younger brothers are simply Chevaliers de Cadignan.

The Cadignans, like two princes of the House of Rohan in other times, have a right to a chair of state in their own house, and may keep a retinue of pages, gentlemen, in their service. This is a necessary piece of explanation, given partly to anticipate absurd criticisms from persons who know nothing of the matter, partly too as a record of an old stately order of things in a world which is said to be passing away, an order of things which some, who understand it but little, are very eager to abolish.

The Cadignans bear *or five fusils sable conjoined in fesse*, with the motto MEMINI, and a close crown, without supporters or lambrequins. What with the prevalent ignorance of heraldry in these days, and a mighty influx of foreigners to Paris, the title of prince is beginning to enjoy a certain vogue ; but it is usually only a courtesy title. There are no real princes in France save those who inherit domains with their name, and are entitled

to be addressed as ' Your Highness.' The disdain felt for
the title by the old noblesse, and the reasons which led
Louis XIV. to give supremacy to the rank of duke, prevented France from claiming the style of Highness for
the few princes in existence (those of Napoleon's crea-
tion excepted). This is how the Princes de Cadignan
came to rank nominally below other princes on the
continent of Europe.

The persons known collectively as the Faubourg
Saint-Germain protected the Princess; treating her with
a respectful discretion due to a name that will always be
honoured, to misfortunes which no longer gave rise to
talk, and to Mme. de Cadignan's beauty, which was all
that remained of her faded glories. The world that she
had adorned gave her credit for thus taking the veil, as it
were, and entering the cloister in her own house. For
her, of all women, such a piece of good taste involved an
immense sacrifice; and in France anything great is
always so keenly appreciated, that the Princess's retreat
gained for her all the ground that she had lost in public
opinion while her splendour was at its height. Of her
old friends among women, she only saw the Marquise
d'Espard; and as yet she was never seen in public on
great occasions, or at evening parties. The Princess
and the Marquise called upon one another, very early in
the morning, and, as it were, in secret; and when the
Princess dined with her friend, the Marquise closed her
doors to every one else.

Mme. d'Espard's behaviour was admirable. She
changed her box at the Italiens, coming down from the
first tier to a *baignoire* on the ground floor, so that
Mme. de Cadignan could come and depart without
being seen. Not every woman would have been capable of a piece of delicacy which deprived her of the
pleasure of dragging a former and fallen rival in her
train, and posing as her benefactress. Thus enabled to
dispense with ruinous toilettes, the Princess went

privately in the Marquise's carriage, which in public she would have refused to take. Nobody ever knew why Mme. d'Espard behaved in this way; but her conduct was sublime, involving a whole host of the little sacrifices which seem mere trifles in themselves, but taken as a whole reach giant's proportions. In 1832 the snows of three years had covered the Duchesse de Maufrigneuse's adventures, whitening them so effectually that nothing short of a prodigious effort of memory could recall the heavy indictments formerly laid to her charge. Of the queen adored by so many courtiers, of the duchess whose levities might furnish a novelist with several volumes, there now remained an exquisitely fair woman of thirty-six, who might have passed for thirty in spite of her nineteen-year-old son.

Georges, Duc de Maufrigneuse, beautiful as Antinous, and poor as Job, was certain of a great career; and his mother's first wish was to see him married to a great fortune. Perhaps she meant to choose an heiress for him some day out of Mme. d'Espard's salon, which was supposed to be the first in Paris; perhaps this was the real reason of her intimacy with the Marquise. The Princess, looking forward, saw another five years of retirement before her; five desolate lonely years; but if Georges was to marry well, her conduct must receive the hall-mark of virtue.

The Princess lived in a modest ground-floor flat in a mansion in the Rue de Miromesnil, where relics of bygone splendour had been turned to account. A great lady's elegance still pervaded everything. She had surrounded herself with beautiful things, which told their own story of a life in high spheres. The magnificent miniature of Charles x. above her chimney-piece was painted by Mme. de Mirbel, and bore the legend, 'Given by the King,' engraved on the frame. The companion picture was a portrait of Madame, who had been so peculiarly gracious to her. The album that shone conspicuous on one of the tables was an almost priceless treasure, which none of the bourgeoises that rule our modern money-making and censorious society would dare to exhibit in public. It was a piece of audacity that paints the Princess's character to admiration. The album was full of portraits, some thirty among them belonging to intimate friends—lovers, the world said. As to numbers, this was a slander; but with regard to some ten of them perhaps, as the Marquise d'Espard said, there was a good, broad foundation for the calumny. However that might be, Maxime de Trailles, de Marsay, Rastignac, the Marquis d'Esgrignon, General de Montriveau, the Marquises de Ronquerolles and d'Ajuda-Pinto, Prince Galathionne, the young Duc de Grandlieu, the young Duc de Rhétoré, the young Vicomte de Sérizy, and Lucien de Rubempré's beautiful face, had all received most flattering treatment from the brushes of the famous portrait-painters of the day. At this time the Princess only received two or three of the originals of the portraits, and pleasantly called the book 'My Collection of Errors.'

Adversity had made a good mother of Mme. la Princesse. Her amusements during the first fifteen years of the Restoration had left her little time to think of her son; but now, when she took refuge in obscurity, this illustrious egoist bethought herself that maternal sentiment pushed to an extreme would win absolution for her. Her past life would be condoned by sentimental people, who will pardon anything to a fond mother, and she loved her son so much the better because she had nothing else left to love. Georges de Maufrigneuse was, for that matter, a son of whom any mother might have been proud. And the Princess had made all kinds of sacrifices for him. Georges had a stable and coach-house, and inhabited three daintily-furnished rooms in the entresol above, which gave upon the street.

His mother stinted herself to keep a horse for him to

ride, a cab-horse, and a diminutive servant. The Duke's
tiger had a hard time of it ! 'Toby,' once in the service
of 'the late Beaudenord'—for in this jocular manner
young men of fashion were wont to allude to that
ruined dandy—Toby, to repeat, now turned twenty-five
years of age, and still supposed to be fourteen, must
groom the horses, clean the cab or the tilbury, go out
with his master, keep his rooms in order, and be on hand
in the Princess's antechamber to admit visitors, if by
any chance a visitor called on her.

When you considered the part that the beautiful
Duchesse de Maufrigneuse had played under the Restoration ; how she had been one of the queens of Paris, a
radiant queen, leading a life so luxurious that even the
wealthiest women of fashion in London might have taken
lessons of her; it was something indescribably touching
to see her in that mere nutshell of a place in the Rue
de Miromesnil, only a few doors away from the huge
hôtel de Cadignan, which nobody was rich enough to
live in, so that the speculative builder's hammer brought
it down. The woman for whom thirty servants were
scarce sufficient, the mistress of the finest salons and the
prettiest *petits appartements* in which she entertained so
splendidly, was now living in a suite of five rooms—an
antechamber, a dining-room, a drawing-room, a bedroom, and dressing-room—with a couple of women
servants for her whole establishment.

'Ah ! she is an admirable mother,' that shrewd woman
the Marquise d'Espard would remark, 'and admirable
without overdoing it. She is happy. Nobody would
have believed that such a frivolous woman would be
capable of taking a resolution and following it up so
persistently as she does. And our good Archbishop has
encouraged her, he is goodness itself to her, he has just
persuaded the dowager Comtesse de Cinq-Cygne to call
upon her.'

In any case, let us own that no one but a queen can

abdicate, and descend nobly from the lofty elevation which is never utterly lost to her. It is only those who are conscious that they are nothing in themselves that will waste regrets on their decline, and pity themselves, and turn to a past that will never return for them. They know instinctively that success will not come twice. The Princess was forced to do without the rare flowers with which she had been wont to surround herself, a setting that enhanced her beauty, for no one could fail to compare her to a flower. Wherefore she had chosen her ground-floor flat with care, so as to enjoy a pretty little garden with flowering trees and a green grass-plot to brighten her quiet rooms all through the year.

Her annual income possibly amounted to twelve thousand francs or thereabouts, but even that modest sum was made up partly by an allowance from the old Duchesse de Navarreins (the young Duke's paternal aunt), partly by contributions from the Duchesse d'Uxelles, who was living on her estate in the country, and saving as none but dowager-duchesses can save; Harpagon was a mere tiro in comparison.

The Prince de Cadignan lived abroad, always at the orders of his exiled masters. He shared their adversity, serving them with a devotion as disinterested, and perhaps rather more intelligent than that of most other adherents of fallen royalty. His position was even now a protection to his wife in Paris. In such obscurity did the Princess live, and so little did her destitution arouse the suspicions of the Government, that a certain Marshal, to whom France owes an African province, used to meet Legitimist leaders at her house and hold counsel with them while Madame was making the attempt in La Vendée.

Foreseeing the approaching bankruptcy of love, and the drawing nigh of that fortieth year beyond which there lies so little for a woman, the Princess launched forth into the realms of politics and philosophy. She

took to reading !—she who for the last sixteen years had
shown the utmost abhorrence of anything serious !
Literature and politics to-day take the place of devout-
ness as the last refuge of feminine affectation.   It was
said in fashionable circles that Diane meant to write a
book.   During this transition period, when the beautiful
woman of other days was preparing to fade into a woman
of intellect, until such time as she should fade away for
good, Diane made of the reception at her house a
privilege in the highest degree flattering for the persons
thus favoured.   Under cover of these occupations she
contrived to hoodwink de Marsay, one of her early
lovers, and now the most influential member of the
Government of the Citizen King.   Several times she
received visits from the Prime Minister in the evening
while the Legitimist leaders and the Marshal were
actually assembled in her bedroom, discussing plans for
winning back the kingdom, and forgetting in their
deliberations that the kingdom was not to be won without the help of ideas—the one means of success overlooked by them.   It was a pretty woman's revenge thus
to inveigle a prime minister and use him as a screen for
a conspiracy against his own government; the Princess
wrote Madame the sprightliest account of an adventure
worthy of the best days of the Fronde.

The young Duc de Maufrigneuse went to La Vendée,
and contrived to come back again quietly and without
committing himself, but not until he had shared Madame's
perils.   When all seemed lost, Madame sent him back,
unfortunately perhaps, for a young man's impassioned
vigilance might possibly have foiled treachery.

Great as Mme. de Maufrigneuse's transgressions
might have been in the eyes of the middle-class matron,
her son's behaviour blotted them all out for the
aristocratic world.   It was something great and noble
surely to risk the life of an only son and the heir to an
historic name in this way.   There are persons, reputed

clever, who redeem the faults of private life by political services, and *vice versâ*. But the Princesse de Cadignan had acted without calculation of any kind. Perhaps there is never calculation on the part of those who so conduct their lives; and circumstances account for a good half of many seeming inconsistencies.

On one of the first fine days in May 1833, the Marquise d'Espard and the Princess were taking a turn, they could scarcely be said to be taking a walk, along the one garden path beside the grass plot. It was about two o'clock in the afternoon, the sun was taking leave of the garden for the day, but the air was warm with heat reflected from the walls, and the air was full of the scent of flowers brought by the Marquise.

'We shall lose de Marsay soon,' Mme. d'Espard was saying, 'and with him goes your last hope of fortune for the Duc de Maufrigneuse; since you played such a successful trick on that great politician, his affection for you has sensibly increased.'

'My son shall never come to terms with the younger branch, even if he must starve first and I should have to work for him,' returned the Princess. 'But Berthe de Cinq-Cygne has no aversion for him.'

'The younger generation is not bound in the same way as the older——'

'Let us say nothing about that. If I fail to tame the Marquise de Cinq-Cygne, it will be quite bad enough to be forced to marry my son to some blacksmith's daughter, as young d'Esgrignon did.'

'Did you love him?' asked the Marquise.

'No,' the Princess answered gravely, 'd'Esgrignon's naïveté was only a kind of provincial's callowness, as I found out a little too late, or too soon, if you prefer it.'

'And de Marsay?'

'De Marsay played with me as if I were a doll. I was almost a girl. We never love the men who take the office of tutor upon themselves; they grate overmuch on our little susceptibilities.'

'And that wretched boy who hanged himself?'

'Lucien? An Antinous and a great poet. I worshipped him in all conscience, and I might have been happy. But he was in love with a girl of the town; and I gave him up to Mme. de Sérizy. . . . If he had cared to love me, should I have given him up?'

'What an odd thing, that you should come into collision with an Esther!'

'She was handsomer than I,' said the Princess.—'Very soon I shall have spent three years in complete solitude,' she went on after a pause. 'Well, there has been nothing painful in the quiet. To you, and you only, I will venture to say that I have been happy. Adoration palled upon me; I was jaded without enjoyment; the surface impressions never went deeper into my heart. All the men that I had known were petty, mean, and superficial, I thought; not one of them did anything in the least unexpected; they had neither innocence, nor greatness, nor delicacy. I should have liked to find some one of whom I could stand in awe.'

'Then, is it with you as it is with me, my dear? Have you tried to love and never found love?'

'Never,' broke in the Princess, laying a hand on her friend's arm. The two women went across to a rustic bench under a mass of jessamine now flowering for the second time. Both had spoken words full of solemn import for women at their age.

'Like you,' resumed the Princess, 'I have been more loved, perhaps, than other women; but through so many adventures, I feel that I have never known happiness. I have done many reckless things, but always with an end in view, and that end receded as I advanced. My heart has grown old with an innocence unfathomed in it. Yes, a credulous first love lies unawakened beneath all the experience; and I feel too that I am

young and fair, in spite of so much weariness, so many
blighting influences. We may love, yet not be happy;
we may be happy when we do not love; but to love and
to be happy both, to know the two boundless joys of
human experience—this is a miracle, and the miracle
has not been worked for me.'

'Nor for me,' said Mme. d'Espard.

'A dreadful regret haunts me in my retreat; I have
found pastimes, but I have not loved.'

'What an incredible secret!'

'Ah! my dear, these are secrets that we can only
confide to each other; nobody in Paris would believe
us.'

'And if we had not both passed our thirty-sixth year,
perhaps we might not make these admissions.'

'No. While we are young, we are stupidly fatuous
on some points,' assented the Princess. 'Sometimes
we behave like the poverty-stricken youths that play
with a toothpick to make others believe that they have
dined well.'

'After all, here we are,' Mme. d'Espard said, with
bewitching grace, and a charming gesture as of innocence
grown wise; 'here we are, and there is still enough life
in us, it seems to me, for a return game.'

'When you told me the other day that Béatrix had
gone off with Conti, I thought about it all night long,'
said the Princess, after a pause. 'A woman must be
very happy indeed to sacrifice her position and her
future, and to give up the world for ever like that.'

'She is a little fool,' Mme. d'Espard returned gravely.
'Mlle. des Touches was only too delighted to be rid of
Conti. Béatrix could not see that it was a strong proof
that there was nothing in Conti when a clever woman
gave him up without making a defence of her so-called
happiness for a single moment.'

'Then is she going to be unhappy?'

'She is unhappy now. What was the good of leaving

her husband? What is it but an admission of weakness in a wife?'

'Then, do you think that Mme. de Rochefide's motive was not a desire to experience a complete love, that bliss of loving and being loved which for us both is still a dream?'

'No. She aped Mme. de Beauséant and Mme. de Langeais, who, between ourselves, would have been as great figures as La Vallière, or the Montespan, or Diane de Poitiers, or the Duchesses d'Étampes or de Chateauroux, in any age less commonplace than ours.'

'Oh, with the king omitted, yes, my dear. Ah! if I could only call up those women, and ask them if——'

'But there is no necessity to call up the dead,' broke in the Marquise; 'we know living women who are happy. A score of times I have begun intimate talk about this kind of thing with the Comtesse de Mont-cornet. For fifteen years she has been the happiest woman under the sun with that little Emile Blondet. Not an infidelity, not a thought from another; they are still as they were at the first. But somebody always comes to disturb us at the most interesting point. Then there is Rastignac and Mme. de Nucingen, and your cousin Mme. de Camps and that Octave of hers; there is a secret in these long attachments; they know something, dear, that we neither of us know. The world does us the exceeding honour to take us for *rouées* worthy of the Court of the Regency, and we are as innocent as two little boarding-school misses.'

'I should be glad to have even that innocence,' the Princess exclaimed mockingly; 'ours is worse, there is something humiliating in it. There is no help for it! We will offer up the mortification to God in expiation of our fruitless quest of love; for it is scarcely likely, dear, that in our Martin's summer we shall find the glorious flower that did not bloom for us in May and June.'

'That is not the question,' rejoined the Marquise after a pause, filled by meditative retrospect. 'We are still handsome enough to inspire love, but we shall never convince any one of our innocence and virtue.'

'If it were a falsehood, it should soon be garnished with commentaries, served up with the pretty art that makes a lie credible, and swallowed down like delicious fruit. But to make a truth credible!—Ah! the greatest men have perished in that attempt,' added the Princess, with a subtle smile that Lionardo's brush alone could render.

'Fools can sometimes love,' said the Marquise.

'Yes; but not even fools are simple enough to believe this,' pointed out the Princess.

'You are right,' the Marquise said, laughing. 'We ought not to look to a fool or a man of talent for the solution of the problem. There is nothing for it but genius. In genius alone do you find a child's trustfulness, the religion of love, and a willingness to be blindfolded. Look at Canalis and the Duchesse de Chaulieu. If you and I ever came across men of genius, they were too remote from our lives, and too busy; we were too frivolous, too much carried away and taken up with other things.'

'Ah! and yet I should not like to leave this world without knowing the joy of love to the full,' exclaimed the Princess.

'It is nothing to inspire love,' said Mme. d'Espard; 'it is a question of feeling it. I see many women that are only pegs on which to hang a passion, and not at once its cause and effect.'

'The last passion that I inspired was something sacred and noble,' said the Princess; 'a future lay before it. Chance, for this once, sent me the man of genius, our due; the due so difficult to come by, for there are more pretty women than men of genius. But the devil was in it.'

'Do tell me about it, dear; this is quite new to me.'

'I only discovered his romantic passion in the winter of 1829. Every Friday at the Opéra I used to see a man of thirty or thereabouts sitting in the same place in the orchestra; he used to look at me with eyes of fire, saddened at times by the thought of the distance between us and the impossibility of success.'

'Poor fellow, we grow very stupid when we are in love,' said the Marquise. The Princess smiled at the friendly epigram.

'He used to slip out into the corridor between the acts,' she went on. 'Once or twice, to see me or to be seen, he pressed his face against the pane of glass in the next box. If people came to my box, I used to see him glued in the doorway to steal a glance. He knew every one in my set by sight at last. He used to follow them to my box, for the sake of having the door left ajar. Poor fellow, he must have found out who I was very soon, for he knew M. de Maufrigneuse and my father-in-law by sight. Afterwards I used to see my mysterious stranger at the Italiens, sitting in a stall just opposite, so that he could look up at me in unfeigned ecstasy. It was pretty to see it. After the Opéra or the Bouffons, I used to see him planted on his two feet in the crush. People elbowed him, he stood firm. The light died out of his eyes when he saw me leaning on the arm of some one in favour. As for anything else, not a word, not a letter, not a sign. This was in good taste, you must admit. Sometimes in the morning, when I came back to my house, I would find him again, sitting on a stone by the gateway. This love-stricken man had very fine eyes, a long, thick fan-shaped beard, a royale, and a moustache and whiskers; you could see nothing of his face but the pale skin over the cheek-bones and a noble forehead. It was a truly antique head.

'The Prince, as you know,' she continued, 'defended the Tuileries on the side of the Quais in July. He came to Saint-Cloud the evening that all was lost. "I was all but killed, dear, at four o'clock," he said. "One of the insurgents had levelled his gun at me, when the leader of the attack, a young man with a long beard whom I have seen at the Italiens, I think, struck down the barrel." The shot hit somebody else, a quarter-master, I believe, two paces away from my husband. So it was plain that the young fellow was a Republican.

'In 1831 when I came to live here I saw him leaning against the house-wall. He seemed to rejoice over my calamities; perhaps he thought that they brought us nearer together. But I never saw him again after the Saint-Merri affair; he was killed that day. The day before General Lamarque's funeral I walked out with my son, and our Republican went with us, sometimes behind, sometimes in front, from the Madeleine to the Passage des Panoramas where I was going.'

'Is that all?' asked the Marquise.

'All,' returned the Princess. 'Oh yes; the morning after Saint-Merri was taken a boy out of the street came and must speak to me; he gave me a letter written on cheap paper, and signed with the stranger's name.'

'Let me see it,' said the Marquise.

'No, dear. The love in that man's heart was something so great and sacred that I cannot betray his confidence. It stirs my heart to think of that short terrible letter, and the dead writer moves me more than any of the living men that I have singled out. He haunts me.'

'Tell me his name?'

'Oh, quite a common one—Michel Chrestien.'

'You did well to tell me of it,' Mme. d'Espard answered quickly; 'I have often heard of him. Michel Chrestien was a friend of a well-known writer whom you have already wished to see—that Daniel d'Arthez who comes to my house once or twice in a winter. This Chrestien, who died, as a matter of fact, at Saint-Merri,

did not lack friends. I have heard it said that he was
one of those great politicians who, like de Marsay, need
nothing but a turn of the wheel of chance to be on a
sudden all that they ought to be.'

'Then it is better that he should be dead,' said the
Princess, hiding her thoughts beneath a melancholy
expression.

'Do you care to meet d'Arthez some evening at my
house?' asked the Marquise. 'You could talk with
him of your ghost.'

'Very willingly, dear.'

Some days after this conversation, Blondet and Rastignac, knowing d'Arthez, promised Mme. d'Espard that
he should dine with her. The promise would scarcely
have been prudent if the Princess's name had not been
mentioned, but the great man of letters could not be
indifferent to the opportunity of an introduction to her.

Daniel d'Arthez is one of the very few men of our day
who combine great gifts with a great nature. He had
at this time won, not all the popularity that his work
deserved, but a respectful esteem to which the chosen
few could add nothing. His reputation certainly would
increase, but in the eyes of connoisseurs he had practically reached his full development. Some writers find
their true level soon or late, and once for all, and
d'Arthez was one of them. Poor, and of good family,
he had rightly guessed the spirit of the age, and trusted
not to his ancestor's name, but the name won by himself. For many years he fought his battle in the arena
of Paris, to the annoyance of a rich uncle, who left the
obscure writer to languish in the direst poverty. Afterwards, when his nephew became famous, he left him all
his money, a piece of inconsistency to be laid to the
score of vanity. The sudden transition from poverty
to wealth made no change whatever in Daniel d'Arthez's
way of life. He continued his work with simplicity

worthy of ancient times, and laid new burdens upon himself by accepting a seat in the Chamber of Deputies, on the benches to the Right.

Since his name became known in the world he had occasionally gone into society. An old friend of his, the great doctor Horace Bianchon, had introduced him to the Baron de Rastignac, an under-secretary of state, and a friend of de Marsay's. These were the two politicians who nobly enough gave Michel Chrestien's friends permission to look for his dead body in the cloisters of Saint-Merri, and to bury the Republican with due honours. Gratitude for a service which contrasted strongly with the rigour used by the administration at a time when party spirit ran so high, formed a bond, as it were, between d'Arthez and Rastignac, a bond which the under-secretary of state and the illustrious minister were too adroit not to turn to account. Several of Michel Chrestien's friends held opposite opinions in politics ; these had been won over and attached to the new government. One of them, Léon Giraud, first received the appiontment of Master of Requests, and afterwards became a Councillor of State.

Daniel d'Arthez's life was entirely devoted to his work. He saw society by glimpses only ; it was a sort of dream for him. His house was a convent. He led the life of a Benedictine, with a Benedictine's sober rule, a Benedictine's regularity of occupation. His friends knew that he had always dreaded the accident of a woman's entry into his life, he had studied woman too well not to fear her ; and by dint of much study he knew less of his subject, much as your profound tactician is always beaten under unforeseen conditions when scientific axioms will not apply. He turned the face of an experienced observer upon the world while he was still at heart a completely unsophisticated boy. The seeming paradox is quite intelligible to any one who can appreciate the immense distance set between faculties and senti-

ments—for the former proceed from the brain, the latter
from the heart.   A man may be great, and yet be a
villain, and a fool may rise to sublime heights of love.
D'Arthez was one of the richly endowed beings in whom
a keen brain and a wide range of intellectual gifts have
not excluded a capacity for deep and noble feeling.   By a
rare privilege he was both a doer and a thinker.   His
private life was noble and pure.   Carefully as he had
shunned love hitherto, he was learned in love ; he knew
beforehand how great an ascendency passion would gain
over him.   But poverty and cold, and the heavy strain of
the preparation of the solid groundwork of his brilliant
after-achievements, had acted marvellously as a preserva-
tive.   Then his circumstances grew easier, and he formed
a commonplace and utterly incomprehensible connection ;
the woman certainly was good-looking enough, but
without manners or education, and socially his inferior.
She was kept carefully out of sight.

Michel Chrestien maintained that men of genius
possess the power of transforming the most massive
women into sylphs ; for them the silliest of the sex have
sense and wit, and the peasant-girl is a marquise ; the
more accomplished the woman, the more (according
to Chrestien) she loses in their eyes, because she leaves
less to the imagination.   He also held that love (a
purely physical craving for lower natures) becomes
for the higher, the greatest achievement of the soul of
man ; the closest and strongest of all ties that bind two
human creatures to each other.   By way of justifying
d'Arthez, he instanced Rafael and the Fornarina.   (He
might have taken himself as a model in that kind, since
he saw an angel in the Duchesse de Maufrigneuse.)
But d'Arthez's strange fancy was explicable in many
ways.   Perhaps at the outset he lost all hope of finding
a woman to correspond to the exquisite visionary
ideal, the fond dream of every intelligent man ; perhaps his heart was too fastidiously sensitive, too delicate

to surrender to a woman of the world; perhaps he preferred to do as nature bade while keeping his illusions
and cultivating his ideal; or had he put love far from
him as something incompatible with work, with the
regularity of a cloistered life, in which passion might
have worked confusion?

For some months past Blondet and Rastignac had
rallied him on this score, reproaching him with knowing
nothing of the world nor of women. To hear them
talk, his works were numerous enough and advanced
enough to permit of some diversion; he had a fine fortune, yet he lived like a student; he had had no pleasure
from his fame or his wealth; he knew nothing of the
exquisite delights of the noble and delicate passion that a
high-born, high-bred woman can inspire and feel. Was it
not unworthy in him to know love only in its gross material
aspects? Love reduced to the thing that nature made
it was, in their eyes, the most besotted folly. It was
the glory of civilisation that it had created Woman,
when nature stopped short at the female; nature cared
for nothing but the perpetuation of the species, whereas
civilisation invented the perpetuation of desire; and, in
short, discovered love, the fairest of man's religions.
D'Arthez knew nothing of charming subtleties of language; nothing of proofs of affection continually given
by the brain and soul; nothing of desire ennobled by
expression; nothing of the divine form that a high-bred
woman lends to the grossest materialism. D'Arthez
might know women, but he knew nothing of the
divinity. A prodigious deal of art, a fair presentment
of body and soul, was indispensable in a woman, if love
was worthy to be called love. In short, the tempters
vaunted that delicious corruption of the imagination
which constitutes a Parisienne's coquetry; they pitied
d'Arthez because he lived on plain and wholesome
fare, and had not tasted luxuries prepared with the
Parisienne's skill in these high culinary arts, and

whetted his curiosity. At length Dr. Bianchon, recipient of d'Arthez's confidences, knew that this curiosity was aroused. The connection formed by the great man of letters with a commonplace woman, far from growing more agreeable with use and wont, had become intolerable to him; but the excessive shyness that seizes upon solitary men was holding him back.

'What?' said Rastignac, 'when a man bears per bend *gules* and *or*, a besant and a torteau counterchanged, why does he not allow the old Picard scutcheon to shine on his carriage? You have thirty thousand livres a year and all that you make by your pen; you have made good your motto—ARS THES*aurusque virtus*, an old punning device such as our ancesters loved—yet you will not air it in the Bois de Boulogne! Good qualities ought not to hide themselves in this age.'

'If you read your work over to that fat Laforêt-like creature who solaces your existence, I would forgive you for keeping her,' put in Blondet. 'But, my dear fellow, if you live on dry bread; materially speaking, mentally you have not so much as a crust.'

These friendly skirmishes between Daniel and his friends had been going on for some months before Mme. d'Espard asked Rastignac and Blondet to induce d'Arthez to dine with her, saying as she did so that the Princesse de Cadignan was extremely anxious to make the famous writer's acquaintance. There are women for whom curiosities of this kind have all the attraction that magic-lantern pictures possess for children; but the pleasure for the eyes is poor enough at the best, and fraught with disenchantment. The more interesting a clever man seems at a distance, the less he answers expectations on a nearer view; the more brilliant he was imagined to be, the duller the figure that he subsequently cuts. And it may be added, parenthetically, that disappointed curiosity is apt to be unjust. D'Arthez was not to be deluded by Rastignac or Blondet, but they told him laughingly that here was a most alluring opportunity of rubbing the rust off his heart, of discovering something of the supreme felicity to be gained through the love of a Parisian great lady. The Princess was positively smitten with him; there was nothing to fear; he had everything to gain from the interview; he could not possibly descend from the pedestal on which Mme. de Cadignan had placed him. Neither Blondet nor Rastignac saw any harm in crediting the Princess with this love-affair; her past had furnished so many anecdotes that she could surely bear the weight of the slander. For d'Arthez's benefit, they proceeded to relate the adventures of the Duchesse de Maufrigneuse. Beginning with Her Grace's first flirtations with de Marsay, they told of her subsequent escapades with d'Ajuda-Pinto (whom she took from his wife, and so avenged Mme. de Beauséant); and of her third *liaison* with young d'Esgrignon, who went with her to Italy, and got himself into an ugly scrape on her account. Then they told how wretched a certain well-known ambassador had made her; how happy she had been with a Russian general; how she had acted since then as Egeria to two Ministers of Foreign Affairs, and so forth, and so forth. D'Arthez told them that he had heard more about her than they could tell him; their poor friend Michel Chrestien had worshipped her in his secret heart for four years, and all but lost his wits for her.

'I often used to go with him to the Italiens or the Opéra,' Daniel said. 'He and I used to rush along the streets to keep up with her horses, while he gazed at the Princess through the windows of her brougham. The Prince de Cadignan owed his life to that love affair; a street-boy was going to fire at him when Michel stopped him.'

'Well, well, you will find a subject ready made,' smiled Blondet. 'Just the woman you want; she will only be cruel through delicacy; she will initiate you into the mysteries of refined luxury in the most gracious way; but take care! She has run through many a fortune. The fair Diane is a spendthrift of the order that costs not a centime, but for whom men spend millions. Give yourself body and soul if you will, but keep a hold of your purse, like the old man in Girodet's picture of the *Deluge*.'

This conversation invested the Princess with the grace of a queen, the corruption of a diplomatist, the mystery of an initiation, the depth of an abyss, and the danger of a siren. D'Arthez's ingenious friends, being quite unable to foresee the results of their hoax, ended by making Diane d'Uxelles the most portentous Parisienne, the cleverest coquette, the most bewildering courtesan in the world. They were right; and yet the woman so lightly spoken of was sacred and divine for d'Arthez. There was no need to work upon his curiosity. He agreed to meet her at the first asking, and that was all his friends wanted of him.

Mme. d'Espard went to the Princess as soon as the invitation was accepted.

'Do you feel that you are in good looks and good form for coquetry, dear?' she asked. 'Come and dine with me in a few days' time, and I will serve you up d'Arthez. Our man of genius is the shyest of the shy; he is afraid of women; he has never been in love. Here is a subject for you. He is extremely clever, and so simple that he disarms suspicion and puts you at a disadvantage. His perspicacity is altogether of the retrospective kind; it acts after the event, and throws out all your calculations. You may take him in to-day; to-morrow he is not to be duped by anything.'

'Ah! if I were only thirty years old, I would have some fun,' said the Princess. 'The one thing wanting in my life hitherto has been a man of genius to outwit. I have always had partners, never an adversary. Love was a game, not a contest.'

'Admit that I am very generous, dear Princess ; for, after all, well-regulated charity——'

The women looked laughingly into each other's faces, and their hands met with a friendly pressure. Surely both of them must have been in possession of important secrets ! They certainly did not take account of a man or a service to render ; and any sincere and lasting friendship between two women is sure to be.cemented by petty crimes. You may see two of these dear friends, each of them quite able to kill the other with the poisoned dagger in her hand ; and a touching picture of harmony they present—till the moment comes when one of them chances to let her weapon drop.

In a week's time, therefore, the Marquise gave one of her small evening parties, her *petits jours*, when a few intimate friends were invited by word of mouth, and the hostess shut her door to other visitors. Five people were asked to dinner : Emile Blondet and Mme. de Montcornet, Daniel d'Arthez, Rastignac and the Princesse de Cadignan—three men and, including the mistress of the house, three women. Never did chance permit of more skilful prearrangement than on this occasion of d'Arthez's introduction to Mme. de Cadignan.

Even at this day the Princess is supposed to be one of the best-dressed women in Paris, and for women dress is the first of arts. She wore a blue velvet gown with large white hanging sleeves. The corselet bodice was cut low at the throat ; but a sort of chemisette of slightly drawn tulle with a blue border—such as you may see in some of Rafael's portraits—covered her shoulders, leaving only about four fingers' breadth of her neck quite bare. A few sprays of white heather, cleverly arranged by her maid, adorned the fair, rippling hair for which Diane had been famous. In truth, at this moment she looked scarcely five-and-twenty. Four years of solitude and repose had restored brilliancy to her complexion ; and there are moments, surely, when

a woman looks more beautiful for the desire to please;
the will counts for something in the changes that pass
over a face.   If persons of sanguine or melancholic
temperament turn sallow, and the lymphatic grow livid
under the influence of violent emotion, surely it must
be conceded that desire and hope and joy are great
beautifiers of the complexion; they glow in brilliant
light from the eyes, kindling beauty in a face with a
fresh brightness like that of a sunny morning.   The
white fairness for which the Princess was so famous had
taken on the rich colouring of mature and majestic
womanhood.   At this period of her life, reflection and
serious thought had left their impression upon her; the
dreamy, very noble forehead seemed wonderfully in
harmony with the slow queenly gaze of her blue eyes.
No physiognomist, however skilled, could have imagined
that calculation and decision lay beneath those preter-
naturally delicate features.   Some women's faces baffle
science by their repose and fineness, and leave observation at fault; the opportunity of studying them while
the passions speak is hard to come by; when the
passions have spoken it is too late; by that time a
woman is old, she does not care to dissimulate.

The Princess was just such an inscrutable feminine
mystery.   Whatever she chose to be she could be.   She
was playful, childlike, distractingly innocent; or subtle,
serious, and disquietingly profound.   When she came to
the Marquise's, she meant to be a simple, sweet woman,
who had known life only by its deceptions; a soulful,
much-slandered, but resigned victim, a cruelly-used
angel, in short.

She came early, so as to take her place beside Mme.
d'Espard on the settee by the fireside.   She would be
seen as she meant to be seen; she would arrange her
attitude with an art concealed by an exquisite ease; her
pose should be of the elaborated and studied kind which
brings out all the beauty of the curving line that begins

at the foot, rises gracefully to the hips, and continues through wonderful sinuous contours to the shoulder, outlining the whole length of the body. Nudity would be less dangerous than draperies so artfully arranged to cover and reveal every line. With a subtlety beyond the reach of many women, Diane had brought her son with her. For a moment Mme. d'Espard beheld the Duc de Maufrigneuse with blank amazement, then her eyes showed that she comprehended the situation. She grasped the Princess's hand with, 'I understand! D'Arthez is to be made to accept all the difficulties at the outset, so that you will have nothing to overcome afterwards.'

The Comtesse de Montcornet came with Blondet, Rastignac brought d'Arthez. The Princess paid the great man none of the compliments with which ordinary people are lavish on such occasions; but in her advances there was a certain graciousness and deference which could scarcely have been exceeded for any one. Just so, no doubt, she had been with the King of France and the Princes. She seemed pleased to see the great man of letters, and glad to have sought him out. People of taste (and the Princess's taste was excellent) are known by their manner as listeners; by an unfeigned interest and urbanity, which is to politeness what practice is to good doctrine. Her attentive way of listening when d'Arthez spoke was a thousand times more flattering than the most highly-seasoned compliments. The introduction was made by the Marquise quite simply, and with regard to the dues of either.

At dinner, so far from adopting the affectations which some women permit themselves with regard to food, the Princess ate with a very good appetite; she made a point of allowing the natural woman to appear without airs of any kind. D'Arthez sat next to her, and between the courses she entered upon a *tête-à-tête* with him under cover of the general conversation.

'My reason for procuring myself the pleasure of a meeting with you, monsieur,' she said, 'was a wish to hear something of an unfortunate friend of yours who died for a cause other than ours. I lay under great obligations to him, but it was out of my power to acknowledge or to requite his services. The Prince de Cadignan shares my regrets. I have heard that you were one of the poor fellow's most intimate friends, and that disinterested staunch friendship between you gives me a certain claim to your acquaintance; so you will not think it strange that I should wish to hear all that you could tell me of one so dear to you. I am attached to the exiled family, and of course hold monarchical opinions; but I am not of the number of those who think that it is impossible for a Republican to be noble at heart. A monarchy and a republic are the only forms of government which do not stifle nobility of sentiment.'

'Michel Chrestien was sublime, madame,' Daniel answered with an unsteady voice. 'I do not know of a greater man among the heroes of old times. You must not think that he was one of the narrow Republicans who want the Convention and the Committee of Public Safety re-established with its pretty ways. No, Michel used to dream of European Federation on the Swiss model. Set aside the magnificent monarchical system which, in my opinion, is peculiarly suited to our country; and let us admit that Michel's project would mean the abolition of war in the old world, and a Europe constituted afresh on a very different basis from that of ancient conquest, modified subsequently by the feudal system. On this showing the Republicans most nearly approached his theories; and for that reason he fought with them in July and at Saint-Merri. In politics we were diametrically opposed, but none the less we were the closest friends.'

'It is the finest possible testimony to both your characters,' Mme. de Cadignan said timidly.

'During the last four years of his life he told me of his love for you. No one else knew about it,' continued d'Arthez. 'We had been like brothers; but that confidence bound us to each other even more closely than before. He alone, madame, would have loved you as you deserve to be loved. Many a wetting I have had, as he and I accompanied your carriage home, running to keep up with the horses, so as not to miss a glimpse of your face—to admire you——'

'Why, monsieur, I shall soon be bound to make compensation——'

'Why is not Michel here?' returned Daniel in a melancholy voice.

'Perhaps he might not have loved me for long,' began the Princess with a sorrowful shake of the head. 'Republicans are even more absolute in their ideas than we Absolutists who sin through indulgence. He would dream of me as a perfect woman no doubt; he would have been cruelly undeceived. We women are persecuted with slander; and, unlike you literary men, we cannot meet calumny and fight it down by our fame and our achievements. People take us, not for the women we are, but simply as others make us out to be. Others would very soon hide the real unknown self that there is in me by holding up a sham portrait of an imaginary woman, the true Mme. de Maufrigneuse in the eyes of the world. He would think me unworthy of the noble love he bore me, he would think I could not understand.' Again the Princess shook her head with its coronet of heather among the bright gold curls. There was something sublime in the movement; it expressed sorrowful misgivings and hidden griefs that could not be uttered. Daniel understood all that it meant. He looked at her with quick sympathy in his eyes.

'Still,' she said, 'when I saw him again one day, a long while after the Revolution of July, I almost gave way to a wish that came over me to grasp him by the

...the pleasure of ... she said, 'was a wish ... ... friend of yours wh... ... other ... ... I hav under gre... ... was out of my power ... ... his services. The Prince ... I have heard that y... ... most intimate friends, a... ... residing between you g... ... your acquaintance; so you ... ... should wish to hear all t... ... I am attac... ... held monarch... ... the number of those ... ... impossible for a Republican to be ... ... monarchy and a republic are the only f... ... mobility of sentim...

... was sublime, madame,' D... ... 'I do not know ... ... the heroes of our times. You ... ... the narrow Republican ... ... the Committee of Public S... ... very ways. No, Michel ... ... Federation on the Swiss ... ... monarchical system whi... ... suited to our country; a... ... project would mean the ... ... and a Europe const... ... different basis from that of a... ... subsequently by the feudal ... ... the Republicans more nearly app... ... of that reason ... ... ht with... ... Merci. I... ... we w... ... but none ... we w...

... possible to ... both you ...

'During the last four years of his life he told me of his love for you. No one else knew about it,' continued the other. 'We had been like brothers; but that confidence bound us to each other even more closely than before. He alone, madame, would have loved you as you deserve to be loved. Many a evening I have had, to him accompanied your carriage home, running in step with the horses, so as not to miss a glimpse of you—to admire you——.'

'Why, madame, I shall soon be bound to make——

'Why is not Michel here?' resumed Daniel in a softer voice.

hand, then and there before every one, in the peristyle of the Théâtre Italien, and to give him my bouquet. And then—I thought that such a demonstration of gratitude would be sure to be misconstrued, like so many generous acts that people call "Mme. de Maufrigneuse's follies"; it will never be in my power to explain them; nobody save God and my son will ever know me as I really am.'

Her murmured words, spoken with an accent worthy of a great actress, in tones so low that no one else could overhear them, must have thrilled any listener. They went to d'Arthez's heart. The famous man of letters was quite out of sight; this was a woman striving to rehabilitate herself for the sake of the dead. Perhaps people had slandered her to him; she wanted to know if anything had tarnished her name for this man who had loved her once. Had he died with all his illusions?

'Michel was one of those men who love wholly and completely,' returned d'Arthez; 'such as he, if they choose amiss, can suffer, but they can never give up her whom they have chosen.'

'Then was I loved like that?' she cried, with a look of high beatitude.

'Yes, madame.'

'And he was happy through me?'

'For four years.'

'No woman ever hears of such a thing without a feeling of proud satisfaction,' she said, and there was a modest confusion in the noble sweet face that turned to his.

One of the cleverest manœuvres known to such actresses is a trick of veiling their manner if words have said too much, or of talking with their eyes when other language falls short. There is an irresistible fascination in these ingenious dissonances that creep into the music of love, or true or feigned.

'To have made a great man happy,' she went on (and

her voice dropped lower and lower when she had assured
herself of the effect that she had produced). 'To have
made a great man happy, and that without committing a
crime—this is the fulfilment of one's destiny, is it not?'

'Did he not write to you?'

'Yes, but I wanted to be quite sure; for, believe me,
monsieur, when he set me so high, he was not mistaken
in me.'

Women have an art of investing their utterances with
a certain peculiar sacramental virtue; they can impart
an indescribable something to their words, a thrill that
gives them a wider significance, a greater depth; and,
unless the charmed auditor subsequently takes it into his
head to ask himself what those words really meant, the
effect is attained—which is the peculiar aim and object
of eloquence. If the Princess had worn the crown of
France at that moment, instead of the high plaited
coronet of bright hair and wreath of delicate heather,
her brows could not have looked more queenly. She
seemed to d'Arthez to be walking over the tide of slander
as our Saviour walked over the sea of Galilee; the shroud
of her dead love wrapped her round as an aureole clings
about an angel. There was not the remotest suggestion
that she felt that this was the one position left to her to
take up; not a hint of a desire to seem great or loving;
it was done simply and quietly. No living man could
have done the Princess the service rendered by the dead.

D'Arthez, worker and recluse, had had no experience
of the world; study had folded him beneath its shelter-
ing wings. Her words, her tones, found a credulous
listener. He had fallen under the spell of her exquisite
ways; he was filled with admiration of her flawless
beauty, matured by evil fortune, freshened by retirement;
he bowed down before that rarest combination—a vivid
intellect and a noble soul. He longed, in short, to be
Michel Chrestien's heir and successor.

The first beginnings of his love may be traced to an

idea—a common case with your profound thinker.
While he looked at his neighbour, while his eyes grew
familiar with the outlines of her head, the disposition of
her delicate features, her shape, her foot, her finely
modelled hands; while he saw her now on a closer view
than in the days when he accompanied his friend on his
wild pursuit of her carriage, he was thinking to himself
that here was an instance of that wonderful thing—the
power of second-sight developed in a man under the
influence of love's exaltation. How clearly Michel
Chrestien had read this woman's heart and soul by the
light of the fire of love! And she too on her side had
divined the Federalist; he might, no doubt, have been
happy! In this way the Princess was invested with a
great charm for d'Arthez; a halo as of poetry shone
about her.

In the course of the dinner, d'Arthez remembered
Michel's confidences, Michel's despair, Michel's hopes
when he fancied that he was loved in return, and his
passionate, lyrical outpourings to the one friend to
whom he spoke of his love. And Daniel the while was
all unconscious that he was to reap the benefit of the
preparations due to chance. It very seldom happens
that a confidant can pass without remorse to the estate
of rival; d'Arthez could do this, and wrong no one now.
In one brief moment he realised the immense distance
that separates the high-bred lady, the flower of the
great world, from the ordinary woman, whom, however,
he only knew by a single specimen. He had been
approached on his weakest side, touched on the tenderest
spots in his soul and genius. His simplicity, his
impetuous imagination urged him to possess this woman;
but he felt that the world held him back, and the
Princess's bearing, her majesty, be it said, raised a barrier
between him and her. It was something new to him
to respect the woman he loved; and this unwonted
feeling acted in a manner as an irritant; the physical

attraction grew all the more potent because he had swallowed the bait, and must keep his uneasiness to himself.

They talked of Michel Chrestien till dessert was served. It was an excuse for lowering their voices on either side. Love, sympathy, intuition—here was her opportunity of posing as a slandered, unappreciated woman ! here was his chance of stepping into the dead Republican's shoes ! Possibly a man of such candid mind may have detected within himself a certain diminution of regret for the loss of his friend.

But when the dessert shone resplendent on the table ; when the light of the candles in the sconces fell upon the rich colours of fruit and sugar-plums among the bouquets of flowers ; then, under shelter of the brilliant screen of blossoms that separated the guests, it pleased the Princess to put an end to the confidences. With a word, a delicious word, accompanied by one of the glances that seem to turn a fair-haired woman into a brunette, she found some subtle way of expressing the idea that Daniel and Michel were twin souls. After this d'Arthez threw himself into the general conversation with boyish spirits, and a slightly fatuous air not unworthy of a youth at school.

The Princess took d'Arthez's arm in the simplest way when they returned to the Marquise's little drawing-room. She lingered a little in the great salon, till the Marquise, on Blondet's arm, was at some little distance from them. Then she stopped d'Arthez.

'It is my wish to be not inaccessible to that poor Republican's friend,' she said. 'I have made it a rule to receive no visitors, but you shall be the one exception. Do not think of this as a favour. Favours are only possible between strangers, and it seems to me that we are old friends. I wish to look on you as Michel's brother.'

D'Arthez could only reply by a pressure of the arm ; he found nothing to say.

Coffee was served. Diane de Cadignan wrapped herself in a large shawl with coquettish grace, and rose to go. Blondet and Rastignac knew too much of the world and of courtiers' tact to try to detain her or to make any ill-bred outcry; but Mme. d'Espard, taking the Princess by the hand, induced her to sit down again.

'Wait till the servants have dined,' she whispered; 'the carriage is not ready.'

She made a sign to the footman who carried out the coffee tray. Mme. de Montcornet, guessing that Mme. d'Espard wished to speak with the Princess, drew off d'Arthez, Rastignac, and Blondet by one of those wild paradoxical tirades which Parisiennes understand to admiration.

'Well?' asked the Marquise. 'What do you think of him?'

'He is simply an adorable child; he is scarcely out of swaddling clothes. Really, even this time there will be a victory without a struggle, as usual.'

'It is disheartening,' said Mme. d'Espard, 'but there is one thing left.'

'And that is?'

'Let me be your rival.'

'That is as you shall decide. I have made up my mind what to do. Genius is a kind of cerebral existence; I do not know how to reach its heart. We will talk of this later on.'

After that last enigmatic remark, Mme. d'Espard made a plunge into the conversation. Apparently she was neither hurt by the words, 'That is as you shall decide,' nor curious to know what might come of the interview. The Princess stayed nearly an hour longer on the settee by the fireside. She sat in a listless, careless attitude, like Dido in Guérin's picture; and while she seemed to be absorbed in listening, she glanced now and again at Daniel with undisguised yet well-controlled admiration. The carriage was announced. She grasped the Marquise d'Espard's hand, bowed to Mme. de Montcornet, and vanished.

The Princess's name was not mentioned in the course of the evening. The rest of the party, however, reaped the benefit of d'Arthez's uplifted mood; he talked his best; and, indeed, in Rastignac and Blondet he had two supporters of the first rank as regards quickness of intellect and mental grasp, while the two women had long since been counted among the wittiest great ladies in Paris. To them that evening was like a halt at an oasis; it was a rare enjoyment keenly appreciated by the quartette, who lived in constant dread of the danger signals of society, politics, or drawing-room cliques. Some people are privileged to shine like beneficent stars upon others, giving light to their minds and warmth to their hearts. D'Arthez's was one of these finer natures. A man of letters, if he rises to the height of his position, is accustomed to think without restraint, and apt, in society, to forget that everything must not be said; still, as there is almost always a certain originality about his divagations, no one complains of them. It was this savour of originality, so rare in mere cleverness, this simple-minded freshness, that made d'Arthez's character something nobly apart; and in this lay the secret of that delightful evening. D'Arthez came away with the Baron de Rastignac. As they drove home, the latter naturally spoke of the Princess, and asked him what he thought of her.

'No wonder Michel loved her,' returned d'Arthez; 'she is no ordinary woman.'

'A very extraordinary woman,' Rastignac returned drily. 'I can tell by the sound of your voice that you are in love with her already. You will call before three days are out; and I am too old a hand in Paris not to know what will pass between you. So, my dear Daniel, I beg you not to fall into any "confusion of interests."

c

Love the Princess by all means if you feel that you can love her, but bear your interests in mind. She has never asked or taken two farthings of any man whatsoever; she is far too much a Cadignan or d'Uxelles for that; but to my certain knowledge she has not only squandered a very considerable fortune of her own, she has made others run through millions of francs. How? why? and wherefore? Nobody can tell. She does not know herself. Thirteen years ago I saw her swallow down a charming young fellow's property and an old notary's savings to boot in twenty months.'

'Thirteen years ago!' exclaimed d'Arthez; 'then how old is she?'

'Why, did you not see her son?' Rastignac retorted, laughing. 'That was her son at table—the Duc de Maufrigneuse, a young fellow of nineteen. And nineteen and seventeen make——'

'Thirty-six!' exclaimed the man of letters in amazement; 'I took her for twenty.'

'She will be quite willing; but you need have no uneasiness on that score, she will never be more than twenty for you. You are setting foot in the most fantastic of worlds.—Good-night. Here you are at home,' added Rastignac, as the carriage turned into the Rue de Bellefond, where d'Arthez lived in a neat house of his own. 'We shall meet at Mlle. des Touches' in the course of the week.'

D'Arthez allowed love to invade his heart after the fashion of my Uncle Toby, *videlicet*, without the least attempt at resistance. He proceeded at once to uncritical adoration, admiring the one woman and excluding all others. The Princess, one of the most remarkable portents in Paris, where everything good or evil is possible—the Princess, fair creature, became for him the 'angel of his dreams,' hackneyed though the expression may be, now that it has fallen on evil days. A full comprehension of the sudden transformation wrought in the illustrious man of letters is impossible, unless you remember how solitude and continual work leave the heart dormant, and how painful a connection with a vulgar woman may become, when physical cravings give place to love, and love develops new desires and fancies and regrets, and calls forth the diviner impulses of the highest regions of a man's nature. D'Arthez was, indeed, the child, the schoolboy that the Princess at once discerned him to be.

And the beautiful Diane herself received an almost similar illumination. At last she had found a man above other men, the man whom all women desire to find, even if they only mean to play with him; the power that they consent to obey for the sake of gaining control of it. At last she had discovered a great intellect, combined with a boy's heart, and this in the first dawn of passion; and she saw, with happiness undreamed of, that all this wealth was contained in a form that pleased her.

D'Arthez was handsome, she thought. Perhaps he was. He had reached the sober age of maturity; he had led a quiet, regular life that had preserved a certain bloom of youth through his thirty-eight years; and, like statesmen and men of sedentary life generally, had attained a reasonable degree of stoutness. As a very young man he bore a vague resemblance to the portraits of the young Bonaparte; and the likeness was still as strong as it might be between a dark-eyed man with thick brown hair and the Emperor with his blue eyes and chestnut locks. But all the high and burning ambition that once shone in d'Arthez's eyes had been softened, as it were, by success; the thoughts that lay dormant beneath the lad's forehead had blossomed; the hollows in his face had filled up. Prosperity had mellowed the sallow tints that once told of a penurious life and faculties braced to bear the strain of incessant and exhausting toil.

If you look carefully at the finest faces among ancient
philosophers, you can always find that those deviations
from the perfect type which give to each face a character
of its own are rectified by the habit of meditation, and
the continual repose demanded by the intellectual life.
The most crabbed visage among them—that of Socrates,
for instance—acquires a well nigh divine serenity at last.
In the noble simplicity that became d'Arthez's imperial
face very well, there was something guileless, something
of a child's unconsciousness of itself, and a kindliness that
went to the hearts of others. He had none of that
politeness in which there is always a tinge of insincerity,
none of the art by which the best-bred and most amiable
people can assume those qualities which they have not,
much to the discomfiture of their late-enlightened dupes.
Some sins of omission he might make as a consequence of
his isolation; but he never jarred upon others, and a
perfume of the wilderness only enhances the gracious
urbanity of the great man who lays aside his greatness
to descend to the social level, and, like Henri IV., will
either lend a hand in children's games or lend his wit to
fools.

If d'Arthez made no attempt at a defence, the Princess,
on her return home, did not open the question again
with herself. There was no more to be said, so far as
she was concerned; with all her knowledge, and all her
ignorance, she loved. She only asked herself if she
deserved such great happiness—what had she done that
heaven should send such an angel to her? She would
be worthy of this love; it should last; it should be hers
for ever; the last years of youth and waning beauty
should be sweet in the paradise that she saw by glimpses.
As for resisting it, as for haggling over herself, or
coquetting with her lover, she did not even think of it.
Her thoughts were of something quite different. She
understood the greatness of genius; she felt instinctively
that genius is not apt to apply the ordinary rules to a

woman of a thousand. So after a rapid forecast, such
as none but great feminine natures can make, she vowed
to herself to surrender at the first summons. Her estimate of d'Arthez's character, based on a single interview,
led her to suspect that there would be time to make
what she wished of herself, to be what she meant to be
in the eyes of this sublime lover, before that summons
would be made.

And herewith begins an obscure comedy, played on
the stage of the inner consciousness of a man and woman,
each to be duped by the other. *Tartuffe* is the merest
trifle compared with such inscrutable comedies as this;
they enlarge the borders of the depravity of human
nature; they lie beyond the domain of dramatic art.
Extraordinary as they are throughout, they are natural,
conceivable, justified by necessity. Such a comedy is a
horrible kind of drama, which should be entitled the
seamy side of vice.

The Princess began by sending for d'Arthez's books.
She had not read a single word of them, but nevertheless
she had kept up a flattering conversation on the subject
for twenty minutes without making a single slip. She
proceeded to read them through, and then tried to compare his work with that of the best contemporary
writers. The result was a fit of mental indigestion on
the day of d'Arthez's visit. Every day that week she
had dressed with unusual care; her toilette expressed an
idea for the eyes to accept, without knowing how or
wherefore. So she appeared in a combination of soft
shades of grey; a listless, graceful half-mourning, an
appropriate costume for a woman who felt weary of life,
and had nothing left to bind her to life save a few
natural ties (her son perhaps). Hers, apparently, was
an elegant disgust that stopped short, however, of
suicide; she was finishing her allotted time in the
earthly prison house.

She received d'Arthez as though she expected his

visit, and had seen him at her house a hundred times, doing him the honour of treating him as an old acquaintance. The conversation began in the most commonplace way. They talked of the weather, of the Cabinet, of de Marsay's bad health, of the hopes of the Legitimist party. D'Arthez was an Absolutist. The Princess could not but know the opinions of a man who sat among the fifteen or twenty Legitimist members of the Chamber of Deputies; so she took occasion to tell the story of the trick she had played de Marsay; she touched on the Prince's devotion to the Royal family and to Madame; and thence, by an easy transition, brought d'Arthez's attention to the Prince de Cadignan.

'There is this at least to be said for him, he is an attached and devoted servant of His Majesty,' said she. 'His public character consoles me for all that I have suffered from his private life. But,' she continued, adroitly leaving the Prince on one side, 'have you not noticed (for nothing escapes you) that men have two sides to their characters? One side they show at home, to their wives; it is their true character that appears in private life; the mask is taken off, dissimulation is at an end; they do not trouble to seem other than they are; they are themselves—often they are horrible. They are great, noble, and generous for the rest of the world, for the King, and the Court, and the salons; they wear a costume embroidered with virtues and bedizened with fine language; they possess exquisite qualities in abundance. What a shocking farce it is! And yet there are people that wonder at the smile some women wear, at their air of superiority over their husbands, their indifference——'

She broke off, but allowed her hand to drop till it rested on the arm of her chair, a gesture that rounded off her discourse to admiration. D'Arthez's eyes were intent upon her lissom figure, upon the lines so gracefully curved against the silken depths of her easy-chair; upon the movements of her dress; upon a certain fascinating little wrinkle that played up and down over her bust, a daring device which only suits a waist so slender that it has nothing to lose by it. The Princess, watching him, took up the order of her thoughts, as though she were speaking to herself.

'I will say no more,' she said. 'For as for women that give themselves out for "misunderstood," and victims of ill-assorted unions who take themselves dramatically and pose as interesting persons—that kind of thing seems to me hopelessly vulgar, and you authors have ended by making such women very ridiculous. One must either submit, and there is no more to be said, or one resists and finds amusement. In either case a woman should keep silence. It is true that I could not make up my mind to do either, but that is so much the more reason, perhaps, for keeping silence now. How silly it is to complain! If a woman is not equal to the circumstances, if she fails in tact, or sense, or subtlety, she deserves her fate. Are not women queens in France? They play with you when they choose, as they choose, and for as long as they choose.'

She swung her scent-bottle, with a marvellous blending of feminine insolence and mocking gaiety in her gesture.

'I have often heard contemptible little creatures regret that they were women,' she continued; 'and I always felt sorry for them. If I had the choice, I would be a woman over again. Ah! the pleasure and pride of owing your triumphs to strength, to all the power put in your hands by laws of your own framing! And when we see you at our feet, doing and saying foolish things for our sakes, is it not intoxicating joy to feel that the woman's weakness triumphs? So, when we succeed, we are bound to keep silence under penalty of losing our ascendency. And after a defeat, a woman's pride bids her be silent. The slave's silence dismays the master.'

While this prattle was piped forth in those winning tones of gentle derision, with an accompaniment of little dainty turns of the head, d'Arthez was spellbound, just as a partridge is fascinated by the sportsman's dog. This kind of woman was something quite new in his experience.

'Tell me, madame, I beg of you, how any man could have made you suffer; be sure that where other women would be vulgar, you would be distinguished, even if you had not a manner of saying things that would make a cookery-book interesting.'

'You are going far in friendship,' she said, so gravely, that d'Arthez grew serious and uneasy.

She changed the subject. It grew late. The man of genius, poor fellow, went away in a contrite frame of mind; he had seemed inquisitive; he had hurt her feelings; and he was convinced that she had suffered as few women suffer. Diane had spent her life in amusing herself; she was neither more nor less than a feminine Don Juan, with this difference—if she had tempted the stone statue it would not have been with an invitation to supper, and she certainly would not have had the worst of the encounter.

It is impossible to continue this history without a word as to the Prince de Cadignan (better known as the Duc de Maufrigneuse), or the whole salt and savour of the Princess's miraculous inventions will be lost upon the reader. An outsider could never understand the atrocity of the comedy which the lady has been playing for the benefit of a man of letters. In person M. le Duc de Maufrigneuse, like his father the Prince de Cadignan, was tall and spare; he was a complete fine gentleman, his urbanity never deserted him; he made charming speeches; he became a colonel by the grace of God, and a good soldier by accident. In other respects the Prince was as brave as a Pole, showed his valour on all occasions without discrimination, and used the jargon of Court circles to hide his mental vacuity. Ever since he attained the age of thirty-six he had been perforce as indifferent to the sex as his royal master King Charles x.; for, like his master, he had found too much favour with the fair in his youth, and now was paying the penalty. He had been the idol of the Faubourg Saint-Germain for eighteen years, during which time he led the dissipated, pleasure-filled life of an eldest son.

The Revolution had ruined his father; and though after the Restoration the late Prince had recovered his post, the governorship of a royal castle, with a salary and diverse pensions, he had kept up the state of a *grand seigneur* of old days, and squandered his fortune during the brief gleam of prosperity to such purpose, that all the sums repaid him by the law of indemnity went in a display of luxury in his immense old mansion. It was the only piece of property left to him, and the greater part of it was occupied by his daughter-in-law. The old Prince de Cadignan died at the ripe age of eighty-seven, some years before the Revolution of July. He had ruined his wife, and for a long time there had been something like a coolness between him and his son-in-law, the Duc de Navarreins; the Duke's first wife had been a Cadignan, and the accounts of the trust of her fortune had never been satisfactorily settled.

The present Prince (then the Duc de Maufrigneuse) had had a *liaison* with the Duchesse d'Uxelles. Towards 1814, when the Duke reached his thirty-sixth year, the Duchess, seeing that he was poor but stood very well at Court, gave him her daughter with a rent-roll of fifty or sixty thousand livres, to say nothing of expectations. In this way Mlle. d'Uxelles became a duchess, her mother knowing that in all probability the newly married wife would be allowed great liberty. An heir was born, after which unexpected piece of good fortune the Duke left his wife complete freedom of action, amused himself by going from garrison to garrison, spent the winters in Paris, contracted debts which his father paid, and professed the most complete indifference for his wife. He always gave the Duchess a week's warning before returning to Paris. Adored by his regiment, in high favour with the Dauphin, an adroit courtier, and something of a gambler, there was no sort of affectation about the Duc de Maufrigneuse; the Duchess never could persuade him to take up an Opéra girl, out of regard for appearances and consideration for her, as she pleasantly said. The Duke succeeded to his father's post at Court, and contrived to please both Louis xviii. and Charles x., which shows that he understood how to turn a colourless character to a tolerable good account; and besides, his life and behaviour were covered over by the most elegant veneer. In language and fine manners he was a perfect model; he was popular even among Liberals. The Cadignans, according to the Prince his father, were famous for ruining their wives; in this respect, however, he found it impossible to keep up the family tradition, the Duchess was running through her fortune too quickly for him.

These little details of the family history were public property at Court and in the Faubourg Saint-Germain; so much so, in fact, that if any one had begun to discuss them, he would have been met with a smile. A man might as well have announced the capture of Holland by the Dutch. No woman ever mentioned the 'charming Duke' without a word of praise. His conduct towards his wife had been perfect; it was not a small thing for a man to behave himself as well as Maufrigneuse had done, he had left the Duchess's fortune entirely at her disposal; he had given her his support and countenance on every occasion. And indeed, from pride, or good nature, or from some chivalrous feeling, M. de Maufrigneuse had many a time come to the Duchess's rescue; any other woman would have gone under, in spite of her connections, in spite of the combined credit of the old Duchesse d'Uxelles, the Duc de Navarreins, the old Prince de Cadignan, and her husband's aunt. The present Prince is allowed to be one of the true nobles among the noblesses. And perhaps, if a courtier is faithful at need, he has won the finest of all victories over himself.

The Duchesse d'Uxelles was a woman of five-and-forty when she married her daughter to the Duc de Maufrigneuse, and therefore she saw her old friend's success not merely without jealousy, but with interest. At the time of the marriage she had showed herself a great lady and saved the situation; though she could not prevent scoffing on the part of spiteful persons at Court, who said that the Duchess's noble conduct cost her no great effort, albeit she had given the past five years to repentance and devotion, after the manner of women who stand in great need of forgiveness.

To return to Diane de Cadignan. The extent of the knowledge of literature which she displayed grew more and more remarkable day by day. She could venture with the utmost boldness upon the most abstruse questions, thanks to studies daily and nightly pursued with an intrepidity worthy of all praise. D'Arthez was bewildered. He was incapable of suspecting that Diane, like a good many writers, repeated at night what she read of a morning. He took her for a woman of no ordinary power. In the course of these conversations they wandered further and further from the end that Diane had in view; she tried to return to the ground of confidential talk, but it was not very easy to bring a man of d'Arthez's temper back to a subject after he had once been warned from it. However, after a month of excursions into literature and beautiful Platonic discourses, d'Arthez grew bolder, and came every day at three o'clock. At six he took leave, only to return three hours later to stay till midnight or one o'clock in the morning. This with the regularity of an impatient lover ; and the Princess, on her side, was always more or less carefully dressed at his hours. The tryst thus kept daily, the pains that they both took with themselves, their whole proceedings, in fact, expressed the feelings to which neither of them dared to confess ; and the Princess divined in some marvellous way that the grown child dreaded the coming contest as much as she herself longed for it. And yet d'Arthez's manner was a constant declaration of love—a declaration made with a respect which was inexpressibly pleasant to the Princess. Every day they felt so much the more closely drawn together, because there was no convention, no sharp line of difference to arrest the progress of their ideas; no barrier was raised, as frequently happens between lovers, by formal demands on the one side, and coquettish or sincere demurs upon the other. Like most men whose youth lasts on into middle age, d'Arthez was consumed by a poignant irresolution caused by vehement desires on the one hand, and the dread of incurring his mistress's displeasure on the other. A young woman understands nothing of all this while she shares the emotion, but the Princess was too experienced not to linger over its delights. So Diane enjoyed to the full the delicious child's-play of love, finding all the more charm in it because she knew so well how to put an end to it. She was like a great artist, dwelling complacently on the vague outlines of a sketch, sure of the coming hour of inspiration that shall shape a masterpiece out of an idea that floats as yet in the limbo of things unborn. How many a time, as she saw that d'Arthez was ready to advance, she amused herself by checking him with her queenly air. She could control the tempest in the man's boyish heart, she could raise the storm and still it again, by a glance, by giving him her hand to kiss, by some commonplace word uttered in a soft, tremulous voice.

This policy of hers had been coolly resolved upon, and she acted it out divinely, gradually deepening the lines of the image engraven upon the heart of a clever man of letters of whom it pleased her to make a child. With her he was trustful, open, almost simple; and yet at times something like a reaction would set in, and she could not but admire the man's greatness, blended with such innocence. The arch-coquette's play was binding her at unawares to her bond-slave. At length Diane grew impatient with her love-sick Epictetus; and as soon as she felt that he was disposed to put a blind faith in her, she set herself to tie a thick bandage over his eyes.

One evening Daniel found the Princess in a pensive mood. She was sitting with one elbow on the table, her bright golden head bathed in the lamplight, while she played with a letter, absently tapping it upon the tablecloth. When d'Arthez had been allowed a full view of the letter, she folded it and thrust it into her belt.

'What is the matter?' asked d'Arthez. 'You look troubled.'

'I have heard from M. de Cadignan,' she replied. 'Deeply as he has wronged me, I have been thinking, since I read this letter, that he is an exile, and alone; he is fond of his son, and his son is away from him.'

Her soul seemed to vibrate through her voice; to d'Arthez it was a revelation of a divine sensitiveness to another's pain. It touched him to the quick. His lover's eagerness to read her became, as it were, a piece of curious literary and scientific inquiry. If he could only know the height of her woman's greatness; the full extent of the injuries forgiven; and learn how near the angels a woman of the world may rise while others accuse her of frivolity and selfishness and hardness of heart! Then he remembered that once before he had sought to know this angel's heart, and how he had been repulsed. He took the slender transparent hand with

its taper fingers in his, and said, with something like a
tremor in his voice, ‘Are we friends enough now for
you to tell me what you have suffered? Old troubles
must count for something in your musings.’

‘Yes,’ said the fair Diane, prolonging the one syllable;
Tulou's flute never sighed forth a sweeter sound. Then
she drifted again into musings, her eyes clouded over;
and as Daniel waited in anxious suspense, the solemnity
of the moment penetrated his being. His poet's imagination beheld the cloud veiling the sanctuary; slowly
the obscurity would clear away, and he should behold
the wounded lamb lying at the feet of God.

‘Well?’ he said softly and quietly.

Diane looked into his face with its look of tender
entreaty, then her eyes fell slowly, and the lashes
drooped; the movement was a revelation of the noblest
delicacy. A man must have been a monster to imagine
that there could be a taint of hypocrisy in the graceful
curve of the throat, as Diane raised her little dainty
head to send a glance into the very depths of those
hungry eyes.

‘Can I? and ought I?’ she began, with a certain
hesitation, and her face wore a sublime expression of
dreamy tenderness as she gazed at d'Arthez. ‘Men
keep faith so little in such things. They feel so little
bound to secrecy.’

‘Ah! but if you cannot trust me, why am I here?’
he cried.

‘Ah! my friend, does a woman calculate when she
binds herself to a friendship for life?’ answered Diane,
and there was all the charm of an involuntary confession
about her words. ‘It is not a question of refusing you
(what can I refuse to you?); but what would you think
of me if I should speak? Willingly I would tell you
of my position, a strange one at my age; but what
would you think of a wife who should lay bare the
wounds dealt to her by her own husband, and betray

the secrets of another ? Turenne kept his word with
thieves ; ought I not to show the honour of a Turenne
towards those who tortured me ? '

' Have you given your word to any one ? '

' M. de Cadignan thought it unnecessary to ask for
secrecy. So you would have more of me than myself ?
Ah ! tyrant, am I to bury my honesty in you ? ' and
her glance made the pretended confidence seem something greater than the gift of her person.

' You rate me rather too low if you can fear any
wrong whatsoever from me,' he said with ill-disguised
bitterness.

' Forgive me, my friend,' she said. She took his hand
in hers, caressing it with a most loving soft touch of her
fingers. 'I know all your worth. You have told me the
story of your life ; it is a noble, a beautiful story ; it is
sublime, it is worthy of your name ; perhaps you think I
owe you mine in return ? But at this very moment I am
afraid of lowering myself in your eyes by telling secrets
that are not mine only. And, poet and lonely thinker as
you are, perhaps you may not believe in the horrors of
worldly life. Oh ! when you invent your tragedies, you
little know what tragedies are going on in many an apparently closely united family ! You do not imagine the
extent of the wretchedness beneath the gilding.'

' I know all,' he cried.

' No, nothing,' she answered. ' Ought a daughter to
betray her mother ? '

At those words of hers, d'Arthez felt as if he had lost
his way in darkness among the Alps, and found, with
the first glimpse of dawn, that he stood on the very edge
of a bottomless precipice. He looked with dazed eyes
at the Princess, and a cold chill crept over him. For a
moment Diane thought that the man of genius was a
weakling ; but a flash in his eyes reassured her.

' And now, you are almost like a judge for me,' she
said despairingly. ' And I may speak, for every

slandered creature has a right to prove its innocence.
I have been, nay—if any one remembers a poor recluse,
a woman forced by the world to renounce the world—I
am still accused of such light conduct, of so many sins,
that I may be forgiven for putting myself in the true
light for the heart in which I find a refuge from which
I shall not be driven forth. It has always seemed to
me that self-justification tells heavily against innocence;
for that reason I have always scorned to defend myself;
to whom, indeed, could I speak? Painful things like
these can only be confided to God, or to some one very
near Him, to a priest or to a second self. Ah, well, if
my secrets are not there,' she added, laying a hand on
d'Arthez's breast, ' as they are here' (bending the busk
of her corset with her fingers), ' you cannot be the
great d'Arthez, and I have been mistaken in you.'

D'Arthez's eyes filled, and Diane drank in those tears;
she gave him a sidelong glance with steady eyes and
unquivering eyelids. It was as deft and neat as a
cat's spring on a mouse. Then, for the first time, after
sixty days of protocols, d'Arthez took the warm, moist
hand, carried it to his lips, and set a kiss upon it—a
slow, long kiss, drawn from the wrist to the finger-tips,
taken with such delicate rapture that the Princess,
bending her head, augured very well of literature. In
her opinion, men of genius ought to love more perfectly
than men of the world, coxcombs, diplomates, or even
military men, though these certainly have nothing else
to do. Diane had had experience. She knew that a
man's character as a lover is revealed by very small
signs and tokens. If a woman is learned in this lore,
she can tell from a mere gesture what she has to
expect; much as Cuvier could examine a fragment of a
fossil foot, and say, ' This belonged to an animal that
lived so many thousand years ago; its habit was amphi-
bious, carnivorous, herbivorous, or what not; it had or
had not horns, and so forth.' She felt sure that the

imagination which d'Arthez put into his literary style would show itself in his love; so she held it expedient to bring him to the highest degree of passion and belief in her. She drew her hand back at once, with a magnificent gesture fraught with emotion. If she had said in words, 'No more of that, you will kill me!' she could not have spoken more forcibly. For a moment her eyes rested upon his; joy and fear and prudery and confidence and languor; a vague longing and something of a maiden's shyness were mingled in their expression. For that moment she was a girl of twenty. She had prepared, you may be sure, for that hour's comedy; never had woman dressed herself with such art; and now, as she sat in her great chair, she looked like a flower ready to open out at the first kiss of the sun. Real or artificial, whichever she was, she intoxicated Daniel.

And here, if it is permissible to hazard a personal opinion, let us confess that it would be delightful to be thus deceived for as long as possible. Talma on the stage certainly rose far above nature many a time; but is not the Princesse de Cadignan the greatest actress of our day? Nothing was wanting to her save an attentive audience. But, unfortunately, women disappear in stormy epochs; they are like water-lilies, they must have a cloudless sky and the softest of warm breezes if they are to blossom and spread themselves before our enchanted eyes.

The hour had come. Diane was about to entangle a great man in the inextricable toils of a romance that had long been growing; and he was to listen to it as a catechumen might have listened to an epistle from one of the apostles in the palmy days of the Christian Church.

'My mother, who is still living at Uxelles, married me in 1814 to M. de Maufrigneuse when I was seventeen years old (you see, my friend, how old I am). She made the match, not out of love for me, but from love of *him*. He was the only man she had ever cared for;

so she repaid him in this way for all the happiness that
he had given her. Oh! do not be shocked by the ugly
combination; it is a thing that often happens. Some
women put their lover before their children, just as
most women are mothers rather than wives. The two
instincts of wifely love and motherhood, developed as
they are by social conditions, often come into conflict
in a woman's heart. One of them must necessarily
supplant the other unless both kinds of love are equally
strong, as sometimes happens with an extraordinary
woman, the glory of our sex. A man of your genius
surely will understand these things; fools wonder at
them, yet they are none the less founded in nature. I
will go further, they are justifiable by differences in
character, temperament, situation, and the nature of the
attachment. If I myself, for instance, at this moment,
—after twenty years of misfortune, and disappoint-
ment, and heavy trials, and hollow pleasures, and slander
which I could not refute—if I were offered a true and
lasting love, might I not feel ready to fling myself at
the feet of the man who offered it? If I did, would
not the world condemn me? And yet, surely twenty
years of wretchedness ought to buy absolution for
twelve years given to a pure and hallowed love—the
twelve years of life that remain before I fade? But it
will not be; I am not foolish enough to diminish my
merits in the eyes of God. I have borne the burden
and heat of the day until evening; I will finish my day;
I shall have earned my reward——'

  'What an angel!' thought d'Arthez.

  'In short, though the Duchesse d'Uxelles cared more
for M. de Maufrigneuse than for the poor Diane whom
you see before you, I have never borne her a grudge.
My mother had scarcely seen me; she had forgotten me;
but her behaviour to me, as between woman and woman,
was bad; and what is bad between woman and woman
becomes hateful between mother and daughter. Mothers

that lead such a life as the Duchesse d'Uxelles led keep their daughters at a distance. I only "came out" a fortnight before my marriage. Judge of my innocence! I knew nothing; I was incapable of guessing the motives that brought the match about. I had a fine fortune—sixty thousand livres a year from forests, which they either could not sell or had forgotten to sell during the Revolution, and the château d'Anzy in the Nivernais to which the forest belonged. M. de Maufrigneuse was burdened with debts. If I afterwards came to understand what debts meant, at the time of my marriage I was too completely ignorant of life to suspect the significance of the word. The accumulated interest of my fortune went to pacify my husband's creditors.

'M. de Maufrigneuse was thirty-eight years old when I was married to him; but those years were like a soldier's campaigns, they should count double. Oh, he was far more than seventy-six years old. My mother at the age of forty had still some pretensions to beauty; and I found that I was between jealousy on either side. What a life I led for the next ten years! . . . Ah! if people but knew how the poor, much-suspected young wife suffered! To be watched by a mother who was jealous of her own daughter! Ah, God! . . . You writers of tragedies will never invent a drama so dark and so cruel! I think, from the little I know of literature, that a play as a rule is a series of events, conversations, and actions which lead to the catastrophe; but this thing of which I am speaking to you is a most dreadful catastrophe without end. It is as if the avalanche that fell this morning should fall again at night—and yet again next morning. A cold shudder runs through me while I speak of it, while I light up the cavern from which there was no escape, the cold, gloomy place where I used to live. If you must know all, the birth of my child—altogether mine, indeed for you must surely have been struck by his likeness

to me ?—he has my hair, my eyes, the outline of my face,
my mouth, my smile, my chin, my teeth—well, my child's
birth was due either to chance or to some agreement
between my mother and my husband. For long after
my marriage I was still a girl ; I was abandoned, so to
speak, directly afterwards ; I was a mother, but a girl
still. The Duchess was pleased to prolong the period
of ignorance, and to attain this end a mother has horrible
advantages. As for me, a poor, little creature brought
up like a mystic rose in a convent, I knew nothing of
married life, I developed late, and felt very happy ; I
rejoiced over the good understanding and the harmony
that prevailed in the family. I did not care much for
my husband, and he took no pains to please me ; and at
length my thoughts were altogether diverted from him
by the first joys of motherhood, joys the more keenly
felt because I had no suspicion that there could be any
others. So much had been dinned into my ears about
the respect that a mother owed herself ! And besides, a
girl always loves to "play at mamma." At that age a
child is as good as a doll. I was so proud too to have
that lovely flower, for Georges was a lovely child—a
wonder ! How could one think of society while one
had the pleasure of nursing and tending a little angel ?
I adore little children while they are quite little and
pink and white. So I saw no one but my baby ; I lived
with him ; I would not allow his nurse to dress or undress him or to change his clothes. The little cares that
grow so wearisome to the mother of a regiment of babes
were all pure pleasure to me. But after three or four
years, as I am not altogether a fool, the light broke in
upon me in spite of all the pains they took to bandage
my eyes. Can you imagine me when the awakening
came, four years afterwards, in 1819 ? *Deux Frères
ennemis* is a rose-water tragedy compared with the
dramatic situation in which the Duchess and I, mother
and daughter, were placed with regard to each other.

Then I defied both her and my husband, by flirting publicly in a way that made people talk. Heaven knows what they did not say. You can understand, my friend, that the men with whom I was accused of light conduct were simply daggers that I used to defend myself against the enemy. My thoughts were so full of revenge that I did not feel the wounds that I dealt myself. I was innocent as a child; people looked upon me as a depraved woman, one of the worst of women. I knew nothing of this.

'The world is very stupid, very ignorant, very blind. People only penetrate into the secrets that interest them and serve their spite; but when the greatest and noblest things are to be seen, they put their hands before their eyes. And yet, it seems to me that the pride that thrilled through me and shook me in those days, the indignant innocence in my expression and attitudes, would have been a godsend to a great painter. The tempest of anger in me must have flashed like lightning through a ballroom; my disdain must have poured out like a flood. It was wasted passion. Nothing save the indignation of twenty years can rise to such sublime tragic heights. As we grow older we cannot feel indignant, we are tired; evil is not a surprise; we grow cowardly, we are afraid. As for me, I made fine progress. I acted like the veriest fool; I bore the blame of wrongdoing, and had none of the pleasure. I enjoyed compromising myself. I played child's tricks.

'I went to Italy with a hare-brained boy; he made love to me, and I threw him over; but when I found out that he had got himself into a scrape on my account (he had forged a bill), I hurried to the rescue. My mother and my husband, who knew the secret of it all, kept a tight hand over me as an extravagant wife. Oh! that time I went to the King. Louis xviii., though he had no heart, was touched. He gave me a hundred thousand francs out of the privy purse. The Marquis d'Esgrignon (you may perhaps have met him in society, he married a very rich heiress afterwards), the Marquis d'Esgrignon was rescued from the depths into which he plunged for me. This adventure, brought about by my heedlessness, made me reflect. I saw then that I was the first to suffer from my revenge. My mother and husband and father-in-law had every one on their side; they stood to all appearance between me and the consequences of my recklessness. My mother knew that I was far too proud, too great, too truly a d'Uxelles, to do anything commonplace; about this time she grew frightened by the mischief she had done. She was fifty-two years old. She left Paris and went to live at d'Uxelles. Now she repents of her sins towards me, and expiates them by the most extravagant devotion and boundless love. But in 1823 she left me alone, face to face with M. de Maufrigneuse.

'Oh, my friend, you men cannot know what an elderly man of pleasure is; nor what a house is like when a man is accustomed to have women of the world burning incense before him, and finds neither censer nor perfumes at home; when he is dead to everything, and jealous for that very reason. When M. de Maufrigneuse was mine alone, I tried, I tried to be a good wife; but I came into conflict with the asperities of a morose temper, with all the fancies of an effete voluptuary; the drivelling puerilities, the vain self-sufficiency of a man who was, to tell truth, the most tedious, maundering grumbler in the world. He treated me like a little girl; it gave him pleasure to humiliate me on every occasion, to crush me with the bludgeon of his experience, and to show me how completely ignorant I was. He mortified me at every moment. He did everything, in fact, to make himself detestable and to give me a right to deceive him; but for three or four years I was the dupe of my own heart and my desire to do right. Do you know what a shameful speech it was that urged me to fresh recklessness? Could you imagine the supreme lengths to which slander is carried in society?—"The Duchesse de Maufrigneuse has gone back to her husband," people said.—"Pooh! out of sheer depravity; it is a triumph to quicken the dead, nothing else remains for her to do," replied my best friend, a relative at whose house I had the pleasure of meeting you.'

'Mme. d'Espard!' exclaimed Daniel, aghast.

'Oh, I have forgiven her, my friend. The speech was extremely clever, to go no further, and I may perhaps have said more cruel things of other unhappy women who were quite as pure as I was.'

Again d'Arthez kissed her hands. The sainted woman had chopped her mother in pieces and served her up to him; the Prince de Cadignan, whose acquaintance we have previously made, had been put forward as an Othello of the blackest dye; and now she was acknowledging her faults and scourging herself vigorously—all to assume, for the eyes of this guileless man of letters, that virgin estate which the simplest woman tries at all costs to offer to her lover.

'You can understand, my friend, that when I went back into the world, it was to make a sensation, and I intended to make a sensation. There were fresh struggles to be gone through; I had to gain independence and to counteract M. de Maufrigneuse. So I began a life of dissipation for new reasons. I tried to forget myself, I tried to forget real life in a life of dreams; I shone in society, I entertained; I was a Princess, and I got into debt. At home I found forgetfulness in sleep. Beautiful, high-spirited, and reckless, I began a new life in the world; but in the weary struggle between dreams and reality, I ran through my fortune.

'The revolt of 1830 came just as this chapter out of the *Arabian Nights* drew to an end; and just at that time I found the pure and sacred love which I longed to

know. (I am frank with you!) It was not unnatural
(admit) that when a woman's heart had been repressed
again and again by fate, it should awaken at last at the
age when a woman sees that she has been cheated of her
due? I saw that so many women about me were happy
through love. Oh! why was Michel Chrestien so much
in awe of me? There again is another irony in my
life. There was no help for it. When the crash came
I had lost everything; I had not a single illusion left;
I had pressed out the last drops of all experience, but of
one fruit I had not tasted, and I had neither taste nor
teeth left for it. In short, by the time I was obliged to
leave the world I was disenchanted. There was something providential in this, as in the insensibility that
prepares us for death,' she added, with a gesture full
of religious unction.

'Everything that happened just then helped me,' she
continued; 'the downfall and ruin of the Monarchy
buried me out of sight. My son makes up to me for
a great deal. Motherhood compensates us for all our
thwarted powers of loving. People are astonished by
my retreat, but I have found happiness. Oh! if you
but knew how happy the poor creature before you has
grown. The joys which I have not known, and shall
never know, are all forgotten in the joy of sacrificing
myself for my son's sake. Who could think that life,
for the Princesse de Cadignan, would be summed up by
a wretched marriage-night, the adventures with which
she is credited, and a childish defiance of two dark
passions? Nobody could believe it. At this day I am
afraid of everything. I remember so many delusions and
misfortunes that I should be sure to repulse genuine
feeling, and pure love for love's sake; just as rich men
repulse the deserving poor because some hypocritical
knave has disgusted them with charity. All this is
horrible, is it not? But, believe me, this that I have
told you is the history of many another woman.'

The last words were spoken in light jesting tones, which recalled the flippant woman of fashion. D'Arthez was dazed. The convict sent to the hulks for robbery and murder with aggravating circumstances, or for forging a signature on a bill, was in his eyes a saintly innocent compared with men and women of the world. The atrocious jeremiad had been forged in the arsenal of falsehood, and dipped in the waters of the Parisian Styx; there was an unmistakable ring of truth in the Duchess's tones. D'Arthez gazed at her for a little while; and she (adorable woman) lay in the depths of her great chair, her white hands resting over the arms like drops of dew at the edge of a flower-petal. She was overcome by her own revelations; she seemed to have lived again through all her past sorrows as she spoke of them, and now sank exhausted. She was an angel of melancholy in fact.

Suddenly she sat upright, and raised her hand, while lightnings blazed in the eyes that were supposed to be purified by twenty years of chastity. 'Judge of the impression that your friend's love must have made on me!' she cried, 'but by the savage irony of fate—or was it God's irony?—he died; he died when (I confess it) I was so thirsty for love that if a man had been worthy of me, he would have found me weak; he died to save the life of another, and that other was—who but M. de Cadignan? Are you surprised to find me pensive?'

It was the last stroke. Poor d'Arthez could bear no more. He fell on his knees before her, he hid his face in her hands, and his tears fell fast—happy tears, such as angels might shed, if angels weep. And since Daniel's face was hidden, Mme. de Cadignan could allow a mischievous smile of triumph to steal across her mouth, a smile such as monkeys might summon up over a piece of superlative mischief, if monkeys laugh.

'Aha! I have him fast!' thought she.

And true enough, she had him fast.

'Then you are——' He began raising that fine head of his to gaze lovingly into her eyes.

'Virgin and martyr,' she finished his sentence for him, smiling at the commonplace phrase, but her cruel smile lent an enchanting significance to the words. 'I laugh,' she said, 'because I am thinking of the Princess as the world knows her, of that Duchesse de Maufrigneuse to whom the world assigns de Marsay as a lover; and the villainous political bravo, de Trailles; and empty-headed little d'Esgrignon, and Rastignac, and Rubempré, and ambassadors and Cabinet ministers and Russian generals,—and all Europe, for anything I know. There has been much gossip about this album that I had made; people believe that all my admirers were my lovers. Oh! it is shocking! I cannot think how I can suffer a man at my feet; I ought to despise them all; that should be my creed.'

She rose and stood in the window; her manner of going was full of magnificent suggestion.

D'Arthez stayed on the hearth-stool where he had been sitting. He did not dare to follow the Princess, but he gazed at her, he heard her use her handkerchief. It was a pure matter of form; what is a princess that blows her nose? Diane tried to do the impossible to confirm d'Arthez's belief in her sensibility. His angel was in tears! He flew to her, put his arm about her waist, and held her tightly to him.

'No, no, leave me,' she murmured faintly. 'I have too many doubts to be good for anything. The task of reconciling me with life is beyond a man's strength.'

'Diane! I will give you love for all the life that you have lost!'

'No, do not talk to me like that,' she answered. 'I feel guilty; I am trembling at this moment as if I had committed the worst of sins.'

Diane had recovered a little maid's innocence, yet nevertheless she stood before him august and great and noble as a queen. It was a clever manœuvre, so clever that she had wheeled round from seeming, and reached the actual truth; and as for d'Arthez, no words will describe the effect produced by it upon his inexperience and open nature. Great man of letters as he was, he stood dumb with admiration, a passive spectator waiting for a word, while the Princess waited for a kiss. But she had grown too sacred to him for that. Diane felt cold in the window; her feet were freezing; she went back to her old position in the chair.

'He will be a long while about it,' thought she, looking at Daniel with a proud forehead and face sublime with virtue.

'Is she a woman?' the profound observer of human nature was asking of himself. 'How should one act with her?'

They spent their time till two o'clock in the morning in the fond, foolish talk that such women as the Princess can turn into adorable intercourse. She was too old, she said, too faded, too much of a wreck; d'Arthez proved to her that she had the most delicate, soft, and fragrant skin; delicious to touch, and white and fair to see, of which things she was fully convinced in her own mind. She was young; she was in her flower. Her beauty was disputed, charm by charm, detail by detail, with—'Do you think so?—You are raving!—This is desire.—In a fortnight you will see me as I am.—In truth, I am verging on forty; how should any one love a woman of my age?'

D'Arthez was impetuous as a schoolboy, his eloquence was sown thickly with the most extravagant words. And the Princess, listening, laughed within herself, while she heard the ingenious writer talking like a love-sick sub-lieutenant, and seemed to drink in the nonsense, and to be quite touched by it.

Out in the street d'Arthez asked himself whether he ought not to have been less in awe of her. As he went through the strange confidences that had been made to him—naturally, they have been much abridged and condensed here, for the mellifluous utterances given in full, with their appropriate commentary of expression and gesture, would fill a volume—as he looked through his memory, the plausibility of the romance, the depths below the surface, and the Princess's tones, all combined to foil the retrospective sagacity of an acute but straightforward man.

' It is true,' he told himself as he lay wide awake, ' it is true that there are tragedies in society. Society hides such horrors as this beneath the flowers of delicate luxury, the embellishments of scandal, and the sparkle of anecdotes. We cannot imagine anything that has not happened. Poor Diane ! Michel caught a glimpse of the enigma when he told us that there were volcanic fires under the ice ! And Bianchon and Rastignac are right too. When a man can find his high ideals and the intoxication of desire both blended in the love of a woman—a woman of quick intelligence and refinement and dainty ways—it must surely be unspeakable bliss.'

He tried to fathom the love in his heart, and found no limits.

Towards two o'clock next day, Mme. d'Espard called on the Princess. An intense curiosity brought her. For more than a month she had neither seen her friend nor received a single tell-tale word. Nothing could be more amusing than the first half hour of the conversation between two daughters of Eve endowed with the wisdom of the serpent. Diane de Cadignan shunned the subject of d'Arthez as she would avoid a yellow dress. And the Marquise wheeled about the question as a Bedouin Arab might hover about a rich caravan. Diane enjoyed the situation ; the Marquise grew furious. Diane was watching her opportunity ; she meant to turn her dear friend to account as a sporting dog. And one of the two celebrated women was more than a match for the other. The Princess rose a head above the Marquise; and Mme. d'Espard in her own mind admitted her inferiority. Herein, possibly, lay the secret of the bond between them. The weaker spirit of the two lay low, feigning an attachment, watching for the moment so long looked for by the weak, the chance of springing at the throat of the strong, and leaving the impress of one joyous bite. Diane saw this perfectly well. The rest of the world was completely deceived by the amenities that passed between the two dear friends.

The Princess waited; and as soon as she saw the question rise to her friend's lips, she said, 'Well, dear; I owe a great, complete, and boundless happiness to you.'

'What do you mean?'

'Do you remember our ruminations three months ago, as we sat out in the garden on the bench under the jessamine in the sun? Ah! well; no one can love like a man of genius. I would willingly say of my great Daniel d'Arthez as Catherine de' Medici said of the Duke of Alva, "One salmon's head is worth all the frogs' heads in the world."'

'I am not at all surprised that you do not come to me,' said Mme. d'Espard.

'Promise me, my angel, if he goes to see you, not to say a word of me,' continued the Princess, as she took the Marquise's hand. 'I am happy—oh! happy beyond words—and you know how far an epigram or a jest may go in society. A word can be fatal; some people can put so much poison in a word. If you only knew how I have wished during the past week that you too might find such a passionate love! And, indeed, it is sweet; it is a glorious triumph for us women if we may finish our lives as women thus, with an ardent, pure, complete, whole-hearted, and devoted love to soothe us at last after so long a quest.'

'Why ask me to be true to my best friend?' said

Mme. d'Espard. 'Can you think me capable of playing you a vile trick?'

'When a woman possesses such a treasure, it is so natural to fear to lose it, that the thought of fear occurs to her at once. I am absurd. Forgive me, dear.'

A few moments later, the Marquise took leave.

'What a character she will give me!' thought the Princess as she watched her departure. 'But I will save her the trouble of tearing Daniel away; I will send him to her at once.'

Daniel came in a few minutes afterwards. In the middle of an interesting conversation the Princess suddenly interrupted him, laying her beautiful hand on his arm.

'Forgive me, my friend, but I might forget to mention something; it seems a silly trifle, yet it is a matter of the utmost importance. You have not set foot in Mme. d'Espard's house since that day—a thousand times blessed!—when I met you for the first time. Go to her; not out of politeness, but for my sake. Perhaps she may be offended with me; she may possibly have chanced to hear that you have scarcely left my house, so to speak, since her dinner-party. And besides, my friend, I should not like you to give up your connections and society, nor your work and occupations. I should be more outrageously slandered than ever. What would they not say of me?—"That I am holding you in a leash, that I am monopolising you, that I am afraid of comparisons, that I want to be talked about even now, and I am taking good care to keep my conquest, for I know that it will be the last"—and so on and so on. Who could guess that you are my one and only friend? If you love me as you tell me you do, you will make people believe that we are to each other as brother and sister and nothing more.—Go on.'

There was an ineffable sweetness in the way in which this charming woman arranged her robes so as to fall gracefully; it always schooled d'Arthez into obedience. A vague, subtle refinement in her discourse touched him even to tears. Other women might haggle and dispute the way inch by inch, in sofa-converse; the Princess rose at once above all ignoble and vulgar bargainings to a height of greatness unknown before. She had no need to utter a word, they understood their union nobly. It should be when they willed it, upon either side; there was no yesterday, to-day, or to-morrow for them; there should be none of the interminable hoisting of the pennon styled 'sacrifice' by ordinary women, doubtless because they know how much they are certain to lose, while a woman who has everything to gain knows that the festival will be her day of triumph.

Diane's words had been vague as a promise, sweet as hope, and binding, nevertheless, as a pledge. Let it be admitted at once, the only women who can rise thus high are illustrious and supreme deceivers like Diane; they are queens still when other women find a lord and master. By this time d'Arthez had learned to measure the distance that separates these few from the many. The Princess was always beautiful, never wanting to herself. Perhaps the secret lies in the art with which a great lady can lay veil after veil aside, till in this position she stands like an antique statue. To retain a single shred would be indecent. The bourgeoise always tries to clothe herself.

Broken to the yoke by tenderness, and sustained by the noblest virtues, d'Arthez obediently went to Mme. d'Espard's. On him she exerted her most charming coquetry. She was very careful not to mention the Princess's name; she merely asked him to dine with her at an early date.

On that day d'Arthez found a large party invited to meet him. The Marquise had asked Rastignac,

Blondet, the Marquis d'Ajuda-Pinto, Maxime de Trailles, the Marquis d'Esgrignon, the two Vandenesses, du Tillet (one of the richest bankers in Paris), the Baron de Nucingen, Nathan, Lady Dudley, one or two of the wiliest attachés from the embassy, and the Chevalier d'Espard. The Chevalier, be it said, was one of the most astute personages in the room, and counted for a good half in the schemes of his sister-in-law.

Maxime de Trailles turned to d'Arthez.

'You see a good deal of the Princesse de Cadignan, don't you?' he asked, with a laugh.

D'Arthez replied with a stiff inclination of the head. Maxime de Trailles was a bravo of a superior order; he feared neither God nor man; he shrank from nothing. Women had loved him, he had ruined them, and made them pledge their diamonds to pay his debts; but his shortcomings were covered by a brilliant veneer, by charming manners, and a diabolical cleverness. Everybody feared him, everybody despised him; but nobody was bold enough to treat him with anything short of extreme civility. He could see nothing of all this, or possibly he lent himself to the general dissimulation. De Marsay had helped him to reach the highest elevation that he could attain. De Marsay, having known Maxime from of old, judged him capable of fulfilling certain diplomatic functions in the secret service, of which Maxime had, in fact, acquitted himself to admiration. D'Arthez had been mixed up in political affairs for some time past; he knew enough of the man to fathom his character; and he alone, it may be, was sufficiently high-minded to say aloud what others thought.

'It is for her, no tout, dat you neklect de Chaimper,' put in the Baron de Nucingen.

'Ah! a man could not set foot in the house of a more dangerous woman,' the Marquis d'Esgrignon exclaimed, lowering his voice. 'My disgraceful marriage is entirely owing to her.'

'Dangerous?' repeated Mme. d'Espard. 'You must not say such things of my best friend. Anything that I have ever heard or seen of the Princess seemed to me to be prompted by the highest motives.'

'Pray, let the Marquis say his say,' said Rastignac. 'When a man has been thrown by a mettled horse, he will pick faults in the animal and sell it.'

The Marquis d'Esgrignon was nettled by the speech. He looked across at Daniel d'Arthez.

'Monsieur is not on such terms with the Princess that we may not speak of her, I hope?'

D'Arthez was silent; and d'Esgrignon, who did not lack wit, retorted on Rastignac with an apologetic portrait of Mme. de Cadignan. His sketch set the table in good-humour; but as d'Arthez was absolutely in the dark, he bent over to Mme. de Montcornet and asked her to explain the joke.

'Well, judging by the good opinion that you have of the Princess, you are an exception; but all the other guests, it would seem, have been in her good graces.'

'I can assure you that that view is totally false,' returned Daniel.

'Yet here is M. d'Esgrignon, of a noble Perche family, who was utterly ruined for her twelve years ago, and all but went to the scaffold besides.'

'I know about it,' said d'Arthez. 'Mme. de Cadignan rescued M. d'Esgrignon from the Assize Court, and this is how he shows his gratitude to-day.'

Mme. de Montcornet stared at d'Arthez; she looked almost dazed with astonishment and curiosity. Then she glanced at Mme. d'Espard, as who should say, 'He is bewitched!'

During this short conversation Mme. d'Espard had defended her friend; but her defence, after the manner of

E

a lightning conductor, had drawn down the tempest. When d'Arthez gave his attention to the general conversation, Maxime de Trailles brought out his epigram.

'In Diane's case, depravity is not the effect but the cause; perhaps her exquisite naturalness is due to this; she does not try after studied effects; she invents nothing. She brings you out the most subtle refinements as the sudden inspiration of the most artless love; and you cannot help believing her too.'

The phrase might have been prepared for a man of d'Arthez's calibre; it came out with such effect that it was like a conclusion. Nobody said any more of the Princess; she seemed to be disposed of. But d'Arthez looked first at de Trailles and then at d'Esgrignon, with a sarcastic expression.

'She took a leaf out of a man's book, that has been her greatest mistake,' he said. 'Like a man, she squanders marriage jewels, she sends her lovers to the money-lenders, she ruins orphans, she devours dowries, she melts down old châteaux, she inspires crimes—and perhaps commits them herself—but——'

Never in their lives had either of the two personages addressed heard language so much to the purpose. When d'Arthez came to a pause on that *but*, the whole table was dumbfounded; the spectators sat, fork in hand, looking from the intrepid man of letters to the Princess's treacherous enemies. There was an awful pause; they waited to see what would come next.

'*But*,' pursued d'Arthez, with satirical flippancy, 'Mme. de Cadignan has this one advantage over men. If any one risks himself for her, she comes to the rescue, and says no ill of any man afterwards. Why should not one woman, among so many, amuse herself with men, as men play with women? Why should not the fair sex take a turn at that game from time to time?——'

'Genius is more than a match for cleverness,' said Blondet, addressing Nathan.

And, indeed, d'Arthez's avalanche of epigrams was like a reply from a battery to a discharge of musketry. They hastened to change the subject. Neither the Comte de Trailles nor the Marquis d'Esgrignon felt disposed to try conclusions with d'Arthez. When coffee was served, Blondet and Nathan went over to him with an alacrity which no one cared to imitate, so difficult was it to reconcile admiration of his behaviour with the fear of making two powerful enemies.

'We knew before to-day that your character is as great as your talent,' said Blondet. 'You bore yourself just now not like a man, but rather as a god. Not to be carried away by one's feelings or imagination, not to blunder into taking up arms in the defence of the woman one loves (as people expected you to do), a blunder which would have meant a triumph for these people, for they are consumed with jealousy of celebrated men of letters—ah! permit me to say that this is the supreme height of statecraft in private life.'

'You are a statesman,' added Nathan. 'It is as clever as it is difficult to avenge a woman without defending her.'

'The Princess is one of the heroines of the Legitimist party,' d'Arthez returned coolly; 'surely it is the duty of every gentleman to champion her on those grounds? Her services to the cause would excuse the most reckless life.'

'He will not show his hand,' said Nathan to Blondet.

'Just as if the Princess were worth the trouble,' added Rastignac, as he joined the group.

D'Arthez went to the Princess. She was waiting for him in an agony of anxiety. She had authorised an experiment which might prove fatal. For the first time in her life she suffered at heart, and a perspiration broke out over her.   Others would tell d'Arthez the truth, she had told him lies; if he should believe the truth, she did not know what she should do; for a character so noble, a man so complete, a soul so pure, a conscience so ingenuous, had never passed through her hands before.   It was because she longed to know a true love that she had woven such a tissue of cruel lies. She felt that poignant love in her heart, she loved d'Arthez, and she was condemned to deceive him, for him she must always be the sublime actress who had played this comedy for his benefit.   She heard d'Arthez's step in the dining-room with a great agitation; a shock quivered through the very springs of existence.   Then she knew that her happiness was at stake; she had never felt such emotion before, yet hers had been a most adventurous life for a woman of her rank.   With eyes gazing into space, she saw d'Arthez in one complete vision, saw through the outward form into his inmost soul. Suspicion had not so much as brushed him with her bat's wing!   The reaction set in after the terrible throes of fear, and joy almost overcame Diane; for every creature is stronger to bear pain than to stand the extreme of happiness.

'Daniel!' she cried, rising to her feet and holding out her arms, 'I have been slandered, and you have avenged me.'

Daniel was utterly astounded by the words, for the roots of them lay far down out of his sight.   He felt two beautiful hands clasp his face, and the Princess kissed him reverently on the forehead.

'How did you know?——'

'Oh, illustrious simpleton! do you not see that I love you madly?'

From that day there was no more question of the Princesse de Cadignan or of d'Arthez.   The Princess has since inherited some property from her mother; she spends her summers with the great man of letters in a villa at Geneva, returning to Paris for a few months during the winter. D'Arthez only shows himself at the Chamber. What is still more significant, he very rarely publishes anything.

Is this the catastrophe of the story? Yes, for those that can understand, but not for people who must have everything told.

Les Jardies, *June* 1839.

BUREAUCRACY

To the Contessa Serafina San Severino,
née *Porcia.*

Being obliged to read everything, in the endea-
vour to repeat nothing, I chanced, the other day,
to turn over the pages of a collection of three
hundred more or less broadly humorous tales
written by Il Bandello, a sixteenth century
writer, but little known in France, whose works
have only lately been republished in extenso in the
compact Florentine edition entitled Raccolta
di Novellieri Italiani. *As I glanced for the*
first time through Il Bandello's original text,
your name, Madame, and the name of the Count,
suddenly caught my eyes, and made so vivid an
impression upon my mind, that it seemed that I
had actually seen you. Then I discovered, not
without surprise, that every story, were it but
five pages long, was prefaced by a familiar letter
of dedication to a king or queen, or to one of the
most illustrious personages of the time. I saw the
names of noble houses of Genoa, Florence, Milan,
and Il Bandello's native Piedmont. Sforze,
Dorie, Fregosi, and Frascatori ; the Dolcini of
Mantua, the San Severini of Crema, the Visconti
of Milan, and the Guidoboni of Tortona, all
appear in his pages ; there is a Dante Alighieri

(some one of that name was then, it seems, in existence), stories are inscribed to Queen Margaret of France, to the Emperor of Germany, the King of Bohemia, the Archduke Maximilian. There are Sauli, Medici, Soderini, Pallavicini, and a Bentivoglio of Bologna; there are Scaligeri and Colonne; there is a Spanish Cardona; and as for France, Anne de Polignac, Princesse de Marcillac, and Comtesse de la Rochefoucauld, the Marignys, Cardinal d'Armagnac, and the Bishop of Cahors—all the great company of the time in short—are delighted and flattered by a correspondence with Boccaccio's successor. I saw, likewise, how much nobility there was in Il Bandello's own character; for while he adorns his pages with such illustrious names as these, he is true to his personal friendships. After the Signora Gallerana, Countess of Bergamo, comes the name of a doctor to whom he inscribes his tale of Romeo e Giulietta; *after the* signora, molto magnifica, Hipolita Visconti ed Attellana *follows the name of Livio Liviana, a simple captain of light cavalry; a preacher succeeds the Duke of Orleans, and next in order after one Riario you find* Messer magnifico, Girolamo Ungaro, mercante Lucchese, *a virtuous personage for whose benefit it is narrated how* un gentiluomo navarese sposa una che era sua sorella e figliuola, non lo sapendo; *the subject being furnished by the Queen of Navarre.*

Then I thought that I, like Il Bandello, might put one of my stories under the protection of una virtuosa, gentilissima illustrissima *Contessa Serafina San Severino, telling her truths that might be taken for flatteries. Why should I not confess that I am proud to bear my testimony here and elsewhere to the fact that fair and noble friendships, now as in the sixteenth century, are and have been the solace of men of letters wherever the fashion of the day may rank them? that in those friendships they have ever found consolation for slander, insult, and harsh criticism, while the approval of such an audience enables them to rise above the cares and vexations of the literary life? And because you found such pleasure in the mental activity of Paris, that brain of the world; because, with your Venetian subtlety of intellect, you understood it so well; because you loved Gérard's sumptuous salon (now closed to us), in which all the European celebrities of our quarter of the century might be seen, as we see them in Il Bandello's pages; because the great and dangerous Siren's fêtes and magical ceremonies struck you with wonder, and you gave me your impressions of Paris so simply—for all these reasons, surely, you will extend your protection to this picture of a sphere of life which you cannot have known, albeit it is not lacking in character.*

I could wish that I had some great poem to offer instead to you whose outward form is the visible expression of all the poetry in your heart and soul; but since a poor writer of prose can only give what he has, the inadequacy of the offering may perhaps be redeemed, in your eyes, by the respectful homage paid by a deep and sincere admiration, such as you can inspire.

De Balzac.

In Paris, where there is a certain family likeness among students and thinkers who live under similar conditions, you must have seen many faces not unlike M. Rabourdin's at the point at which this history takes up his career. M. Rabourdin at that time was a chief clerk in a most important Government department. He was

a man of forty, with hair of so pretty a shade of grey,
that women really might love to have it so; it was just
the tint that softens the expression of a melancholy
face. There was plenty of light in the blue eyes; his
complexion, though still fair, was sanguine, and there
were little patches of bright red in it; his mouth was
grave; his nose and forehead resembled those features
in portraits of Louis xv. In person he was tall and
spare, as thin, indeed, as if he had but recently recovered
from an illness; his gait suggested something of a
lounger's indolence, something too of the meditative
mood of a busy man.

If this portrait gives the man's character by anticipa-
tion, his costume may contribute to set it further in
relief; Rabourdin invariably wore a long blue overcoat,
a black stock, a double-breasted waistcoat *à la Robespierre*,
black trousers without straps, grey silk stockings, and
low shoes. At eight every morning, punctual as the
clock, he sallied forth duly shaven and ballasted with a
cup of coffee, and went, always along the same streets,
to the office, looking so prim and tidy that you might
have taken him for an Englishman on the way to his
embassy. By these tokens you discern the father of a
family, a man that has little of his own way in his own
house, and plenty of business cares to worry him at the
office; and yet withal sufficient of a philosopher to take
life as it is; an honest man, loving and serving his
country without blinking the difficulties in the way of
getting the right thing done; a prudent man, since
he knows something of human nature; a man whose
manner to women is exquisitely polite because he
expects nothing of them. Lastly, he was a man of
very considerable attainments, kindly to his inferiors,
apt to keep his equals at a distance, and to stand on his
dignity with his chiefs.

At this period of his life you would have noticed that
he wore a certain resigned, indifferent air; he seemed

to have buried his youthful illusions, and renounced personal ambitions; certain signs indicated that though discouraged he had not yet given up his early projects in disgust, but he persisted in his work rather for the sake of employing his faculties than from any hope of a doubtful triumph. He wore no ' decorations,' and occasionally blamed himself for the weakness of wearing the Order of the Lily in the early days of the Restoration.

There were certain mysterious elements in Rabourdin's life. His father he had never known. His mother had lived in luxury and splendour; she had a fine carriage, she was always beautifully dressed, her life was a round of gaiety; her son remembered her as a marvellously beautiful and seldom-seen vision. She left him scarcely anything when she died; but she had given him the ordinary imperfect school education which develops great ambitions and little capacity for realising them. Then he left the Lycée Napoléon only a few days before her death to enter a Government office as a supernumerary at the age of sixteen. Some unknown influence promptly obtained the position for him. At twenty-two, Rabourdin became senior clerk; he was chief clerk at twenty-five. After this, the patronage which had brought the young fellow thus far on in life showed itself in but one more instance. It procured him an entrance to the house of one M. Leprince, a retired auctioneer, reputed to be wealthy. M. Leprince was a widower with an only daughter. Xavier Rabourdin fell over head and ears in love with Mlle. Célestine Leprince, then aged seventeen, and endowed (so it was said) with two hundred thousand francs for her portion. Men in the highest position might well turn their eyes in the direction of this young lady. A tall, handsome girl with an admirable figure, she had inherited the gifts of an artist mother, who brought her up carefully. Mlle. Leprince spoke several languages, and had acquired some smatterings of learning—a dangerous advantage, which compels a woman to be very careful if she would avoid any appearance of pedantry. And Célestine's mother, blinded by unwise tenderness, had held out hopes that could not be realised; to hear her talk, nobody short of a duke, an ambassador, a marshal of France, or a cabinet minister could give her Célestine her rightful social position. And, indeed, Mlle. Leprince's manners, language, and ways were fitted for the best society. Her dress was too handsome and elegant for a girl of her age; a husband could give Célestine nothing but happiness. And, what was more, the mother (who died a year after her marriage) had spoiled her with such continual indulgence, that a lover had a tolerably difficult part to play.

A man had need have plenty of courage to undertake such a wife! Middle-class suitors took fright and retired. Xavier, an orphan with nothing but his salary as chief clerk in a Government office, was brought forward by M. Leprince, but for a long time Célestine would not hear of him. Not that Mlle. Leprince had any objection to her suitor himself; he was young, handsome, and very much in love, but she had no mind to be called Mme. Rabourdin.

In vain M. Leprince told his daughter that Rabourdin was of the stuff of which cabinet ministers are made. Célestine retorted that a man of the name of Rabourdin would never rise to be anything under the Bourbons, with much more to the same purpose. Driven thus from his intrenchments, her parent was guilty of a grave indiscretion; he hinted to Célestine that her suitor would be Rabourdin *de* somewhere or other before he could reach the age that qualifies for the Chamber. Xavier was sure to be a Master of Requests before very long, and Secretary-General of his department. After those two steps, the young fellow would be launched into the upper regions of the administration some day;

besides, Rabourdin would inherit a fortune and a name by a certain will, as he (Leprince) knew of his own knowledge. The marriage took place.

Rabourdin and his wife believed in the mysterious power discovered to them by the old auctioneer. Hope and the improvidence counselled by love in the early days of married life led the young couple into expense; and in five years M. and Mme. Rabourdin had spent nearly a hundred thousand francs of their principal. Célestine not unreasonably took alarm when promotion did not come, and it was by her wish that the remaining hundred thousand francs of her portion were put into land. The investment only paid a very low interest; but then some day or other old M. Leprince would leave his money to them, and their prudent self-denial would receive the reward of a pleasant competence.

But old M. Leprince saw that his son-in-law had lost his interest, and tried, for his daughter's sake, to repair the secret check. He risked a part of his capital in a very promising speculation; but the poor man became involved in one of the liquidations of the firm of Nucingen, and worried over his losses until he died, leaving nothing behind him but some ten fine pictures which adorned his daughter's drawing-room, and a little old-fashioned furniture which she consigned to the attics.

After eight years of vain expectation, Mme. Rabourdin at last grasped the idea that her husband's fatherly providence must have died suddenly, and that the will had been mislaid or suppressed. Two years before Leprince's death, when the place of the head of the division fell vacant, it was given to one M. de la Billardière, a relative of a deputy on the Right-hand benches, who became a member of the Government in 1823. It was enough to drive a man to resign. But how could Rabourdin give up a salary of eight thousand francs (to say nothing of an occasional bonus) when he was living up to his income, and three-fourths of it came from this source ? Besides, would he not have a right to a pension after a few years of patience ? But what a fall was this for a woman whose high pretensions at the outset were almost justifiable, a woman who was supposed to be destined for great things !

Mme. Rabourdin fulfilled the promise of Mlle. Leprince. She possessed the elements of an apparent superiority which pleases in society ; her great acquirements enabled her to speak to every one in his own language. And her ability was genuine ; she had an independent mind of no common order ; her conversation was as charming for its variety as for the originality of her ideas. Such qualities would have shone to advantage and profit in a queen or an ambassadress ; they were worth little in the inevitably humdrum routine of domestic life. If people talk well, they are apt to want an audience ; they like to talk at length, and sometimes they grow wearisome. To satisfy her intellectual cravings, Mme. Rabourdin received her friends one day in the week, and went a good deal into society, for the sake of the admiration to which she was accustomed.

Those who know life in Paris will understand what a woman of this stamp must suffer when she continually feels the pinch of straitened means at home. In spite of all the senseless rhetorical abuse of money, you must take your stand, if you live in Paris, at the foot of a column of figures ; you must bow down before arithmetic, and kiss the cloven foot of the Golden Calf.

Given an income of twelve thousand francs a year, to meet all the expenses of a household consisting of father, mother, and two children, with a housemaid and a cook, and to live on a second-floor flat in the Rue Duphot at a rent of a hundred louis—what a problem was this ! Before you begin to estimate the gross expenditure of the house, you must deduct the wife's expenses for dress and hired carriages (for dress is the first thing to con-

sider); then see how much remains to pay for the education of two children (a girl of seven and a boy of nine,
who already cost two thousand francs, in spite of a free
scholarship), and you will find that Mme. Rabourdin
could barely allow her husband thirty francs a month.
Most married men in Paris are, in fact, in the same predicament if they do not wish to be thought monsters of
cruelty.

And so it had come to pass that the woman who
believed that she was born to shine as one of the queens
of society was obliged to exert her intellect and all her
powers in a sordid struggle for which she was quite un-
prepared—a daily wrestling-match with account books.
And even so there had been bitter mortifications to
suffer. She had dismissed her man-servant after her
father's death. Most women grow weary of the daily
strain. They grumble for a while, and then yield to
their fate; but Célestine's ambition, so far from declin-
ing, was only increased by the difficulties. If she could
not overcome obstacles, she would clear them from her
path. Such complications in the machinery of existence ought to be abolished; and if the Gordian knot
could not be untied, genius should cut it. So far from
accepting the shabby lot of the lower middle-class
housewife, Célestine grew impatient because her great
future career was delayed. Fate had not done fairly by
her, she thought.

For Célestine honestly believed that she was meant
for great things. And perhaps she was right. Perhaps
in great circumstances she might have shown herself
great. Perhaps she was not in her place. Let us
admit that among women, as among men, there are
certain types that can mould society to their own wish.
But as, in the natural world, not every young sapling
shoots up into a tree, and small fry are more numerous
than full-grown fish, so, in the artificial world called
society, many a human creature who might have done

great things, many an Athanase Granson,[1] is doomed to perish undeveloped like the seeds that fall on stony ground. Of course there are domesticated women, agreeable women, and costly feminine works of art; there are women born to be ˙mothers, wives, or mistresses; there are wholly intellectual and wholly material women; even as among men there are soldiers, artists, craftsmen, mathematicians, merchants, poets, and men who understand nothing beyond money-making, agriculture, or public business. And then the irony of fate comes in and works strange contradictions; many are called, but few chosen, and the law of spiritual election holds equally good in worldly concerns.

Mme. Rabourdin, in her own opinion, was eminently fitted to counsel a statesman, to kindle an artist's soul, to further the interests of an inventor, and to help him in his struggles, or to devote herself to the half-political, half-financial schemes of a Nucingen, and to make a brilliant figure with a large fortune. Perhaps this was how she tried to account to herself for the disgust that she felt for laundress's bills, for the daily schemes of kitchen expenditure and the small economies and cares of a small establishment. In the life that she liked she took a high place. And since she was keenly sensitive to the prickings of the thorns in a lot which might be compared with the position of St. Lawrence upon a gridiron, some outcry surely was only to be expected of her. And so it befell that in paroxysms of thwarted ambition, during sharp throbs of pain, given by wounded vanity, Célestine threw the blame upon Xavier Rabourdin. Was it not incumbent upon her husband to give her a suitable position? If she had been a man, she certainly would have had energy enough to realise a fortune quickly and make a much loved wife happy. He was 'too honest,' she said; and this reproach in the mouths of some women is as good as a certificate of idiocy.

[1] See *La Vieille Fille.*

Célestine would sketch out magnificent plans for him, ignoring all the practical difficulties put in the way by men and circumstances; and, after the manner of women when under the influence of intense feeling, she became, in theory, more machiavellian than a Gondreville, and Maxime de Trailles himself was hardly such a scoundrel. At such times Célestine's imagination conceived all possibilities; she saw herself in the whole extent of her ideas. Rabourdin, meanwhile, with his practical experience, was unmoved from the outset by these glorious dreams. And Célestine, somewhat dashed, came to the conclusion that her husband was a narrow-minded man, whose views were neither bold enough nor comprehensive enough. Unconsciously she began to form an utterly false idea of her companion in life. She snuffed him out continually, to begin with, by her brilliant arguments; and when he began to explain matters to her, she was apt to cut him short. Her own ideas were wont to occur to her in flashes, and she was afraid to lose the spark of wit.

She had known from the very first days of their married life that Rabourdin admired and loved her; and therefore she treated him with careless security. She set herself above all the laws of married life, and the courtesies of familiarity, leaving all her little shortcomings to be pardoned in the name of Love; and as she never corrected herself, she always had her way. A man in this position is, as it were, confronting a schoolmaster who cannot or will not believe that the boy whom he used to keep in order has grown up. As Mme. de Staël once received a remark made by a 'greater man' than herself, by exclaiming before a whole roomful of people, 'Do you know that you have just said something very profound?' so Mme. Rabourdin would say of her husband, 'There is sometimes sense in what he says!' Gradually her opinion of Xaxier began to show itself in little ways. There was a lack of respect

in her manner and attitude towards him. And all unconsciously she lowered him in the eyes of others, for everybody all the world over takes a wife's estimate into account
in forming an opinion of a man ; it is the universal rule
in taking a precognition of character ; *un préavis*, as the
Genevese say, or, to be more accurate, *un préavisse.*

When Rabourdin saw the mistake that he had made
through love, it was too late. The bent had been taken;
he suffered in silence. In some rare natures the power
to feel is as great as the power of thought, a great soul
supplements a highly organised brain ; and, after the
manner of these, Rabourdin was his wife's advocate at
the bar of his judgment. Nature (he told himself) had
given her a rôle to play ; it was entirely by his fault
that she had been cheated of her part. She was like a
thoroughbred racer harnessed to a cart full of flints—
she was not happy. He took the blame upon himself,
in short. His wife had inoculated him with her belief
in herself by dint of repeating the same things over and
over again. Ideas are infectious in family life. The
9th Thermidor, like many other portentous events, was
brought about by feminine influence.

Urged on in this way by Célestine's ambition,
Rabourdin had long been meditating how to satisfy it ;
but he hid his hopes from her to save her the torment
of suspense. He had made up his mind, good man that
he was, to make his way upwards in the administration
by knocking a very considerable hole in it. He wanted,
in the first place, to bring about a revolution in the
civil service, a radical reform of a kind that puts a man
at the head of some section of society ; but as he was
incapable of scheming a general overturn for his particular benefit, he was revolving projects of reform in
his own mind and dreaming of a triumph to be nobly
won. The idea was both generous and ambitious.
Perhaps few employés have not thought of such plans ;
but among officials, as among artists, there are many

F

abortive designs for one that sees the light. Which
saying brings us back to Buffon's apophthegm, 'Genius
is patience.'

Rabourdin's position enabled him to study the French
administrative system and to watch its working. Chance
set his speculative faculties moving in the sphere of his
practical experience (this, by the way, is the secret of
many a man's achievements), and Rabourdin invented a
new system of administration. Knowing the men with
whom he had to do, he respected the machinery then in
existence, still in existence, and likely to remain in
existence for a long while to come, every generation
being scared by the thought of reconstruction; but
while Rabourdin respected the mechanism as a whole,
nobody, he thought, could refuse to simplify it.

How to employ the same energy to better purpose—
here, to his thinking, lay the problem. Reduced to its
simplest expression, his plan consisted in redistributing
the burden of taxation in such a way that it should fall
less heavily on the nation, while there should be no
falling off in the revenues of the State; and, furthermore, in those days when the budget provoked such
frantic discussion, he meant to make the undiminished
national income go twice as far as before.

Long practical experience had made it clear to
Rabourdin that perfection is gradually attained by a
succession of simple modifications. Economy is simpli-
fication. If you simplify, you dispense with a superfluous
wheel; and, consequently, something must go. His
system, therefore, involved changes which found expression in a new administrative nomenclature. Herein,
probably, you may find the reason of the unpopularity of
the innovator. Necessary suppressions are taken amiss
from the outset; they threaten a class which does not
readily adapt itself to a change of environment.
Rabourdin's real greatness lay in this—he restrained the
inventor's enthusiasm, while he sought patiently to gear

one measure into another so as to avoid unnecessary friction, and left time and experience to demonstrate the excellence of each successive modification. This idea of the gradual nature of the change must not be lost sight of in a rapid survey of the system, or it will seem impossible to bring about so great a result. It is worth while, therefore, incomplete as Rabourdin's disclosures were, to indicate the starting-point from which he meant to embrace the whole administrative horizon. The account of his scheme, moreover, brings us to the very core of the intrigues of which it was the cause, and may throw a light besides upon some present day evils.

Rabourdin had been deeply impressed by the hardships of the lives of subordinate officials. He asked himself why they were falling into discredit. He searched into the causes of their decline, and found them in the little semi-revolutions, the back eddies, as it were, of the great storm of 1789. Historians of great social movements have never examined into these, though, as a matter of fact, they made our manners and customs what they are.

In former times, under the monarchy, armies of officials did not exist. They were then few in number and under the direct control of a prime minister, who was always in communication with the crown. In this way the official staff might be said to serve the King almost directly. The chiefs of these zealous servitors were simply plain *premiers commis*—first clerks. In all departments not under His Majesty's direct control—such as the taxes, for instance—the staff were to their chiefs pretty much as the clerks in a counting-house are to their employer; they were receiving a training which was to put them in the way of getting on in life. In this way every point in the official circumference was in close connection with the centre, and received its impetus therefrom. Consequently, there was devotion on one side and trust on the other in those days.

Since 1789 the State, or if you like to have it so,

La Patrie has taken the place of the sovereign. The clerks no longer take their instructions directly from one of the first magistrates in the realm. In our day, in spite of our fine ideas of La Patrie, they are government employés, while their chiefs are drifted hither and thither by every wind that blows from a quarter known as the ministry, and the ministry cannot tell to-day whether to-morrow will find it in existence. As routine business must always be dispatched, there is always a fluctuating number of supernumeraries who cannot be dispensed with, and yet are liable to dismissal at a moment's notice. All of these naturally are anxious to be 'established clerks.' And thus Bureaucracy, the giant power wielded by pigmies, came into the world. Possibly Napoleon retarded its influence for a time, for all things and all men were forced to bend to his will; but none the less the heavy curtain of Bureaucracy was drawn between the right thing to be done and the right man to do it. Bureaucracy was definitely organised, however, under a constitutional government with a natural kindness for mediocrity, a predilection for categorical statements and reports, a government as fussy and meddlesome, in short, as a small shopkeeper's wife. Cabinet ministers' lives became a continual struggle with some four hundred petty minds led by a dozen or so of restless and intriguing spirits. It was a delightful spectacle for the rank and file of the service. They hastened to make themselves indispensable, hampering energy with documents, thereby creating a *vis inertiæ*, styled the Report. Let us explain the Report.

When kings had ministers, and they only began this practice under Louis xv., they were wont to have a report drawn up on all important questions, instead of taking counsel as before with the great men of the realm. Imperceptibly, ministers were compelled by their understrappers to follow the royal example. They

were so busy holding their own in the two Chambers
or at Court, that they allowed themselves to be guided
by the leading-string of the Report. If anything of consequence came up in the administration, the minister
had but one answer to the most pressing question—'I
have asked for a report.' In this way the Report became
for men in office, and in public business generally, pretty
much what it is for the Chamber of Deputies and the
Legislature, a sort of consultation in the course of which
the reasons for and against a measure are set forth with
more or less impartiality. The minister, like the Chamber, after reading it, is very much where he was before.

Any kind of decision must be made instantaneously.
Whatever the preliminary process, the moment comes
when you must make up your mind, and the bigger the
array of arguments, the harder it is to come by a wise
decision. The greatest deeds were done in France
before reports were invented and decisions were made
out of hand. The supreme rule for statesman, lawyer,
or physician is the same—he must adopt a definite
formula to suit each individual case. Rabourdin, who
thought within himself that 'a minister is there to
give decisions, to understand public business, and to
despatch it,' beheld the report carrying all before it,
from the colonel to the marshal, from the commissary
of police to the king, from the prefect to the cabinet
minister, from the Chamber to the police-courts.

Since 1808 everything had been on its trial; everything was weighed and pondered in conversation, books,
and newspapers, and every discussion took literary shape.
France was making dissertations instead of acting, and
came to the brink of ruin in spite of these fine reports.
A million of them would be drawn up in a year in
those days! Wherefore bureaucracy got the upper
hand. Portfolios, letter-files, wastepaper, documents,
and vouchers, without which France would be lost, and
circulars which she could not do without, increased and

multiplied and waxed imposing. Bureaucracy for its own ends fomented the ill-feeling between the receipts and expenditure, and calumniated the administration for the benefit of the administrator. Bureaucracy devised the Lilliputian threads which chain France to Parisian centralisation; as if from 1500 to 1800 France had managed to do nothing without thirty thousand government clerks! And no sooner had the official fastened on the government as mistletoe takes root on a pear-tree, than he ceased to take any interest in his work, and for the following reasons :—

The Princes and the Chambers compelled the ministers to take their share of responsibility in the budget, by insisting that their names and the amounts of salaries paid by and to them should appear in detail therein. They were likewise obliged to keep a staff of clerks. Therefore they decreased the salaries, while they increased the number of clerks, in the belief that a government is so much the stronger for the number of people in its employ. The exact converse of this is an axiom written large for all eyes to see. The amount of energy secured varies inversely with the number of agents. The Ministerialism of the Restoration made a mistake, as the event proved, in July 1830. If a government is to be firmly rooted in the heart of the nation, it must be, not by attaching individuals, but by identifying itself with the interests of the country.

The official class was led to despise the government which curtailed their salaries and lowered their social position; in retaliation they behaved as a courtesan behaves with an elderly adorer. They gave the crown an adequate return for their salaries. If the government and those in its employ had dared to feel each other's pulses; if the big salaries had not stifled the voices of the little ones, the situation would have been recognised as equally intolerable on either side. An official gave his whole mind to making a living; to draw a salary till he could reach a pension was his one object; and to attain that great result, anything (in his opinion) was permissible. Such a state of things made a serf of a clerk; it was a source of never-ending intrigues in the departments; and to make matters worse, a degenerate aristocracy tried to find pasture on the bourgeois common lands, using all its influence to get the best places for spendthrift sons; and with these the poor civil servant was obliged to compete. A really able man is hardly likely to try to make his way in these tortuous mazes; he will not cringe and wriggle and crawl through muddy by-paths where the appearance of a man of brains creates a general scare. An ambitious man of genius may grow old in the effort to reach the triple tiara, but he will not follow in the footsteps of a Sixtus v., to be a chief clerk for his pains. If a man came into the department and stopped there, he was either indolent or incompetent, or excessively simple.

And so, by degrees, the administration was reduced to a dead level of mediocrity, and an official hierarchy of petty minds became a standing obstruction in the way of national prosperity. A project for a canal, which would have developed the industries of a province, might lie in a pigeon-hole for seven years. Bureaucracy shirked every question, protracted delays, and perpetuated abuses the better to protract and perpetuate its own existence. Every one, even to the minister in office, was kept in leading-strings; and if any man of ability was rash enough to try to do without bureaucracy, or to turn the light upon its blunders, he was incontinently snuffed out. The list of pensions had just been published. Rabourdin discovered that a retired office messenger was drawing a larger sum from the Government than many a disabled colonel. The history of bureaucracy might be read at large in the pension list.

Rabourdin attributed the lurking demoralisation in part to another evil, which has its roots in our modern manners ; there is no real subordination in the service. A complete equality prevails from the head of the division to the lowest copying clerk ; and one man is as good as another in the arena, though when he leaves it, he takes a high place outside. A poet, an artist, and an ordinary clerk are all alike employés ; they make no distinctions among themselves. Education dispensed indiscriminately brings about the natural results. Does not the son of a minister's hall-porter decide the fate of a great man or some landed proprietor for whom his father used to open the door ? The latest comer therefore can compete with the oldest. A wealthy supernumerary driving to Longchamp in his tilbury with a pretty woman by his side, points out the head of his office to his companion with his whip. 'There goes my chief !' he says, and his wheels splash the poor father of a family who must go on foot through the streets. The Liberals call this sort of thing Progress ; Rabourdin looked upon it as Anarchy in the core of the administration. Did he not see the results of it ? —the restless intriguing as of women and eunuchs in the harem of an effete sultan, the pettiness of bigots, the underhand spite, the schoolboy tyranny, the feats on a level with the tricks of performing fleas, the slave's petty revenges taken on the minister himself, the toil and diplomacy from which an ambassador would shrink dismayed—and all undertaken to gain a bonus or an increase of salary ? And meanwhile the men who really did the work, the few whose devotion to their country stood out in strong contrast against the background of incompetence,—these were the victims of parasites, these were forced out of the field by sordid trickery. As all high places were no longer in the gift of the crown, but went by interest in parliament, officials were certain, sooner or later, to become wheels in the

ployé was to the national expenditure what the gambler is to the gambling saloon—whatever he takes away in his pocket he brings back again. A good salary, in his opinion, was a good investment. If you only pay a man a thousand francs a year, and ask for his whole time, do you not as good as organise theft and misery? A convict costs you very nearly as much, and does rather less work. But if the Government pays a man a salary of twelve thousand francs, and expects him to devote himself in return to the service, the contract would pay both sides, and the prospect ought to attract really capable men.

These reflections thereupon led Rabourdin to reconstitute the staff; to have fewer clerks, salaries trebled or doubled, and pensions suppressed. The Government should follow the example set by Napoleon, Louis XIV., Richelieu, and Ximenes, and employ young men; but the young men should grow old in the service. The higher posts and distinctions should be the rewards of their career. These were the capital points of a reform by which the government and the official staff would alike be benefited.

It is not easy to enter into details, to take heading by heading, and go through a scheme of reform which embraced the whole of the budget and descended into all the smallest ramifications of the administration, so that the whole might be brought into harmony. Perhaps, too, an indication of the principal reforms will be enough for those who know the administrative system—and for those who do not. But though the historian ventures upon dangerous ground when he gives an account of a scheme that has very much the look of armchair policy, he is none thè less bound to give a rough idea of Rabourdin's projects for the sake of the light which a man's work throws on his character. If all account of Rabourdin's labours were omitted, if this historian contented himself with the simple statement that the chief clerk in a government office possessed talent or audacity, you would scarcely feel prepared to take his word for it.

Rabourdin divided up the administration into three principal departments. He thought that if in former times there were heads capable of controlling the whole policy of the government at home and abroad, the France of to-day surely would not lack a Mazarin, a Suger, a Sully, a Choiseul, a Colbert, to direct far larger departments than those of the actual system. From a constitutional point of view, moreover, three ministers would work better together than seven, and the chances of going wrong in the choice are reduced ; while, as a last consideration, the crown would be spared the jolts of those perpetual changes of ministry which make it impossible to adhere to any consistent course of foreign policy, or to carry through reforms at home. In Austria, where different nationalities present a problem of different interests to be reconciled and furthered by the crown, two statesmen carry the weight of public business without being overburdened. Was France poorer in political capacity than Germany ? The sufficiently silly farce, entitled 'Constitutional Institutions,' has since been carried to an unreasonable extent ; and the end of it, as everybody knows, has been a multiplication of ministerial portfolios to satisfy the widespread ambition of the bourgeoisie.

In the first place, it seemed natural to Rabourdin to reunite the Admiralty and the War Office. The navy, like the artillery, cavalry, infantry, and ordnance, was a spending department of the War Office. It was surely an anomaly to keep admirals and marshals on a separate footing, when all worked together for a common end—to wit, the defence of the country, the protection of national property, and wars of aggression. The Minister of the Interior was to preside over the Board of Trade, the Police, and the Exchequer, the better to deserve his name ; while the Minister of Foreign Affairs controlled the administration of justice, the royal household, and everything in the interior which concerned arts, letters, or the graces. All patronage was to flow directly from the crown. The last-named minister, by virtue of his office, was also President of the Council of State. The work of each of these departments would require a staff of two hundred clerks at most at headquarters ; and Rabourdin proposed to house them all in one building, as in former days under the monarchy. Reckoning the salaries at an average of twelve thousand francs, the expense of this item in the budget would a little exceed seven millions, as against twenty millions on the actual system.

By reducing the number of the departments to three, Rabourdin suppressed whole divisions, and saved the enormous expense of their maintenance in Paris. He proved that an arrondissement ought to be worked by ten men, and a prefecture by a dozen at most ; on which computation the total number of government officials employed all over France (the army and courts of law excepted) would only amount to about five thousand—a number then exceeded by the staff in Paris alone. On this plan, however, mortgages became the province of the clerks of the various courts ; the staff of counsel for the crown (*ministère public*) in each court would undertake the registration of titles and the superintendence of the crown lands.

In this way Rabourdin concentrated similar functions. Mortgages, death-dues, and registration of titles remained within judicial spheres, while three supernumeraries in each court, and three in the Court-Royal, sufficed for the extra work.

By the consistent application of the same principle, Rabourdin proceeded to financial reform. He had amalgamated all Imperial taxes in one single tax, levied, not upon property, but upon commodities consumed. An assessed tax upon consumption, in his opinion, was the only way of raising the national revenue in times of peace, the land-tax being reserved for times of war. Then, and then alone, the State might demand sacrifices of the owners of the soil for the defence of the soil; at other times it was a gross political blunder to vex the land with burdens beyond a certain limit; something should be left to fall back upon in great crises. On the same principle, loans were to be negotiated in time of peace, because they can then be issued at par, and not (as in hard times) at fifty per cent. discount. If war broke out, the land-tax remained as a resource.

'The invasion of 1814 and 1815 did what neither Law nor Napoleon could do,' Rabourdin used to say to his friends; 'it proved the necessity of a National Debt, and created it.'

Rabourdin held that the true principles of this wonderful mechanism were, unfortunately, not sufficiently understood at the time when he began his work, which is to say, in 1820. He proposed to lay a direct tax upon commodities consumed by the nation, and in this way to make a clean sweep of the whole apparatus for the collection of indirect taxes. He would do away with the vexatious barricades at town gates, securing at the same time a far larger return by simplifying the extremely costly system of collection in actual use. The receipts from the one Imperial tax should be regulated by a tariff comprising various articles of consumption, and the amount fixed in each case by assessment. To diminish the burdensomeness of a tax does not necessarily mean in matters financial that you diminish the tax itself; it is only more conveniently assessed. If you lighten the burden, business is transacted more freely, and while the individual pays less, the State gets more.

Tremendous as this reform may seem, it was carried out in a very simple fashion. Rabourdin took for a

basis the assessments made by the Inland Revenue
Department and the licenses, as the fairest way of com-
puting consumption. House rent in France is a
remarkably accurate guide in the matter of the incomes
of private individuals; and servants, horses, and carriages
lend themselves to estimates for the Exchequer. Houses
and their contents vary very little in yearly value, and
do not easily disappear. Rabourdin pointed out a method
of obtaining more veracious returns than those given by
the system in use; then he took the total revenue
derived by the Exchequer from (so-called) indirect taxation, divided it up, and assessed his single tax at so much
per cent. on each individual taxpayer.

An Imperial tax is a preliminary charge paid on things
or persons, and paid under more or less specious disguises. Such disguises were well enough for purposes
of extortion; but surely they are absurd in these days
when the classes which bear the burden of taxation
know perfectly well why the money is wanted and how
it is raised. As a matter of fact, the budget is not a
strong-box, rather it is a watering-pot; as it is filled and
the water distributed, the country prospers. Suppose,
for instance, that there were six millions of taxpayers
in easy circumstances—and Rabourdin was prepared to
show that so many existed, if the rich taxpayers were
included in the number—would it not be better, instead
of putting a vexatious tax on wine by the gallon, to ask
the consumer to pay a fixed sum per annum to the Government? Such 'wine-dues' would not be more odious
than the door and window tax, while they would bring
in a hundred millions to the Exchequer. If other taxes
on consumption were likewise assessed in proportion to
the house rent, each individual would actually pay less;
the Government would save in the costs of collection;
and the consumer would benefit by an immense reduc-
tion in the prices of commodities which no longer would
be subjected to endless vexatious regulations.

Rabourdin reserved a tax on vineyards, by way of a safeguard against over-production. And, the better to reach the poor consumer, the charge for retailers' licenses was made in proportion to the population of the district. In these three ways the Exchequer would raise an enormous sum without heavy expense, and do away with a tax which was not only vexatious and burdensome, but also very expensive to collect. The burden would fall on the rich instead of tormenting the poor.

Take another instance. Suppose that the duty on salt took the form of one or two francs levied on each taxpayer; the modern *gabelle* would be abolished, the poor population and agriculture generally would feel the relief, the revenue would not be diminished, and no taxpayer would complain. Every taxpayer indeed, whether farmer or manufacturer, would be quick to recognise the improvement if the conditions of living grew easier in country places, and trade increased. And, in fact, the State would see an increase in the number of taxpayers in easy circumstances. The Exchequer would save enormously by sweeping away the extremely costly apparatus for the collection of indirect taxation (a government within a government); and both the Treasury and private individuals would benefit by the economy. Tobacco and gunpowder were to be put under a *régie*, beneath State superintendence. The *régie* system, developed not by Rabourdin, but by others, after the renewal of the legislation on tobacco, was so convincing that that law would have had no chance of passing the Chamber if the Government of the day had not driven them to it. But, then, it was a question of finance rather than of government.

The State should own no property; there should be no Crown domains, no woods and forests, no State mines, no State enterprise. The State as a landowner was an administrative anomaly, in Rabourdin's opinion.

The State farms at a disadvantage, and receives no taxes; there is a double loss. The same anomaly reappeared in the commercial world in the shape of State manufactures. No government could work as economically as private enterprise; the processes were slower; and, besides, the State took a certain proportion of raw materials off the market, and left so much the less for other manufacturers who pay taxes. Is it the duty of a government to manufacture or to encourage manufactures? to accumulate wealth, or to see instead that as many different kinds of wealth as possible are created?

On Rabourdin's system, officials were no longer to pay caution-money in cash; they should give security instead. And for this reason: the State either keeps the money in specie (withdrawing it needlessly from circulation), or puts it out to interest at a rate either higher or lower than the rate of interest paid to the official; making an ignoble profit out of its servants in the former case, or paying more than the market price for a loan in the latter, which is folly. Lastly, if at any time the State disposes of the mass of caution-money, it prepares the way, in certain contingencies, for a terrible bankruptcy.

The land-tax was not to be done away with altogether. Rabourdin allowed a very small amount to remain for the sake of keeping the machinery in working order in case of a war. But clearly produce would be free, and manufacturers, finding cheap raw materials, could compete with the foreigner without the insidious aid of protection.

The administration of the departments would be undertaken gratuitously by the well-to-do, a possible peerage being held out as an inducement. Magistrates, and their subaltern, and the learned professions, should receive honours as a recompense. The consideration in which government officials were held would be immensely increased by the importance of their posts and considerable salaries. Each would be thinking of his career, and France would no longer suffer from the pension cancer.

As the outcome of all this, Rabourdin estimated that the expenditure would be reduced to seven hundred millions, while the receipts would amount, as before, to twelve hundred millions of francs. An annual surplus of five millions could be made to tell more effectually on the Debt than the paltry Sinking Fund, of which the fallacy had been clearly shown. By establishing a Sinking Fund, the State became a fundholder, as well as a landowner and manufacturer. Lastly, to carry out his project without undue friction, and to avoid a St. Bartholomew of employés, Rabourdin asked for twenty years.

These were the matured ideas of the man whose place had been given to the incompetent M. de la Billardière. A scheme so vast in appearance, yet so simple in the working, a project which swept away more than one great official staff, and suppressed many an equally useless little place, required continual calculation, accurate statistics, and the clearest proofs to substantiate it. For a long while Rabourdin had studied the budget in its double aspect, that of ways and means on the one side, and expenditure on the other. His wife did not know how many nights he gave to these thoughts.

And yet to have conceived the project and superimposed it on the dead body of the administration was as nothing ; Rabourdin had still to find a minister capable of appreciating his reforms. His success clearly depended upon a quiet political outlook, and the times were still unsettled. He only considered that the Government was finally secure when three hundred deputies had the courage to form themselves into a solid systematic ministerialist majority. An administration established on that basis had been inaugurated since Rabourdin com-

pleted his scheme. The splendour of the time of peace
due to the Bourbons eclipsed the military splendours of
the brilliant days when France was one vast camp
and victories abroad were followed by expenditure and
display at home. After the Spanish campaign, the
Government seemed as if it were surely entering upon
a peaceful era in which good might be done; and,
indeed, but three months before, a new reign had begun
unhampered by any obstacles, and the Liberals of the
Left hailed Charles x. with as much enthusiasm as the
party of the Right. It was enough to deceive the most
clearsighted. Consequently, the moment seemed pro-
pitious to Rabourdin; for if an administration took up
so great a scheme of reform, and undertook to carry it
through, it must of necessity ensure its own continuance
in office.

Never before had Rabourdin seemed more thoughtful
and preoccupied as he walked to his office of a morning,
and came back again at half-past four in the afternoon.
And Mme. Rabourdin, on her side, despairing over her
spoilt life, and weary of working in private for some few
luxuries of dress, had never seemed so sourly discontent.
Still she was attached to her husband; and the shameful
intrigues by which the wives of other officials supple-
mented an inadequate salary, were, in her opinion,
unworthy of a woman so much above the ordinary level.
For this reason she refused to have anything to do with
Mme. Colleville, who was intimate with François
Keller, and gave entertainments which eclipsed the
parties in the Rue Duphot. Célestine took the impassive manner of the political thinker, the mental pre-
occupation of a hard worker for the listless apathy of an
official drudge whose spirit has been broken by routine;
she thought her husband was submitting to the yoke
of the most hateful poverty of all—the poverty of
straitened means that just enables a man to live. She
sighed to think that she should have married a man of

so little energy. And so, about this time, she determined that she would make her husband's fortune for him; at all costs, she would launch him into a higher sphere, and she would hide all the springs of action from him. She set about this task with the originality of conception which distinguished her from other women; she prided herself on rising above their level, on totally disregarding their little prejudices; the barriers that society raises about her sex should not impede her. She would fight fools with their own weapon, so she vowed in her frenzy; she would stake herself upon the issue if there was no other way. In short, she saw things from a height.

The moment was favourable. M. de la Billardière was hopelessly ill, and must die in a few days. If Rabourdin succeeded to the place, his talents (Célestine admitted his administrative ability) would be so well appreciated that the post of Master of Requests (promised before) would be given to him. Then he would be Royal Commissary, and bring forward the measures of the government in the Chamber. How she would help him then! She would be his secretary; if necessary, she would work all night. All this that she might drive a charming calèche in the Bois de Boulogne, and stand on a footing of equality with Mme. Delphine de Nucingen, and raise her salon to a level with Mme. Colleville's, and be invited to high Ministerial solemnities, and gain an appreciative audience. People should call her 'Mme. Rabourdin *de* Something-or-other' (she did not know yet where her estate should be), just as they said Mme. d'Espard, Mme. d'Aiglemont, or Mme. de Carigliano. In short, of all things she would put the odious-sounding name of Rabourdin out of sight.

These secret aspirations produced certain corresponding changes in the house. Mme. Rabourdin began by walking resolutely into debt. She engaged a man-servant and put him into an inconspicuous livery, brown with red pipings. She renewed some of the furniture; papered her rooms afresh, decorated them with a constant succession of flowers, and strewed them with knicknacks then in fashion; while she herself, who used to feel occasional conscientious qualms as to her expenses, no longer hesitated to dress in a manner worthy of her ambitions. The various tradesmen who supplied her with the munitions of war discounted her expectations. She gave a dinner-party regularly every Friday, the guests being expected to call to take a cup of tea on the following Wednesday. And her dinner guests were carefully chosen from among influential deputies and personages who might directly or indirectly promote her interests. People enjoyed those evenings very much; or they professed to do so at any rate, and that is enough to attract guests in Paris. As for Rabourdin, he was so intently occupied with the conclusion of his great labours that he never noticed the outbreak of luxury in his house.

And so it came to pass that the husband and wife, all unknown to each other, were laying siege to the same place and working on parallel lines.

Now there flourished in those days a certain secretary-general, by name Clément Chardin des Lupeaulx, a personage of a kind that is sometimes brought much into evidence for a few years at a time by the tide of political events. Subsequently, if a storm arises, he and his like are swept away again; you may find them stranded on the shore heaven knows how far away. But even so the hulk has a certain air of importance. The traveller wonders whether the wrecked vessel contained valuable merchandise, whether it played a part on some great occasion, took a share in a great sea-fight, or carried the velvet canopy of a throne, or the dead body of a king. At this precise juncture Clément des Lupeaulx (the Lupeaulx had absorbed the Chardin) had reached his apogee. In every life, however illustrious or obscure, in the careers of dumb animals as of secretaries-general, is there not a zenith and a nadir ?—a period when glossiness and sleekness reach a climax, and prosperity reaches its utmost radiance of glory ? In the nomenclature of the fabulist, des Lupeaulx belonged to the Bertrand genus, and his whole occupation consisted in discovering Ratons. As he happens to be one of the principal characters in this drama, he deserves to be described therein, and so much the more fully because the Revolution of July abolished his place; and a secretary-general was an eminently useful institution for a constitutional minister.

It is the wont of the moralist to pour forth his indignation upon transcendent abominations. Crimes for him are deeds that bring a man into the police-courts, social subtleties escape his analysis; the ingenuity which gains its ends with the Code for a weapon is either too high or too low, he has neither magnifying glass nor telescope; he must have good, strong-coloured horrors, abundantly visible to the naked eye. And as he is always occupied, as one may say, with the carnivora, he had no attention to spare for reptiles; so, luckily for the satirists, the fine shades of a Chardin des Lupeaulx are left to them.

Selfish and vain; supple and proud; sensual and gluttonous; rapacious (for he had debts); discreet as a tomb which keeps its own secrets and allows nothing to issue forth to give the lie to the inscription meant to edify the passing traveller; undaunted and fearless in asking favours; amiable and witty in every sense of the latter word; tactful and ironical at need;—the secretary-general was one among the crowd of mediocrities which form the kernel of the political world. As a politician, he was ready to leap gracefully over any stream, however broad; he was the kind of man that can do you more harm with a kiss than by a thrust with

the elbow ; he was a brazen-fronted sceptic that would
go to mass at Saint Thomas d'Aquin's if there was a
fashionable congregation there.   Des Lupeaulx's knowledge consisted in knowing what other people knew ; he
had chosen the profession of eavesdropper, and never did
any of the confraternity pay a more strict attention to
business.   In his care not to arouse suspicion he was
nauseatingly fulsome ; subtle as a perfume, caressing as
a woman in his manners.

Chardin des Lupeaulx had just completed his fortieth
year.   His youth had long been a source of affliction to
him, for he felt instinctively that only as a deputy could
he lay a sure foundation for his fortune.   Does any one
ask how he had made his way ?   In a very simple manner.
Des Lupeaulx was a political Bonneau.   He undertook
commissions of the delicate kind which can neither be
given to a man that respects himself, nor yet to a man
that has lost his self-respect.   Errands of that sort are
usually undertaken by serious persons of somewhat
doubtful authority, whom it is easy to disavow should
occasion require it.   He was continually compromised,
that was his calling ; and whether he failed or succeeded,
he got on equally fast.

The Restoration was a time of compromise ; compromise between man and man, and between accomplished facts and coming events.   In all public business,
in short, there was a perpetual process of give and take.
Des Lupeaulx grasped the idea that authority stood in
need of a charwoman.

Let an old woman once get a footing in a house ;
let her learn how to make the beds and turn them down
to satisfaction ; let her know where the spoons are kept,
where to sweep refuse, where to put the soiled linen,
and where to find it ; let her acquire the arts of pacify-
ing duns and distinguishing the right kind of person to
admit ; let her once gain her footing, I repeat, and such
a woman may have her faults, yet were she toothless,

crooked, uncleanly in her person and habits—nay, were she addicted to the lottery and in the habit of appropriating thirty sous daily for her stakes therein,—her employers are used to her ways, and do not care to part with her.   They will hold counsel on the most delicate family affairs in her presence ; she is on hand to remind them of resources and to scent out secrets ; she brings the rouge-pot and the shawl at the psychological moment; she allows them to scold her, to bundle her downstairs ; but, lo ! next morning, at their awakening, she enters gaily with an excellent cup of broth.   However great a statesman may be, he too needs a charwoman, a factotum with whom he can show himself weak and irresolute ; somebody in whose presence he can carp at his destiny, put questions to himself, and answer them, and screw his courage up to the sticking-point.   Does not the savage get sparks by rubbing a bit of hard wood against a softer piece ?   Many a bright genius is kindled on the same principle.   Napoleon found such a partner of his joys and cares in Berthier, Richelieu in Père Joseph ; des Lupeaulx took up with anybody and everybody. Did a minister fall from power ?   Des Lupeaulx kept on good terms with him, acting as intermediary between the outgoing and incoming member of the government, soothing the former with a parting piece of flattery, and perfuming a first compliment for the latter.   Des Lupeaulx, moreover, understood to admiration those little trifles of which a statesman has no leisure to think. He could recognise a necessity ; he was apt in obedience. He enhanced the value of his knavery by being the first to laugh at it, the better to gain its full price ; and he was always particularly careful to perform services of a kind which were not likely to be forgotten.   When, for instance, people were obliged to cross the gulf fixed between the Empire and the Restoration ; when everybody was looking about for a plank ; while all the curs in the Imperial service were rushing over to the other side with

voluble professions of devotion, des Lupeaulx had raised
large sums of the money-lenders, and was crossing the
frontier. He staked all to win all. He bought up the
most pressing minor debts contracted in exile by His
Majesty Louis xviii.; and being the first in the field, he
contrived to discharge nearly three millions at twenty
per cent., for he had the good luck to operate in the
thick of the events of 1814 and 1815. The profits
were swallowed down by Messieurs Gobseck, Werbrust,
and Gigonnet, the croupiers of the enterprise; but des
Lupeaulx had promised as much to them. He was not
playing a stake, he was venturing the whole bank,
knowing well that Louis xviii. was not the man to
forget such a white-washing.

Des Lupeaulx received the appointment of Master of
Requests; he was made a chevalier of St. Louis and an
officer of the Legion of Honour. Having once gained a
footing, the adroit climber cast about for a way of main-
taining himself on the ladder. He had gained an entrance
into the stronghold, but generals are not wont to keep any
useless mouths for long. And then it was that to his
professions of useful help and go-between he added a
third—he gave gratuitous advice on the internal diseases
of power.

He discovered that the so-called great men of the
Restoration were profoundly unequal to the occasion.
Events were ruling them. He overawed mediocre
politicians by going to them in the height of a crisis
and selling them those watchwords which men of talent
hear as they listen to the future. You are by no means
to suppose that such watchwords originated with des
Lupeaulx himself; if they had, he would have been a
genius, whereas he was simply a clever man. Bertrand
Clément des Lupeaulx went everywhere, collecting
opinions, fathoming men's inner consciousness, and
catching the sounds they gave forth. Like a genuine
and indefatigable political bee, he gathered knowledge

from all sources. He was a *Bayle's Dictionary* in flesh
and blood, but he improved upon his famous prototype;
he gathered all opinions, but he did not leave others to
draw their own conclusions, and he had the instinct
of the blue-fly; he dropped down straightway upon
the most succulent morsels of meat in the kitchen.

For which reasons des Lupeaulx was supposed to be
indispensable to statesmen. Indeed, the idea took so
deep a root in people's minds, that ambitious and successful men judged it expedient to compromise des Lupeaulx,
lest he should rise too high, and indemnified him for his
lack of importance in public by using their interest for
him in private.

Nevertheless, as soon as this fisher of ideas felt that
he was generally supported, he had insisted upon earnest-
money. He drew his pay as a staff officer of the National
Guard, in which he held a sinecure at the expense of the
city of Paris; he was a government commissioner for the
superintendence of a joint-stock company, and an in-
spector in the Royal Household. His name appeared
twice besides in the civil list as a Secretary-General and
Master of Requests. At this moment it was his ambition
to be a commander of the Legion of Honour, a gentleman of the bed-chamber, a count, and a deputy; but for
this last position he had not the necessary qualifications.
A deputy in those days was bound to pay a thousand
francs in taxes, and des Lupeaulx's miserable place in
the country was scarcely worth five hundred francs
a year. Where was he to find the money to build
a country-house; to surround it with respectable estates,
and throw dust in the eyes of his constituents?

At the opening of this Scene he had scarce anything
to call his own save a round thirty thousand francs
worth of debts, to which nobody disputed his title.
Des Lupeaulx dined out every day. For nine years
he had been housed at the expense of the State, and
the ministers' carriages were at his disposal. Marriage

might set him afloat again, if he could bale out the
waters that threatened to submerge him; but a good
match depended upon advancement, and advancement
depended upon a seat in the Chamber of Deputies.
Casting about for some way of breaking through this
vicious circle, he saw but one expedient—to wit, some
great service to be rendered to the government, or some
profitable bit of jobbery. But conspiracies (alas!) were
played out. The Bourbons, to all appearance, had
triumphed over faction. And as for jobbery!—the Left
benches, unluckily, were doing all that in them lay to
make any government impossible in France; for several
years past their absurd discussions had thrown such a
searching light upon the doings of the government that
good bits of business were out of the question. The last
had been done in Spain, and what a fuss they had made
about it! To crown all, des Lupeaulx had multiplied
difficulties for himself. Believing in the ministers'
friendship for him, he imprudently expressed his desire
to be seated on the ministerial benches. The Ministry
was not slow to perceive the origin of this desire. Des
Lupeaulx meant to strengthen a precarious position, and
to be no longer dependent upon them. It was the revolt
of the hound against the hunter. Wherefore, the
Ministry gave him now a cut or two with the whip,
and now a caress. They raised up rivals unto him. But
des Lupeaulx behaved towards these as a clever courtesan treats new-comers in her profession: he spread
snares, they fell into them, and he made them feel
the consequences pretty promptly. The more he felt
that his position was unsafe, the more he coveted a
permanent berth; but clearly he must not show his
hand. In one moment he might lose everything. A
single stroke of the pen would clip away his colonel's
epaulettes, his controller's place, his sinecure with the
joint-stock company, and his two posts besides, with
their advantages—six salaries in all, cunningly pre-

served in the teeth of the law against cumulative holdings!

Not unfrequently des Lupeaulx would hold out a threat over his minister, as a mistress frightens her lover; he was 'about to marry a rich widow,' and then the minister would coax the dear des Lupeaulx. It was during one of these renewals of love that the secretary-general received a promise of the first vacancy at the Académie des Inscriptions et Belles Lettres. It was enough to keep a horse upon, he said. Clément Chardin des Lupeaulx flourished like a tree set in congenial soil. He found satisfaction for his vices and virtues, his fancies and defects.

Now for the burdens of his day. First of all, out of half a dozen invitations to select the best dinner. This being decided, he went the first thing in the morning to amuse the minister and his wife, and fondle and play with the children. Then he usually worked for an hour or two; which is to say, he spread himself out in a comfortable armchair to read the papers, dictate the gist of a letter, receive all comers in the minister's absence, lay down the rough outline of the day's routine, receive and give promises that meant nothing, and run over petitions with his eyeglass. To these he sometimes affixed his signature, which, being interpreted, meant, 'Do as you like about this; I don't care.' Everybody knew that if des Lupeaulx were really interested in a matter, he would interfere in person. Some confidential chat on delicate topics was vouchsafed to the upper clerks, and he listened to their gossip in return. Every now and again he went to the Tuileries to take orders; then he waited till the minister came back from the Chamber to see if there was any new manœuvre to invent and superintend. Then this ministerial sybarite dressed and dined, and made the round of twelve or fifteen salons between eight in the evening and three in the morning. He talked with journalists

at the Opéra, for with them he was on the best of terms.
There had been a continual exchange of small services.
He gave out his false news and swallowed down theirs;
he prevented them from attacking such and such a
minister on such and such a point—it would give real
pain, he said, to their wives or mistresses.

'Say that the proposed measure is no good, and prove
it if you can; but you must not say that Mariette
danced badly. Put the worst construction, if you like,
upon our love of our neighbour in petticoats, but do not
expose the pranks we played in our salad days. Hang
it all! we have all cut our capers, and we never know
what we may come to as times go. You that are
spicing your paragraphs in the *Constitutionnel* may be a
minister yourself some of these days——'

And des Lupeaulx did the journalists a good turn at
a pinch; he withdrew obstacles put in the way of pro-
ducing a piece; presents or a good dinner were forthcoming at the right moment, and he would promise to
facilitate the conclusion of a piece of business. He
had a liking for literature and patronised the arts. He
had autographs and splendid albums and sketches and
pictures, *gratis*. And he did artists much service by
refraining from doing harm, and supporting them on
occasions when their vanity demanded a satisfaction which
cost him little or nothing. Wherefore he was popular
in the world of journalists, artists, and actors. Both he
and they, to begin with, were infected by the same
vices and the same indolence; and they cut jokes so
merrily at other people's expense over their cups or between two opera dancers—how they should not have
been friends? If des Lupeaulx had not been a secretary-
general, he would have been a journalist; for which
reason des Lupeaulx never received so much as a scratch
through those fifteen years, while epigram was battering
the breach through which insurrection would enter in.

The small fry of the department used to see him

playing at ball in the garden with his lordship's children, and would rack their brains to discover what he did and the secret of his influence; while the *talons rouges*, the courtiers of men in office, looked upon des Lupeaulx as the most dangerous kind of Mephistopheles, and bowed the knee to him, and paid him back with usury the flatteries that he himself was wont to lavish on his betters. Indecipherable as a hieroglyph though he might be for small men, the secretary-general's uses were as plain as a proportion sum to those who had any interest in discovering them. A Prince of Wagram on a small scale to a ministerial Napoleon, he knew all the secrets of party politics; it was his business to sift advice and ideas, and make preliminary reports; he also confirmed week-kneed supporters; he brought in pro-positions and carried them out and buried them; he uttered the 'Yes' or 'No' which the minister was afraid to pronounce. He bore the brunt of the first explosion of despair or anger; he laughed and mourned with his chief. A mysterious link in a chain that con-nected many peoples' interests with the Tuileries, he was discreet as the confessional; sometimes he knew every-thing, sometimes he knew nothing; sometimes he said for the minister what the minister could not say for himself.

With this Hephæstion, in short, the minister might dare to show himself as he was; he could lay aside his wig and false teeth, state his scruples, put on dressing-gown and slippers, unbosom himself of his sins, and lay bare the ministerial conscience.

Not that des Lupeaulx lay exactly on a bed of roses. It was his duty to flatter and advise, to give advice in the guise of flattery, and flattery in the form of advice. Politicians in his profession were apt to look yellow enough; and the constant habit of nodding to signify approval, or to appear to do so, gives a peculiar air to the head. Such men would approve indifferently all that was said before them. Their language bristled with 'buts,' 'howevers,' and 'nevertheless,' and formulas such as 'for my own part,' and 'in your place,' which pave the way to a contrary opinion; they were particularly fond, be it noted, of the expression 'in your place.'

In person, Clément des Lupeaulx might be described as the remains of a fine man: five feet four inches in height, not unconscionably fat, with a complexion warmed by good living, a jaded air, a powdered *Titus*, and small eyeglasses set in a slender frame. He was pre-eminently a blond, as his hand indicated; it was a plump hand like an old woman's, a little too blunt perhaps, and short in the nails—a satrap's hand. His feet were not wanting in distinction.

After five o'clock in the afternoon des Lupeaulx always wore black silk open-work stockings, low shoes, black trousers, a kerseymere waistcoat, an unscented cambric handkerchief, a coat of royal blue, with engraved buttons, and a bunch of orders at his buttonhole. In the morning he appeared in a short closely-buttoned jacket (not inappropriate to an intriguer), and a pair of creaking boots hidden by grey trousers. In this costume his bearing suggested a crafty attorney rather than the demeanour of a minister. His eyes had grown glassy with the use of spectacles, till he looked uglier than he really was, if by accident he removed those aids to weak sight. Shrewd judges of human nature and straightforward men who only feel at ease when truth is spoken, found des Lupeaulx intolerable. His gracious manners skimmed the surface of falsehood; his friendly protestations, and the stale pretty speeches which always seemed fresh for imbeciles, were growing threadbare. Any clearsighted man could see that this was a rotten plank on which it was most desirable not to set foot. And when the fair Célestine Rabourdin deigned to turn her thoughts to making her husband's fortune, she gauged Clément des Lupeaulx pretty accurately, and fell to studying him. Was there still a little sound fibre left ? Would the thin lath bear if one crossed ever so lightly over it, from the office to the division, from eight thousand to twelve thousand francs a year ? She was no ordinary woman. She fancied that she could hold a blackguard politician in play. And so it came to pass that M. des Lupeaulx was to some extent a cause of the extravagant expenditure of the Rabourdin household.

The Rue Duphot, built in the time of the Empire, is remarkable for a good many houses of elegant appearance, and as a rule their interiors are convenient. Mme. Rabourdin's flat was excellently arranged, an advantage which does much to raise the dignity of household life. From a pretty and sufficiently spacious ante-chamber, lighted from the courtyard, you entered the large drawing-room which looked upon the street. Rabourdin's room and his study lay at the further end of this room to the right, and beyond at a right angle was the dining-room which lay to your left as you entered the ante-chamber. A door to the left of the great drawing-room gave admittance to Mme. Rabourdin's bedroom and dressing-room, and behind, at a right angle, was a little room in which her daughter slept. When Mme. Rabourdin was At Home, her bedroom and Rabourdin's cabinet were thrown open. The space enabled her to receive visitors without drawing down ridicule upon herself; her receptions were not like certain unfortunate attempts at evening parties, when the luxury is too evidently assumed for the occasion, and involves a sacrifice of daily habits.

The drawing-room had been newly hung with yellow silk and brown ornaments. Mme. Rabourdin's room was decorated with real Eastern chintz, and the furniture was in the rococo style. Rabourdin's study inherited the discarded drawing-room hangings, which had been

cleaned, and Leprince's fine pictures adorned the walls.
The late auctioneer had picked up some enchanting
Eastern carpets for trifling sums; his daughter now
turned them to account in the dining-room, framing
them in priceless old ebony.   Wonderful Boule side-
boards, also purchased by the late auctioneer, surrounded
the walls, and in the midst stood a tortoise-shell clock-
case inlaid with gleaming brass scroll-work; the first
example of a square-shaped clock which reappeared to
do honour to the seventeenth century.   The air was
fragrant with the scent of flowers; the rooms were
tasteful and full of beautiful things; every little thing
in them was a work of art in itself; everything was
placed to advantage, and in appropriate surroundings.
And Mme. Rabourdin herself, dressed with the simplicity and originality which artists can devise, looked
as though all these pleasant things were a part of her
life; she never spoke of them, she left the charm of
her conversation to complete the effect produced by
the whole.   Thanks to her father, since rococo came
into fashion, Célestine had acquired celebrity.

Des Lupeaulx was accustomed to all sorts of splendour,
sham and real, but Mme. Rabourdin's house was a surprise to him.   An illustration may explain the nature
of the charm that worked upon this Parisian Asmodeus.
Suppose that a traveller had seen all the best beauty of
Italy, Brazil, and India, till he was weary; suppose
that on his return to France his way brought him past
some lovely little lake, the Lake of Orta, under Monte
Rosa, for instance, with its island set in the midst of
quiet waters—a spot coyly hidden and left to nature, a
wild garden, a lonely but not solitary island with its
shapely groves of trees and picturesquely placed statues.
The shores all round about it are half-wild, half-
cultivated; grandeur and unrest encircle it; but within
everything takes human proportions.   Here in miniature
is the world that our traveller has seen already; but

that world has grown modest and pure; its influences
soothe his soul; the delicate charm of the place affects
him as music might; it awakens all kinds of associations
and harmonious echoes. It is a hermitage, and yet it
is life.

It had happened a few days previously that Mme.
Firmiani had spoken to des Lupeaulx of Mme.
Rabourdin. Mme. Firmiani, one of the most charming
women of the Faubourg Saint-Germain, liked Mme.
Rabourdin, and used to receive her at her house, and on
this occasion she had asked des Lupeaulx simply for the
purpose of saying, 'Why do you not call on Mme.
Rabourdin?' (indicating Célestine.) 'Her evening
parties are delightful; and, what is more, her dinners
are—better than mine.' Des Lupeaulx accordingly
allowed a promise to be extracted from him by the fair
Mme. Rabourdin (who raised her eyes to his face for
the first time as she spoke), and went to the Rue
Duphot. Is there any need to say more? Women
have but one stratagem, as Figaro cries; but it never
fails.

Des Lupeaulx dined with this mere chief clerk, and
registered a vow to go again. Thanks to the decorous
and ladylike strategy of the charming woman whom Mme.
Colleville dubbed 'the Célimène of the Rue Duphot,'
he had dined there regularly every Friday for a month
past, and went of his own accord for a cup of tea on
Wednesdays. Only during the last few days, after
much delicate and skilful trying of the ground, Mme.
Rabourdin had come to the conclusion that she had
found the safe and solid spot in the plank. She was sure
now of success. The joy she felt in the depths of her
soul can only be understood in households that know
what it is to wait three or four years for promotion,
and to plan out an increase of comfort when the fondly-
cherished hope shall be realised. What hardships that
hope makes bearable! What prayers are put up to

H

the powers that be! What visits paid to gain the desired end! At last, thanks to her spirited policy, Mme. Rabourdin was to have an income of twenty thousand francs instead of eight. The hour had struck.

'And I shall have managed it very well,' she told herself. 'I have gone to some little expense, but people are not on the look-out for hidden merits in these days; on the contrary, if a man puts himself in evidence by going into society, keeping up his connections and making new ones, he is sure to get on. After all, the ministers and their friends only take an interest in people whom they see, and Rabourdin knows nothing of the world. If I had not got hold of these three deputies, they might very likely have wanted La Billardière's place; but now that they come here, they would feel ashamed to try to take it. They will be our supporters, not our rivals. I have had to flirt a little; it is lucky for me that there was no need to go farther than the first stage with the sort of folly that amuses men.'

But a contest, as yet unforeseen, was about to begin for the place; and its actual commencement may be dated from a ministerial dinner, followed by an evening party of a kind which ministers regard as public. The Minister's wife was standing by the fire, and des Lupeaulx was at her side. As he took his cup of coffee, it occurred to him to include Mme. Rabourdin among the seven or eight really remarkable women in Paris. He had done this before; Mme. Rabourdin, like Corporal Trim's Montero cap, was always coming up in conversation.

'Don't say too much about her, my dear friend, or you will spoil it all,' the Minister's wife returned, half laughingly.

No woman likes to listen to another woman's praises; they one and all keep a word in reserve, so as to put a little vinegar to the panegyric.

'Poor La Billardière won't last long,' remarked His Excellency; 'Rabourdin is the next in succession, he is one of our cleverest men. Our predecessors did not behave well to him, although one of them owed his prefecture of police under the Empire to a certain personage who was paid to use his influence for Rabourdin. Frankly, my dear fellow, you are still young enough yet to be loved for your own sake——'

'If La Billardière's place is Rabourdin's for a certainty, I may be believed if I hold up his wife as a remarkable woman,' returned des Lupeaulx, the irony in His Excellency's tones had not escaped him; 'still, if Mme. la Comtesse cares to judge for herself——'

'I can ask her to my next ball, that is it, is it not? Your remarkable woman would come when certain ladies will be here to quiz us; they will hear "Mme. Rabourdin" announced.'

'But do not they announce Mme. Firmiani at the house of the Minister of Foreign Affairs?'

'A born Cadignan!——' the newly-made Count broke in quickly, with a withering glance at his secretary-general. Neither His Excellency nor his wife was noble. A good many persons thought that something important was going forward. Those who had come to ask favours kept to the other end of the room. When des Lupeaulx came out, the new-made Countess turned to her husband with, 'Des Lupeaulx must be in love, I think.'

'Then it will be for the first time in his life,' returned the Minister, shrugging his shoulders, as who should say that des Lupeaulx was not taken up with such trifles.

Then the Minister beheld a deputy of the Right Centre entering the room, and left his wife to coax over a faltering vote. But it so happened that the deputy was overwhelmed by an unforeseen disaster, and wanted to secure the Minister's influence by coming to announce in strict confidence that he would be forced to send in his resignation in a few days' time. And His Excellency, warned in time, could get his batteries into play before the Opposition had a chance.

The Minister (which is to say, des Lupeaulx) had included among the dinner guests a personage who is practically appointed for life in every government department. This individual, being not a little puzzled to know what to do with himself, and anxious to give himself a countenance, happened to stand planted on both feet with his legs close together, very much after the manner of an Egyptian terminal. He was waiting, near the hearth, for an opportunity of expressing his thanks to the secretary-general; indeed, the abrupt retreat made by that worthy took him by surprise just as he was about to formulate his little compliment. The functionary in question was, in fact, none other than the cashier of the department, the one employé who never shook in his shoes over a change of government. In those days the Chamber did not higgle over the budget as it is wont to do in the present degenerate times; it did not cut down the emoluments of office to effect what may be called 'cheese-paring economies' in kitchen phraseology. Every minister on coming into office received a fixed sum for 'expenses of removal.' It costs as much, alas! to come in as to go out of office; and the installation entails expenses of every sort and description which need not be recorded here. The allowance for expenses used to consist of twenty-five pretty little thousand-franc notes.

When the ordinance appeared in the *Moniteur*, while all officials, great and small, were grouped about their stoves or open hearths, as the case might be, revolving the questions—'What is this one going to do? Will he increase the number of clerks? Or will he dismiss two and take on three?——' while all this was going forward, I say, the placid cashier used to bring out

twenty-five notes and pin them together, engraving a joy-
ful expression meanwhile upon his beadle's countenance.
This done, he skipped up the staircase to the residence, and
was admitted to His Excellency's presence the first thing
in the morning; for servants are wont to confuse the
notions of the power of money with the custodian thereof,
the cash-box with its contents, the idea and its outward
and visible manifestation. The cashier, therefore, always
came upon the ministerial couple in that first blush of
rapture when a statesman is in a benign humour, and a
good fellow for the nonce. In reply to the Minister's
inquiry, 'What do you want?' the cashier produced his
bits of paper, with a speech to the effect that he had
hastened to bring His Excellency the customary indemnity; he then explained the why and wherefore of
the allowance to the astonished and delighted lady, who
never failed to take some portion, and not unfrequently
took the whole. An indemnity for expenses of removal
comes within the province of housekeeping. The
cashier turned his compliment, slipping in a few phrases
for the Minister's benefit. 'If His Excellency vouchsafed to confirm him in his appointment, if he was
satisfied with the purely mechanical service which, etc.,
etc.' And as the man who brings twenty-five thousand
francs is always a good public servant, the cashier never
failed to receive the desired confirmation in a post
whence he watched ministers come and go and come
again for a quarter of a century. Then he would put
himself at madame's disposal; he would bring the
thirteen thousand francs every month at the convenient
time, a little earlier or later as required, and thus, to use
the ancient monastic expression, 'he kept a vote in the
chapter.'

The Sieur Saillard had been a book-keeper at the
Treasury while the Treasury kept books on a system of
double-entry; but the plan was afterwards given up, and
they gave him a cashier's place by way of compensa-

tion. Book-keeping was his one strong point; he was little good at anything else. He was a burly, fat old gentleman, round as a figure o, and simple in the extreme; he walked like an elephant at a measured pace to and from the Place Royale, where he lived in a house of his own. He had a companion on his daily way, in the shape of his son-in-law, M. Isidore Baudoyer, the chief clerk in M. de la Billardière's division, and in consequence Rabourdin's colleague. Baudoyer had married Saillard's only daughter Elizabeth, and, naturally, took up his abode on a floor above his father-in-law. Nobody in the whole department doubted Saillard's stupidity, but nobody at the same time knew how far his stupidity would go; it was so dense that no one could insinuate a question into it; it had no hollow sounding spots; it absorbed everything, and gave nothing out. Bixiou (a clerk of whom mention will presently be made (had drawn a caricature of the cashier, a bewigged head surmounting an egg, with two tiny legs beneath, and the inscription—'Born to pay and receive money without making a mistake. A little less luck, and he would have been a porter at the Bank of France; a little more ambition, and the Government would have thanked him for his services.'

To return to the Minister. At this present moment he was looking fixedly at his cashier, much as he might have gazed at a hat-peg or at the ceiling, without imagining, that is to say, that the peg could hear what he said, or understand a single word.

'I am so much the more anxious that everything should be arranged with the prefect with the utmost secrecy,' His Excellency was saying to the retiring deputy, 'because des Lupeaulx has some idea of the kind. His bit of a place is somewhere in your part of the country, and we don't want him in the House.'

'He has not the electoral qualifications, and he is not old enough,' said the deputy.

'That is so, but you know how Casimir Périer decided with regard to the age limit. As to annual income, des Lupeaulx has something, though it doesn't amount to much; but the law made no provision for increase of landed property, and he might buy more.— Committees give a good foothold to a deputy of the Centre, and we could not openly oppose the goodwill that people would show to serve our dear friend.'

'But where would he find the money to buy land?'

'How did Manuel become the possessor of a house in Paris?' retorted the Minister.

The hat-peg meanwhile was listening, and listening very reluctantly. The two men had lowered their voices and spoke rapidly; but every sound, by some as yet unexplained law of acoustics, reached Saillard's ears. And what were the feelings of that worthy, do you suppose, while he listened to these political confidences? He experienced the most poignant alarm. There are guileless people who are reduced to despair if they appear to be listening to remarks that they are not intended to hear, if they intrude where they are not wanted, or seem to be inquisitive when they are really discreet; and Saillard was one of them. He glided over the carpet in such a sort that when the Minister became aware of his existence, he was half-way across the room. Saillard was a fanatical official. He was incapable of the slightest indiscretion. If His Excellency had but known that the cashier was in his counsel, he would have had no need to do more than say 'Mum.' Saillard saw that the rooms were beginning to fill with courtiers of office, went down to a cab hired by the hour for such costly occasions as this, and returned to the Place Royale.

While old Saillard was making his way across Paris, his beloved Elizabeth and his son-in-law were engaged in playing a virtuous game of boston with the Abbé Gaudron, their director, and a neighbour or two.

Another visitor was also present. This was a certain Martin Falleix, a brassfounder of the Faubourg Saint-Antoine, whom Saillard had set up in business. Falleix, an honest Auvergnat, had come to Paris with his cauldron on his back, and promptly found work with the Brézacs, a firm that bought old châteaux to pull down. At the age of twenty-seven, Martin Falleix, being eager, like every one else, to get on in life, had the good fortune to be taken into partnership by M. Saillard. He was to be the active partner, he was to exploit a patent invention in brassfounding (gold medal awarded at the Exhibition in 1825).

Mme. Baudoyer, whose only daughter was just at the tail-end of her twelfth year (to quote old Saillard), had views of her own upon Falleix, a thick-set, swarthy young fellow, active, sharpwitted, and honest. She was forming him. According to her ideas, the education consisted in teaching the good Auvergnat to play boston, to hold his cards properly, to allow no one to see his hand; to shave and wash his hands with coarse common soap before he came to them; to refrain from swearing, to speak French as they spoke it, to brush his hair erect instead of flattening it down, and to discard shoes for boots, and sackcloth shirts for calico. Only a week since, Elizabeth Baudoyer succeeded in persuading Falleix to give up two huge flat earrings like cask-hoops.

'You are going too far, Mme. Baudoyer,' said he, as she rejoiced over this sacrifice; 'you are getting too much ascendency over me. You make me brush my teeth (which loosens them); before long you will make me brush my nails and curl my hair, and that will never do. They don't like foppery in our line of business.'

Elizabeth Baudoyer, *née* Saillard, was a type that always escapes the artist by the very fact that it is so commonplace. Yet, nevertheless, such figures ought to be sketched, for they represent the lower middle class in Paris, the rank just above the well-to-do artisan.

Their merits are almost defects, and there is nothing lovable about their faults; but their way of life, humdrum and uninteresting though it is, does not lack a certain character of its own.

Elizabeth had a certain puny unwholesome look, which was not good to see. She was barely four feet high, and so thin that her waist measured scarcely half an ell. Her thin features were crowded into the middle of her face; a certain vague resemblance to a weasel was the result. She was thirty years old and more, but she looked more like a girl of sixteen or seventeen. There was little brightness in the china-blue eyes under heavy eyelids and lashes that met the arch of eyebrows. Everything about Elizabeth was insignificant; she had pale flax-coloured hair; the flat shiny surfaces of her forehead seemed to catch the light; her complexion was grey, almost livid in hue. The lower part of her face was triangular rather than oval in shape, but her features, generally speaking, were crooked, and the outlines irregular. Lastly, she had a sub-acid voice, with a pretty enough range of intonations. Elizabeth Baudoyer was the very type of the lower middle-class housewife who counsels her husband at night from her pillow; there is no merit in her virtues, no motive in her ambition, it is simply a development of domestic egoism. If Elizabeth had lived in the provinces, she would have tried to round out the property; as her husband happened to be in a Government office, she wanted advancement. The story of Elizabeth's childhood and girlhood will bring the whole woman before you; it is the history of the Saillard couple.

M. Saillard had married the daughter of a second-hand furniture dealer, one Bidault, who set up business under the arcades of the Great Market. M. and Mme. Saillard had a hard struggle in those early days; but now, after thirty-three years of married life and twenty-nine of work at the office, the fortune of 'the Saillards' (as they

.were called by their acquaintances) consisted of sixty thousand francs in Falleix's business; the big house in the Place Royale, purchased for forty thousand francs in 1804; and thirty-six thousand livres paid down as their daughter's marriage portion. About fifty thousand francs of their capital had come to them on the death of Widow Bidault, Mme. Saillard's mother. Saillard's post had brought in a steady income of four thousand five hundred francs; no one coveted his place for a long while, because there were no prospects of promotion. This money had been saved up, sou by sou, by sordid frugality, and very carefully put out to interest. As a matter of fact, the Saillards knew of but one way of investing money; they used to take their savings, five thousand francs at a time, to their notary, M. Sorbier, Cardot's predecessor, and he arranged to lend it on mortgages. They were always careful to take the first mortgage, with a further guarantee secured on the wife's property if the borrower were a married man.

At this point of their history their big house was worth a hundred thousand francs, and brought them in eight thousand. Falleix paid seven per cent. on his capital before reckoning up the profits, which were equally divided. Altogether, the Saillards possessed an income of seventeen thousand francs at the least. To have the Cross and retire on a pension was old Saillard's one ambition.

Elizabeth's youth had been spent in continual drudgery in a family with such laborious habits and such narrow ideas. Great was the discussion before the purchase of a new hat for Saillard; the career of a coat was reckoned by years; umbrellas were carefully hung up from a brass ring.

No repairs had been made in the house since 1804. The Saillards' ground-floor flat was precisely in the condition in which the previous owners left it; but the gilding had departed from the frames of the pier-glasses, and the painted friezes over the doors were almost invisible beneath the accumulated grime of years. The great spacious rooms, with carved marble chimney-pieces and ceilings worthy of Versailles, were filled with the furniture left by the Widow Bidault. This consisted of easy-chairs of walnut wood, covered with tapestry, rosewood chests of drawers, old-fashioned stands with brass rims and cracked white marble-tops; and a chaos of bargains, in short, picked up by the furniture-dealer in the Great Market. Among these was a superb Boule bureau, to which fashion had not yet restored its proper value. The pictures had been selected entirely for their handsome frames; the chinaware was distinctly heterogeneous; a set of splendid Oriental china dessert plates, for instance, was eked out with porcelain from every possible factory; the silver was a collection of odd lots; the cut-glass was old-fashioned; the table linen fine damask. They slept in a tomb-shaped bedstead with chintz curtains hung from a coronal.

Amid all these relics of the past, Mme. Saillard used to live in her low, modern mahogany armchair with her feet on a footwarmer, every hole in the latter article of furniture charred and blackened. Her chair was drawn up to the grate, where a heap of dead ashes took the place of a fire. On the chimney-piece there stood a clock-case, one or two old-fashioned bronze ornaments, and some flowered candle-sconces. These last were empty however. Mme. Saillard had a *martinet* for her own use, a small, flat brass candlestick with a long handle; and the candles she used were long tallow dips that guttered as they burned. In Mme. Saillard's countenance, in spite of wrinkles, you could read wilfulness, severity, and narrowmindedness; together with a fair and square honesty, a pitiless creed, an undisguised stinginess, and the quiet of a clear conscience. You may see faces thus composed by nature among portraits of the wives of Flemish burgomasters; but these latter are clad in splendid velvets and precious stuffs. Mme. Saillard wore no such robes. She adhered to the old-fashioned garments known as *cottes* in Picardy and Touraines, and as *cotillons* over the rest of France—a petticoat gathered in thick overlying pleats at the back and sides. The upper part of her person was buttoned into a short jacket, another bit of old-world costume, like the butterfly caps and high-heeled shoes which she still continued to wear. She knitted stockings for herself and her husband and for an uncle as well. And although she was fifty-seven years old, and fairly entitled to live at ease after her laborious struggles with domestic economy, she used to knit, after the manner of countrywomen, as she talked or went about the house, or strolled round the garden, or took a peep into the kitchen to see how things were going there.

Niggardliness, at first compelled by painful necessity, had become a habit with the Saillards. When old Saillard came home from the office he took off his coat and worked in his garden. It was a pretty garden divided off from the yard by an iron railing; he had reserved it and kept it in order himself. Elizabeth had gone marketing with her mother in the morning; and, indeed, the two women did all the work of the house. The mother could cook a duck with turnips to admiration; but old Saillard maintained that for serving up the remains of a leg of mutton with onions, Elizabeth had not her equal. 'You could eat your uncle that way and never find it out.'

As soon as Elizabeth could hold a needle, her mother made her mend her father's clothes and the house linen. The girl was always busy as a servant over a servant's work; she never went out alone. They lived but a few paces away from the Boulevard du Temple; consequently, the Gaîté, the Ambigu-Comique, and Franconi's were close at hand, and the Porte Saint-Martin not very far away, yet Elizabeth had never been 'to the play.' When the fancy took her ' to see what it was like,' M. Baudoyer, by way of doing things handsomely, took her to the Opéra so that she might see the finest play of all (M. Gaudron having, of course, given permission). They were giving *Le Laboureur Chinois* at that time. Elizabeth thought 'the play' as dull as ditchwater. She did not want to go again. On Sundays, after she had gone four times to and fro between the Place Royale and the Church of St. Paul (for her mother saw that she was punctual in the practice of religious duties and precepts), her father and mother took her to the Café Turc, where they seated themselves on chairs placed between a barrier and the wall. The Café Turc at that time was the resort of all the beauty and fashion of the Marais, the Faubourg Saint-Antoine, and adjacent neighbourhoods ; the Saillards always went early to secure their favourite place, and then amused themselves by watching the passers-by.

Elizabeth had never worn anything but print gowns in summer, and merino in winter. She made her own dresses. Her mother only allowed her twenty francs a month; but her father was very fond of her, and tempered this rigour with occasional presents. Of ' profane literature,' as the Abbé Gaudron (curate of Saint Paul's and the family oracle) was pleased to qualify it, Elizabeth knew nothing whatsoever. The system had borne its fruits. Compelled to find an outlet for her feelings in some passion, Elizabeth grew greedy of gain ; not that she was lacking in intelligence or perspicacity, but ignorance and her creed had shut her in with a circle of brass. She had nothing on which to exercise her faculties, save the most trivial affairs of daily life ; and as she had few things to think about, the whole force of her nature was brought to bear on the matter in hand. Her natural intelligence, being shackled by her religious opinions, could only exert itself within the limits imposed by casuistry, and casuistry becomes a very storehouse of subtleties from which self-interest selects shifts and evasions. Elizabeth was quite capable of asking her neighbour to do evil that she herself might reap the full benefit thereof; resembling in this respect various saintly personages in whom religion has not altogether extinguished ambition—with these, indeed, she had other points in common; she was relentless in pursuit of her end, underhand in her measures. When offended, she watched her antagonists with feline patience till she had accomplished a complete and cold-blooded revenge to be put down to the account of Providence.

Until the time of Elizabeth's marriage, the Saillards saw no visitors except the Abbé Gaudron, the Auvergnat priest, nominated to the curacy of St. Paul's since the re-establishment of religious worship. This churchman had been friendly with the late Mme. Bidault. Mme. Saillard's paternal uncle was also an occasional visitor. He had been a paper merchant, but he had retired in the year II. of the Republic, at the age of sixty-nine. He never came except on Sundays, because no business could be done on that day.

As for Bidault's personal appearance, there was not much room in the little old man's olive-hued visage for anything but a red bibulous nose and two little vulture-like slits of eyes. His grizzled locks were allowed to hang loose under the brim of his cocked hat. The tabs of his knee-breeches projected grotesquely beyond the buckles. He wore cotton stockings knitted by his niece (la petite Saillard he used to call her), thick shoes with silver buckles, and a greatcoat of many colours. Altogether he looked very much like the sexton-beadle-bellringer-gravedigger-chanter of some village church; a sort of person whom you might take for some freak of the caricaturist, until you met him in real life. Even at this day he used to come on foot to dine with them, and walk back afterwards to the Rue Grenétat, where he lived on a third floor. Bidault was a bill-discounter. The Quartier Saint-Martin, the scene of his professional activity, had nicknamed him Gigonnet, from his peculiar jerky, feverish manner of picking his way in the streets. M. Bidualt went into the bill-discounting line in the year II. of the Republic with a Dutchman, the Sieur Werbrust, a crony of Gobseck's, for his partner.

These, it has been said, were at one time the Saillards' only visitors; but afterwards, old Saillard struck up an acquaintance with M. and Mme. Transon in the church-warden's pew at St. Paul's. The Transons, wholesale earthenware dealers in the Rue de Lesdiguières, took an interest in Elizabeth, and it was with a view to find-ing a husband for her that they introduced young Isidore Baudoyer to the Saillards. The good under-standing between M. and Mme. Baudoyer and the Saillard family was confirmed by Gigonnet's approba-tion. He had employed Mme. Baudoyer's brother, the Sieur Mitral, as his bailiff for many years; and about this time Mitral was thinking of retiring to a pretty house at Ile-Adam. M. and Mme. Baudoyer, Isidore's father and mother, respectable leather-dressers in the Rue Censier, had put by a little money year by year in a jog-trot business. When they had married their only son and made over fifty thousand francs to him, they also thought of going to live in the country; it was they, indeed, who had fixed upon Ile-Adam, and attracted Mitral to that spot; but they still came fre-quently to Paris, where they had kept a *pied-à-terre* in the house in the Rue Censier which Isidore received on his marriage. The Baudoyers had an income of a thousand crowns still left after providing for their son.

M. Mitral, owner of a sinister-looking wig, and a visage the colour of Seine water, illuminated by eyes of the hue of Spanish snuff, was as cool as a well-rope; he was a secretive, mouse-like creature; no one knew

about his money; but he probably did in his corner as
Gigonnet did in the Quartier Saint-Martin.

But if the family circle grew wider, their ideas and
habits underwent no corresponding change. They kept
all the family festivals; birthdays and wedding-days;
all the saints' days of father and mother, son-in-law,
daughter and granddaughter; Easter, Christmas, New
Year's Day, and Twelfth Night. And as these occasions
always demanded a great sweeping and general cleaning
of the house, they might be said to combine practical
utility with the joys of domestic life. Then out came
the presents; useful gifts produced with much pomp
and circumstance and accompaniment of bouquets; a
pair of silk stockings or a velvet skull-cap for Saillard;
gold earrings, or silver plate for Elizabeth or her husband
(for whom they were making up a complete service by
degrees), or a new silk petticoat for Mme. Saillard, who
kept the stuff laid by in the piece. And before the
presents were given, the recipient was always made to
sit in an armchair, while the rest bade him —

'Guess what we are going to give you!'

Finally, they sat down to a grand dinner, which lasted
for five hours. M. Gaudron was invited, and Falleix
and Rabourdin and M. Gothard (formerly M. Baudoyer's
deputy), and M. Bataille, captain of the company in
which Baudoyer and his father-in-law were enrolled.
M. Cardot had a standing invitation, but, like Rabourdin,
he only appeared one time in six. They used to sing
over the dessert, and embrace each other with enthusiasm amid wishes for all possible good luck; and then
the presents were on view, and all the guests must give
their opinion of them. On the day of the velvet skull-
cap, Saillard wore the article in question on his head
during the dessert, to the general satisfaction. In the
evening more acquaintances came in, and a dance followed. A single violin did duty for a band for a long
while; but for the last six years, M. Godard, a great

amateur of the flute, had contributed the shrill sounds of a flageolet to the festivity. The cook, Mme. Baudoyer's general servant, and old Catherine, Mme. Saillard's maid, stood looking on in the doorway with the porter and his wife; and a crown of three livres was given to them to buy wine and coffee.

The whole family circle regarded Baudoyer and Saillard as men of transcendent ability; they were in the employ of the Government; they had made their way by sheer merit; they worked in concert with the Minister, so it was said; they owed their success entirely to their talents. Baudoyer was generally considered to be the more capable man of the two, because his work as chief clerk was allowed to be more arduous and complex than book-keeping. And besides, Isidore had had the genius to study, although he was the son of a leather dresser in the Rue Censier; he had had the audacity also to give up his father's business to enter a Government office, and had reached a high position. As he was a man of few words, he was supposed to be a deep thinker; 'he would perhaps represent the eighth arrondissement some day,' said the Transons. And as often as Gigonnet heard this kind of talk, he would purse up lips that were sufficiently pinched already, and glance at his grand-niece Elizabeth.

As to physique, Isidore was a big heavy man of seven-and-thirty; he perspired easily; his head suggested hydrocephalus. It was an enormous head covered with closely cropped chestnut hair, and joined to the neck by a thick fleshy roll that filled up his coat collar. He had the arms of a Hercules, the hands of a Domitian, and a waist girth which sober living kept 'within the limits of the majestic,' to quote Brillat-Savarin. In face he was very much like the Emperor Alexander. You recognised the Tartar type in the little eyes, in a nose depressed in the middle and raised at the tip, in the silly lips and short chin. His forehead was narrow

I

and low. Isidore was of lymphatic temperament, but time had no whit abated an excessive conjugal attachment. In spite of his likeness to the handsome Russian Emperor and the terrific Domitian, Isidore Baudoyer was nothing but a slave of red-tape; he was not very fit for the post of chief clerk, but he was thoroughly accustomed to the routine work, and his vacuity lay beneath such a thick covering that no scalpel as yet had probed it. He had displayed the patience and sagacity of the ox during those days of hard study; and this fact, together with his square head, had deceived his relatives. They took him for a man of extraordinary abilities.

At the office he was punctilious, pedantic, pompous, and fussy; a perfect terror to his clerks. He was always making observations for their benefit, always insisting upon commas and full stops, always a stickler for rules and regulations, and so terribly punctual that not one of the clerks failed to be in his place before he came in.

Baudoyer used to wear a coat of cornflower blue with yellow buttons, a buff waistcoat, grey trousers, and a coloured stock. He had big feet, and his boots fitted him badly. His watch chain was adorned with a huge bunch of seals and trinkets, among which he still retained the 'American seeds' which used to be the fashion in the year VII.; and this in 1824!

The restraints of religion and rigid habits of life were forces that bound this family together; they had, moreover, one common aim to unite them—the thought of making money was the compass which guided their course. Elizabeth Baudoyer was obliged to commune with herself for lack of any one to comprehend her ideas; for she felt that she was not among equals who could understand them. Facts had compelled her to form her own conclusions of her husband, but as a woman of rigid principle she did her best to keep up M. Baudoyer's reputation; she showed profound respect for him, honouring in him the father of her child and her husband; the 'temporal power,' in short, as the Abbé Gaudron put it. For which reason she would have thought it a deadly sin to allow a stranger to read her real opinion of her vapid mate in any glance, or gesture, or word. She even professed a passive obedience to his will in all things. Rumours of the outer world reached her ears, she noted them and made her own comparisons; and so sound was her judgment of men and affairs, that she became an oracle in private for the two functionaries. Indeed, at the time when this history begins, they had unconsciously reached the point of doing nothing without consulting her.

'She is a sharp one, is Elizabeth!' old Saillard used to say ingenuously. But Baudoyer was too much of a fool not to be puffed up by his ill-founded reputation in the Quartier Saint-Antoine. He would not allow that his wife was clever, while he turned her cleverness to account. Elizabeth felt convinced that her uncle Bidault, *alias* Gigonnet, must be a rich man, a capitalist with an enormous turnover. By the light of self-interest, she read des Lupeaulx better than the Minister read him. She saw that she was mated with a fool; she shrewdly suspected that life might have been something very different for her; but she preferred to leave that might-have-been unexplored. All the gentle affections of Elizabeth's nature found satisfaction in her daughter; she spared her little girl the drudgery that she had known; she loved her child, and thought that this was all that could be expected of her. It was for that daughter's sake that she had persuaded her father to take the extraordinary step of going into partnership with Falleix. Falleix had been introduced to the family by old Bidault, who lent him money on pledges. But Falleix found his old fellow countryman too dear; he complained with much candour before the Saillards that Gigonnet was asking eighteen per cent. of an Auvergnat. Old Mme. Saillard went so far as to reproach her relative.

'It is just because he is an Auvergnat that I only ask eighteen per cent. !' retorted Gigonnet. It was about that time that Falleix, aged twenty-eight, had hit upon a new invention. It seemed to Saillard, to whom he explained it, that the young man 'talked straight' (to use an expression from Saillard's dictionary), and that there was a fortune to be made out of his idea. Elizabeth at once conceived the notion of keeping Falleix to 'simmer' for her daughter, and forming her son-in-law herself. She was looking seven years ahead. Martin Falleix's respect for Mme. Baudoyer knew no bounds; he recognised her intellectual superiority. If he had made millions, he would still have been devoted to the house, where he was made one of the family circle. Elizabeth's little girl had been taught already to fill his glass prettily and to take his hat when he came.

When M. Saillard came home after the Minister's dinner party, the game of boston was in full swing. Elizabeth was advising Falleix; old Mme. Saillard, knitting in the fireside corner, was looking over the curate's hand; and M. Baudoyer, impassive as a milestone, was exerting his intelligence to discover where the cards were. Mitral sat opposite. He had come up from Ile-Adam for Christmas. Nobody moved when Saillard came in. For several minutes he walked up and down the room, his broad countenance puckered by unwonted mental exercise.

'It is always the way when he dines with the Minister; luckily, it only happens twice a year, or they would just kill him outright,' remarked Mme. Saillard. 'Saillard was not made to be in the government——' Aloud she added, 'Saillard, I say, I hope you are not going to keep your best clothes on, your silk breeches, and Elbeuf cloth coat? Just go and take your things off; don't wear them out here for nothing; *ma mère.*'

'There is something the matter with your father,' Baudoyer remarked to his wife, when the cashier had gone to change his clothes in his fireless room.

'Perhaps M. de la Billardière is dead,' Elizabeth returned simply; 'he is anxious that you should have the place, and that worries him.'

'If I can be of service to you in any way, command me,' said the curate of Saint Paul's, with a bow; 'I have the honour to be known to Mme. la Dauphine. In our times all offices should be filled by devoted subjects and men of staunch religious principle.'

'Oh come!' said Falleix; 'do men of merit want patronage if they are to get on in your line? I did the right thing when I turned brassfounder; custom comes to find you out if you make a good article.'

'The Government, sir, is the Government,' interrupted Baudoyer; 'never attack it here.'

'You are talking like the *Constitutionnel*, in fact,' said the curate.

'Just the sort of thing the *Constitutionnel* always says,' assented Baudoyer, who never saw the paper.

The cashier fully believed that his son-in-law was as much Rabourdin's superior in intellect 'as God was above St. Crispin' (to use his own expression); still, the good soul's desire for the step was a guileless wish. He wanted success; he wanted it as all employés want their step, with a vehement, intense, unreflecting, brutal desire to get on; but, at the same time, he must have it, as he wished to have the Cross of the Legion of Honour, to wit, entirely through his own merits, and with a clear conscience. To his way of thinking, if a man had sat for twenty-five years behind a grating in a public office, he might be said to have given his life for his country, and had fairly earned the Cross. He could think of no way of serving the interests of his son-in-law, save by putting in a word for him with the Minister's wife when he took her the monthly stipend.

'Well, Saillard, you look as if you had lost all your relatives! Speak out, my boy, pray tell us something,' cried Mme. Saillard when he came in again.

Saillard turned on his heel, with a sign to his daughter, intimating that politics were forbidden while visitors were present.

When M. Mitral and the curate had taken their departure, Saillard pushed back the table, and sat down in his armchair. He had a way of seating himself which meant that a piece of office gossip was about to be communicated; a sequence of movements as unmistakable as the three raps on the stage at the Comédie-Française. First of all, he pledged his wife and daughter and son-in-law to the most profound secrecy (for however mild the gossip might be, their places, so he was wont to say, depended upon their discretion); then he brought out his incomprehensible riddle. How a deputy was about to resign; how the secretary-general, very reasonably, wanted to be nominated to succeed him; how the Minister was privately thwarting the wish of one of his firmest supporters and most zealous servants; and lastly, how the age limit and pecuniary qualifications had been discussed. Then came an avalanche of conjectures, washed away by a torrent of arguments on the part of the two officials, who kept up an exchange of ponderous banalities. As for Elizabeth, she asked but three questions.

'If M. des Lupeaulx is for us, can he carry Baudoyer's nomination?'

'*Quien!* Begad, he could!' cried the cashier.

Elizabeth pondered this. 'In 1814, Uncle Bidault and his friend Gobseck obliged him,' she thought. Aloud she asked, 'Is he still in debt?'

'Yes-s-s,' said the cashier, with a doleful prolongation of the final sibilant. 'They tried to attach his salary, but they were stopped by an order from headquarters, an injunction at sight.'

'Then, where is his estate of the Lupeaulx?'

'*Quien!* begad! Your grandfather and great-uncle Bidault came from the place, so did Falleix; it is not far from the arrondissement of this deputy that is coming off guard——'

When her colossus of a husband was in bed, Elizabeth bent over him, and though he had sneered at her questions for 'crotchets,' she said—

'Dear, perhaps you are going to have M. de la Billardière's place.'

'There you are again with your fancies!' cried Baudoyer. 'Just leave M. Gaudron to speak to the Dauphiness, and don't meddle with the office.'

At eleven o'clock, just as all was quiet in the Place Royale, M. des Lupeaulx left the Opéra to go to the Rue Duphot. It chanced to be one of Mme. Rabourdin's most brilliant Wednesdays. A good many frequenters of her house had come in after the theatre to swell the groups already assembled in her rooms, and many celebrities were there: Canalis the poet, the painter Schinner, Dr. Bianchon, Lucien de Rubempré, Octave de Camps, the Comte de Granville, the Vicomte de Fontaine, du Bruel, writer of vaudevilles, Andoche Finot the journalist, Derville, one of the longest-headed lawyers of the day; the Comte du Châtelet, and du Tillet the banker, were all present, with several young men of fashion like Paul de Manerville and the young Vicomte de Portenduère.

Célestine was dispensing tea when the secretary-general came in. Her dress suited her well that evening. She wore a perfectly plain black velvet gown and a black gauze scarf; her hair was carefully smoothed beneath a high coronet of plaits, ringlets in the English fashion fell on each side of her face. Her chief distinction was an artist's Italian negligence, the ease with which she understood everything, and her gracious way of welcoming her friends' least wishes. Nature had given her a slender figure, so that she could turn swiftly at the first questioning word; her eyes were Oriental in shape, and obliquely set in Chinese fashion, so that they could glance sidewards. Her soft, insinuating voice was so well under control, that she could throw a caressing charm into every word, even her most spontaneous utterances; her feet were such as you only see in portraits, for in this one respect painters may flatter their sitters without sinning against the laws of anatomy. Like most brunettes, she looked a little sallow by day-light, but at night her complexion was dazzling, setting off her dark eyes and hair. Lastly, the firm, slender outlines of her form put an artist in mind of the Venus of the Middle Ages discovered by Jean Goujon, the great sculptor favoured by Diane de Poitiers.

Des Lupeaulx stopped in the doorway, and leant his shoulder against the frame. He was accustomed to spy out men's ideas; he could not refuse himself the pleasure of spying a woman's feelings; for Célestine interested him far more than any woman had done before. And des Lupeaulx had reached an age when men claim much from women. The first white hairs are the signal for the last passions; and these are the most tumultuous of all, for they are stimulated by the last heat of youth and the sense of exhaustion. The fortieth year is the age for follies, the age when a man desires to be loved for his own sake. To love at forty is no longer sufficient in itself, as it used to be when he was young, and could be happy in falling in love at random in Cherubino's fashion. At forty nothing less than all will satisfy a man, and he is afraid lest he should obtain nothing; whereas at five-and-twenty, he has so much, that it is not worth while to exert his will. There is so much strength to spare at five-and-twenty, that it may be squandered with impunity; but at forty a man takes abuse of strength for vigour. The thoughts that filled des Lupeaulx's mind at this moment were surely melancholy ones, for the elderly beau's countenance had visibly lengthened; the agreeable smile which lent expression to his face, and did duty as a mask, had ceased to contract his features; the real man was visible; it was not a pleasant sight. Rabourdin noticed it.

'What has come to him?' he wondered. 'Is he in disgrace?' But the secretary-general was merely reflecting that he had been dropped once before somewhat too promptly by pretty Mme. Colleville, whose intentions had been precisely the same as Célestine's own. Rabourdin also saw that the would-be statesman's eyes were fixed upon his wife; and he made a note of their expression in his memory. Rabourdin was too clearsighted an observer not to see through des Lupeaulx; indeed, he felt the most thorough contempt for the secretary-general; but if a man is much engrossed by some pursuit, his feelings are less apt to rise to the surface, and mental absorption in the work that he loves is equivalent to the cleverest dissimulation of his attitude of mind. For this reason, Rabourdin's opinions were like a sealed book to des Lupeaulx. The chief clerk was displeased by the upstart politician's presence in his house; but he had not cared to cross Célestine's will. He happened to be chatting confidentially at the moment with a supernumerary, a young clerk destined to play a part in the intrigue set on foot by La Billardière's approaching death, so that it was but a wandering attention that he gave to Célestine and des Lupeaulx.

Some account of the supernumerary ought perhaps to be given here for the benefit of our nephews, and, at the same time, for the edification of foreign readers.

The supernumerary is to the administration what the chorister boy is to the church; what the child of the company is to the regiment, or the 'rat' to the theatre — an ingenuous, innocent being, a creature blinded by illusions. How far should we go without illusions? On the strength of illusions we struggle with the difficulties of art while we scarce keep the wolf from the door, we digest the rudiments of the sciences with faith drawn from the same source. Illusions mean unbounded faith, and the supernumerary has faith in the administration. He does not take it for the unfeeling, cold-blooded, hard-hearted system that it is.

Of supernumeraries, there are but two kinds—the well-to-do and the poor. The poor supernumerary is rich in hope, and needs a berth; the well-to-do super-numerary is poor in spirit, and has need of nothing. No well-to-do family is so simple as to put a man of brains into the administration. The well-to-do supernumerary is usually committed to the care of a senior clerk, or placed under the eye of a director-general, to undergo his initiation into the 'pure comedy' of the civil service, as it would be styled by that profound philosopher Bilboquet. The horrors of probation are mitigated for him until he receives a definite appointment. Government offices are never afraid of the well-to-do super-numerary. The clerks all know that he is not at all dangerous; he aims at nothing short of the highest places in the service.

At this time many families were asking, 'What shall we do with our boys?' There were no chances of getting on in the army. Special careers, such as the navy, the mines, civil and military engineering, and professorships, are either hedged about with regula-tions, or closed by competition; whereas the rotatory movement which metamorphoses clerks in a government office into prefects, sub-prefects, or receivers and controllers of taxes, and the like (in much the same way as the little figures revolve in a magic-lantern),—this movement, to repeat, is subject to no rules, and there are no terms to keep. Through this hole in the administrative system, therefore, behold the well-to-do supernumeraries emerge; these are young men who drive cabs about town, and wear good clothes and moustaches, and behave, one and all of them, as insolently as any self-made upstart. The well-to-do supernumerary was almost invariably a nephew or a cousin or a relative of some minister, or civil servant, or of a very influential peer. Journalists used to be pretty hard upon him; not so the established clerks; they aided and abetted the young gentleman, and made interest with him.

But the poor supernumerary (the only genuine kind) is, in nearly every case, a widow's son. His father before him probably was a clerk in a government office; his mother lives on a meagre pension, and starves herself to support her boy till he can get a permanent post as copying clerk; she dies while he is within sight of that marshal's bâton of the profession—the post of draughting clerk, with a prospect of drawing up reports and formulating orders for the term of his natural life, or even a problematical chance of becoming a senior clerk. This kind of supernumerary always lives in some neighbourhood where rents are low, and leaves it at an early hour. For him the state of the weather is the real Eastern Question. He must walk the whole way to the office, and keep his boots clean, and take care of his clothes; he must make allowance for the time that he is like to lose if a heavy shower forces him to take shelter. The supernumerary has plenty to think about! Pavements in the streets and flagstones along the quays and boulevards were boons indeed for him. If any strange chance should bring you out into the streets of Paris between half-past seven and eight o'clock of a winter morning, when there is a sharp frost, or the weather is generally unpleasant; and if, furthermore, you happen to see a pallid, timorous youth walking along without a cigar in his mouth—look at his pocket; you are pretty sure to discover the outlines of the roll which his mother gave him when he left home, so that he might hold out, without damage to his internal economy, through the nine long hours that separate breakfast from dinner. The period of unsophisticated innocence is, however, but short. By the light of a very little knowledge of life in Paris, a lad soon acquires a notion of the awful distance between a supernumerary and a copying clerk; a distance which neither Archimedes, nor Newton, nor Pascal, nor Leibnitz, nor Kepler, nor Laplace, nor any other mathematician can compute. It is the difference between zero and the unit, between a problematical bonus and a regularly paid salary. The supernumerary accordingly is pretty quick to see the impossibilities of the career; he hears the talk of the clerks; they explain to him how So-and-so was promoted over their heads. By and by he discovers the intrigues of government offices; he finds out how his superiors were promoted, and the extraordinary circumstances that led to their success. One, for instance, married a young lady with a past; another took to wife the natural daughter of a minister; yet another took a heavy responsibility upon his shoulders; while a fourth, an extremely able man, imperilled his health with working like a galley-slave; but this last employé had the perseverance of a mole, and not every man feels himself capable of performing such feats. Everything is known in the office. Sometimes an incompetent man has a wife with plenty of brains; she brought him thus far; it was she who secured his nomination as a deputy; and though he has no capacity for work, he can intrigue in a small way in the Chamber. So-and-so has an intimate friend in a statesman's wife. Such-an-one is in league with a formidable journalist.

Then the supernumerary is disgusted and hands in his resignation. Three-fourths of the supernumeraries leave before they secure permanent berths. Those that remain are either dogged young men or simpletons that say to themselves, 'I have been here for three years, I shall get a berth if I stay on long enough!' or those that feel conscious of a vocation. Clearly the supernumerary is, in the administration, pretty much what the novice is in religious orders. He is passing through his probation, and the trial is severe. In the course of it the State discovers the men that can bear hunger and thirst and want without giving way under the strain; men whom drudgery does not disgust; the temperament that will accept the horrible life, the disease, if you prefer it, of a Government office. The supernumerary system from this point of view, so far from being a scandalous attempt on the part of the Government to get work done for nothing, might fairly be regarded as a beneficent institution.

The young fellow with whom Rabourdin was speaking was a poor supernumerary, by name Sébastien de la Roche. He had walked on tiptoe from the Rue du Roi Doré, in the Marais, but there was not the slightest speck of mud on his clothes. He spoke of his 'mamma,' and dared not lift his eyes to look at Mme. Rabourdin. Her house seemed to him to be a second Louvre. His poor mother had given him a five-franc piece in case it should be absolutely necessary to play; admonishing him, at the same time, to take nothing, to stand the whole time, and to be very careful not to upset a lamp or any of the pretty trifles on the whatnots. He was dressed entirely in black; his gloves had been cleaned with indiarubber, and he exhibited them as little as possible. His fair complexion and bright hazel eyes, with gleams of gold in them, suited well with his thick red-brown hair. Now and again the poor boy would steal a glance at Mme. Rabourdin. 'What a beautiful woman!' he said to himself; and when he went home that night, he thought of the fairy till sleep closed his eyes.

Rabourdin saw that Sébastien had the making of a good clerk in him; and as he took his position of supernumerary seriously, the chief clerk was very much

interested in the poor boy. And not only so, he had
made a pretty correct guess at the poverty in the home
of a poor widow with a pension of seven hundred francs;
Sébastien had not long left school, his education must
necessarily have eaten into her savings. So Rabourdin
had been quite like a father to the supernumerary; he
had often gone out of his way at the board to get a
bonus for him; sometimes, indeed, he had paid the
money out of his own pocket when the argument had
grown too warm with the distributors of favour.

Then he heaped work upon Sébastien; he was training
him; he made him fill du Bruel's place; and du Bruel,
a playwright known to the dramatic world and the
public by the pseudonym of de Cursy, paid Sébastien a
hundred crowns out of his salary. Mme. de la Roche
and her son regarded Rabourdin as a great man, a
guardian angel and a tyrant blended in one; all their
hopes depended on him. Sébastien always looked forward to the time when he should be an established
clerk. Ah! it is a great day for the supernumerary
when he signs his receipt for his salary for the first time.
Many a time he has fingered the money for the first
month, and the whole of it is not paid over to the
mother. Venus smiles upon these first payments from
the ministerial cash-box. This hope could only be
realised for Sébastien by M. Rabourdin, his only protector; and accordingly, the lad's devotion to his chief
was unbounded. Twice a month he dined in the Rue
Duphot; but only with the family, and Rabourdin
always brought him home. Madame never gave him
an invitation except to balls, when dancing young men
were wanted. At the sight of the awful des Lupeaulx
his heart beat fast. One of the Minister's carriages
used to come for des Lupeaulx at half-past four, just
as he himself was opening his umbrella under the
archway before setting off for the Marais. His fate
depended upon the secretary-general; one word from

the man in the doorway could give him a berth and a salary of twelve hundred francs. (Twelve hundred francs! It was the height of his ambition; he and his mother could live in comfort on such a stipend.) And yet, the secretary-general did not know him. Des Lupeaulx was scarcely aware there was such a person as Sébastien de la Roche. If La Billardière's son, a well-to-do supernumerary in Baudoyer's office, chanced to be under the archway at the same time, des Lupeaulx never failed to give him a friendly nod; but then M. Benjamin de la Billardière was the son of a minister's cousin.

At this particular moment Rabourdin was giving poor little Sébastien a scolding. Sébastien was the only person wholly in the secret of Rabourdin's vast labours; Sébastien had copied and recopied the famous memorial on a hundred and fifty sheets of foolscap, to say nothing of tabulated statistics in support of the argument, abstracts on loose leaves, whole columns of bracketed calculations, headings in capital letters, and sub-headings in round hand. The mechanical part that he played in a great design had kindled enthusiasm in the lad of twenty; he would copy out a whole table again after a single erasure; he took a pride in the handwriting that counted for something in so great an enterprise.

Sébastien had been so thoughtless as to take the most dangerous rough draft of all to the office in order to finish the fair copy. This was a list of all the men in the head offices in Paris, with notes of their prospects, their present circumstances, and private occupations after hours.

Most civil servants in Paris eke out their salaries by some supplementary method of gaining a livelihood; unless, like Rabourdin, they possess patriotic ambition or mental superiority. Like M. Saillard, they become sleeping partners in a business, and go through the books at night. A good many clerks, again, marry

seamstresses, or manageresses of lottery offices, or their
wives keep tobacconists' shops or reading-rooms. Some,
like Mme. Colleville's husband (Mme. Colleville, it
may be remembered, was Célestine's rival), have a place
in a theatre orchestra. Yet others, like du Bruel, for
instance, write plays, comic operas, and melodramas,
or take to stage-management. Witness Messrs. Sewrin,
Pixérécourt, Planard, and others as instances in point.
Pigault-Lebrun, Piis, and Duvicquet held posts in the
civil service in their time ; and M. Scribe's first publisher
was a Treasury clerk.

Rabourdin's inventory contained other details. It was
an inquiry into the personal characteristics of individuals.
Some statement of their mental and physical capacities
must of necessity be included in the survey if the
Government was to recognise those who combined
intelligence and aptitude for work with good health,
for these are three indispensable qualifications in men
who must bear the burden of public business and do
everything well and quickly.   The inventory was a
great piece of work ; it was the outcome of ten years
of labour, and a long experience of men and affairs
acquired in the course of intimacies with the heads of
other departments ; but still it would savour somewhat
of espionage, if it fell into the hands of those who did
not understand the drift of it.   If other eyes saw a
single sheet, M. Rabourdin might be ruined. Sébastien's
admiration for his chief was unbounded, and he knew
nothing as yet of the petty spite of bureaucracy. He
had all the disadvantages of simplicity as well as its
charm.   So, although he had just been scolded for
taking the sheet to the office, he had the courage to
make a full confession. The rough draft and the fair
copy were at the office at that moment; he had put
them away in a case where no one could possibly find
them. But as he saw the gravity of his mistake, the
tears came into his eyes.

'Come, come, sir,' Rabourdin added good-naturedly, 'let us have no more imprudence; but do not distress yourself. Go down to the office very early to-morrow morning. Here is the key of a box in my cylinder desk; it has a letter lock; open it with the word *ciel*, and put the rough draft and the copy safely away.'

This piece of confidence dried the lad's tears. His chief tried to induce him to take tea and cake.

'Mamma told me not to take tea because of my digestion,' said Sébastien.

'Very well, my dear boy, here are some sandwiches and cream; come and sit beside me,' said the awe-inspiring Mme. Rabourdin, ostentatiously gracious. She made Sébastien sit by her at the table; and the light touch of the goddess's dress as it brushed his coat brought the poor boy's heart into his mouth. But at this moment the fair lady saw des Lupeaulx, and instead of waiting till he came to her, she went smiling towards him.

'Why do you stay there as if you were sulking with us?' she asked.

'I was not sulking,' he replied. 'But when I came to bring you a bit of good news, I could not help thinking to myself that you would be more cruel now than ever. I foresaw that six months hence I should be almost a stranger to you. No; we cannot dupe each other—you have too much intelligence, and I on my side have had too much experience—I have been taken in too often, if you like it better. Your end is attained; it has cost you nothing but smiles and a few gracious words——'

'Dupe each other!' she repeated, apparently half offended; 'what do you mean?'

'Yes. M. de la Billardière is worse again to-day; and from what the Minister said to me, your husband is certain to be head of the division.'

He gave her the history of his 'scene' with the

K

Minister (for so he was pleased to call it), of the Countess's jealousy, and what she had said with regard to the invitation.

'Monsieur des Lupeaulx,' the lady returned with dignity, 'permit me to point out to you that my husband is the most capable chief clerk; that he stands first in seniority; that old La Billardière's appointment over his head made a sensation all through the service; that he has done the work of the head of the division for the past twelve months; and that we have neither competitor nor rival.'

'That is true.'

'Well,' she continued, with a smile that displayed the prettiest teeth in the world, 'can my friendship for you be spotted with any thought of self-interest? Can you think me capable of it?'

Des Lupeaulx signified his admiring incredulity.

'Ah!' cried she, 'a woman's heart will always be a secret for the cleverest of you men. Yes, I have seen your visits here with the greatest pleasure, and there was a thought of self-interest at the back of the pleasure.'

'Oh!'

'You have an unbounded future before you,' she continued, lowering her voice for his ear; 'you will be a deputy and a minister some day!' (How pleasant it is to an ambitious man to have such words as these murmured in his ear by a pretty woman with a charming voice!) 'Ah! 1 know you better than you know yourself! Rabourdin will be immensely useful to you in your career; he will do the work while you are at the Chamber. And while you are dreaming of taking office, I want Rabourdin to be a state-councillor and a director-general. Here were two men who might be very useful to one another, while their interests could never clash, so I took it into my head to bring them together. That is a woman's part, is it not? You will both get on faster as friends, and it is time that you both should sail ahead. I have burnt my boats,' she added, smiling at him. 'You are not as frank with me as I am with you.'

'You will not listen to me,' he returned in a melancholy tone, in spite of the satisfaction that her words gave him in the depths of his heart. 'What good will your promises of promotion do me if you dismiss me here?'

She turned on him with a Parisienne's quickness.

'Before I listen to you, we must be in a position to understand each other,' she said. And she left the elderly coxcomb and went to talk to Mme. de Chessel, a provincial countess, who made as though she meant to go.

'She is no ordinary woman!' thought des Lupeaulx. 'I am not myself when I am with her.'

And it is a fact that this reprobate who had kept an opera-dancer six years ago, and since then, thanks to his position, had made a seraglio of pretty women for himself among the wives of the employés, and lived in the world of actresses and journalists,—this jaded man of forty, I repeat, was charming with Célestine all that evening, and the very last to leave her salon.

'At last!' thought Mme. Rabourdin, as she went to bed. 'At last we shall have the place. Twelve thousand francs a year, besides extras and the rent of the farm at Grajeux; twenty-five thousand francs altogether. It is not comfort, but still it is not poverty.'

Célestine thought of her debts till she fell asleep. They could be paid off in three years by putting aside six thousand francs a year. She was far from imagining, as she took Rabourdin's promotion for granted, that somewhere in the Marais a little shrewish, self-seeking, bigoted bourgeoise that had never set foot in a salon, a woman without influence or connections, was thinking of carrying the place by storm. And if Mme. Rabourdin could have seen Mme. Baudoyer, she would have

despised her antagonist; she did not know the power of
pettiness, the penetrating force of the grub that brings
down the elm-tree by tracing a ring under the bark.

If it were possible in literature to make use of the
microscope of a Leuwenhoek, a Malpighi, or a Raspail,
as Hoffmann of Berlin attempted to do; if, furthermore,
you could magnify and draw the teredo that brought
Holland within a finger's breadth of extinction by gnaw-
ing through the dykes, perhaps you might see something
within a little resembling the countenances of Messieurs
Gigonnet, Mitral, Baudoyer, Saillard, Gaudron, Falleix,
Transon, Godard and Company. These human
teredos, at any rate, showed what they could do in the
thirtieth year of this nineteenth century. And now is
the time for displaying the official teredo, as he burrows
in the public offices where most of the scenes in this
history will take place.

At Paris all public offices are alike. No matter to
what department you may betake yourself to ask for the
redress of a grievance, or for the smallest favour, you
will find the same gloomy corridors, the same dimly-
lighted backways, the same rows of doors each with an
enigmatical inscription, and an oval, glazed aperture like
an eye; and if you look through those windows, you may
see fantastic scenes worthy of Callot. When you discover the object of your search, you pass first of all
through an outer room, where the office messenger sits,
into a second, the general office; the senior clerk's
sanctum lies to the right or left at the further end of it,
and either beyond, or up above, you find the room appropriated to the use of the chief clerk himself. As for the
immense personage styled the head of the division under
the Empire, the director under the Restoration, and the
head of the division once more in our day, he is housed
either up above or down below his two or three suites
of offices; but occasionally his room lies beyond that of

one of the chief clerks. As a rule it is remarkable for its spaciousness, an advantage not a little prized in these curious honeycomb cells of the big hive known as a government department, or a director-general's department, if there can be said to be such a thing as a director-general.

At the present day almost every department has absorbed all the lesser administrations which used to be separate. By this concentration the directors-general have been shorn of all their splendour in the shape of hôtels, servants, spacious rooms, and little courtyards. Who would recognise the Commissioner of Woods and Forests, or the Comptroller of Excise, in a man that comes to the Treasury on foot and climbs the stairs to a second floor? Once these dignitaries were councillors, or ministers, or peers of France, they were housed in a splendid hôtel in the Rue Sainte-Avoye or the Rue Saint-Augustin. Messieurs Pasquier and Molé, among others, were content with a comptroller-general's post after they had been in office, thus illustrating the remark made by the Duc d'Antin to Louis XIV., 'Sire, when Jesus Christ died on a Friday, He was sure that on Sunday He should rise from the dead.' If the comptroller-general's sphere of activities had increased in extent when his splendour was curtailed, perhaps no great harm would have been done; but nowadays it is with great difficulty that this personage becomes a Master of Requests with a paltry twenty thousand francs a year. He is suffered to retain a symbol of his vanished power in the shape of an usher in small clothes, silk stockings, and a cut-away coat, if, indeed, the usher has not latterly been reformed out of existence.

The staff of an office consists, in administrative style, of a messenger, a number of supernumeraries who work for nothing for so many years, and the established clerks; to wit, the writers or copying-clerks, the draughting-clerks, and first or senior clerks, under a chief and his assistant the *sous-chef*. A *division* usually comprises two or three such offices, and sometimes more. The names of the functionaries vary with the different departments; in some the senior clerk may be replaced by a head book-keeper or an auditor.

The floor of the outer room, inhabited by the office messenger, is tiled like the passage, the walls are covered with a cheap paper; the furniture consists of a stove, a big black table, an inkstand and pens, with sundry bare benches for the accommodation of the public that dances attendance there (the office messenger sits in a comfortable armchair, and rests his feet on a hassock). Sometimes, in addition, there is a water-cistern and a tap. The general office is a large and more or less well-lighted apartment. Wooden floors are very rare; parquetry and open fireplaces, like mahogany cupboards, tables, and desks, red and green leather-covered chairs, silken curtains, and other departmental luxuries are appropriated to the use of chief clerks and heads of divisions. The general office is supplied with a stove, the pipe enters the chimney-opening, if there happens to be a flue. The wallpaper is usually plain green or brown. The tables are of black wood.

A clerk's industry may be pretty accurately gauged by his manner of installing himself. A chilly subject will have a kind of wooden foot-rest; the man of bilious-sanguine temperament is content with a straw mat; the lymphatic man that lives in fear of draughts, open doors, or other causes of a fall in the temperature, will intrench himself behind a little screen of pasteboard cases. There is a cupboard somewhere in which office-coats, over-sleeves, eye-shades, caps, fezs, and other gear of the craft are kept. The chimney-piece is almost always loaded with water-bottles and glasses and the remains of luncheons; a lamp may be found in some dark corners. The door of the assistant's sanctum usually stands ajar, so that that gentleman may keep an eye on the general office, prevent too much talk, and come out to confer with the clerks in great emergencies.

You can tell the quality of the official at a pinch from the furniture of the room. The curtains vary, some are of white or coloured stuff, some are cotton, some silk; the chairs are of cherry-wood or mahogany, and straw-seated, or upholstered or cushioned with leather; the wall-papers are more or less clean. But to whatever department this kind of public property may chance to belong, nothing can look more strange, when removed from its surroundings, than a collection of furniture that has seen so many changes of government and come through so much rough treatment. Of all removals in Paris, the migration of a public office is the most grotesque to witness. The genius of Hoffmann, that high priest of the impossible, could not invent anything more whimsical. Some unaccountable change is wrought in the hand-carts. The yawning pasteboard cases leave a track of dust along the street; the tables appear with their castors in the air. There is something dismaying in the aspect of the ramshackle armchairs and inconceivably odd gear with which the administration of France is carried on. In some ways it reminds you of a turnout of the properties of a theatre, in others of the stock-in-trade of an acrobat. Even so, upon some obelisk you may behold traces of intelligent purpose in the shadowy lettering which troubles your imagination, after the wont of most things of which you cannot discern the end. And lastly, these utensils from the administrative kitchen are all so old, so battered, so faded, that the dirtiest array of pots and pans would be an infinitely more pleasing spectacle.

If foreign and provincial readers would form an accurate idea of the inner life of a public office at Paris, it may, perhaps, suffice to describe M. de la Billardière's division, for its chief characteristics are common, no doubt, to all European administrations.

First and foremost, picture, to suit your fancy, the personage thus set forth in large type in the *Annuaire*:—

'HEAD OF THE DIVISION: M. le Baron Flamet de la BILLARDIÈRE (Athanase Jean François Michel), formerly Grand Provost of the Department of the Corrèze; Gentleman in Ordinary of the Chamber; Master of Requests Extraordinary, President of the Electoral College of the Department of the Dordogne, officer of the Legion of Honour; Chevalier of St. Louis, and of the foreign orders of Christ, of Isabella, of St. Vladimir, etc., etc; Member of the Académie of Gers and of many other learned Societies, Vice-President of the Société des Bonnes-Lettres; Member of the Association of St. Joseph, and of the Prisoners' Aid Society; one of the Mayors of Paris, and so forth, and so forth.'

The man that took up so much space in print was occupying at that moment some five feet and a half by two feet six inches on the bed whereon he lay, his head adorned with a cotton nightcap tied with flame-coloured ribbons; with Desplein, the King's surgeon, and young Dr. Bianchon to visit him, and two elderly kinswomen to mount guard over him on either side; a host of phials, bandages, syringes, and other instruments of death encompassing him about, and the curé of Saint-Roch ever on the watch to insinuate a word or two as to the salvation of his soul.

Every morning his son Benjamin de la Billardière would meet the two doctors with the formula, 'Do you think that I shall be so fortunate as to keep my father?' It was only that very day that, by a slip of the tongue, he had brought out the word 'unfortunate' instead.

La Billardière's division was situated below the latitude of the attics by seventy-one degrees of longitude, measured by the steps of the staircase, in the departmental ocean of a great and imposing pile of buildings. It lay on the north-east side of a courtyard, a space formerly taken up by the stables, and now occupied by Clergeot's division. The two distinct sets of offices were divided by the breadth of the stairhead. All the doors were labelled along a spacious corridor illuminated by borrowed lights. The offices and ante-chambers belonging to the two chief clerks, Messrs. Rabourdin and Baudoyer, were below on the second floor; and M. de la Billardière's ante-chamber, sitting-room, and two private offices lay immediately beyond M. Rabourdin's rooms.

The first floor was divided in two by an entresol, and here M. Ernest de la Brière was established. M. Ernest de la Brière was an occult power which shall be described in a few words, for he certainly deserves a parenthetic mention. So long as the Minister was in office, this young man was his private secretary. For which reason his room communicated by a secret door with His Excellency's sanctum. His Excellency, be it said, had two private cabinets; one of these was in keeping with the state apartments in which he received visitors, and here he conferred with great personages in the absence of his secretary; the other was the study in which he retired to work with his private secretary and without witnesses. Now a private secretary is to a single minister what des Lupeaulx was to a whole government. Between young La Brière and des Lupeaulx there was just the difference that separates the aide de camp from the chief of the staff. The private secretary is a minister's apprentice; he takes himself off and reappears with his patron. If the minister is still in favour, or if he has hopes when he goes out of office, he takes his secretary with him, only to bring him back again. If it is otherwise, he puts his *protégé* out to grass in some administrative pasture—in the Audit Department, for example, that hostelry where secretaries wait till the storm passes over. A young gentleman in this position is not precisely a statesman; he is a man of politics; sometimes, too, he represents the politics of a man. When you come to think of the quantity of letters which he must open and read, to say nothing of his other occupations, is it not evident that such a commodity would be extremely expensive under an absolute monarchy? At Paris a victim of this sort can be had for an annual sum varying from ten to twenty thousand francs; but the young man has the benefit of the minister's carriages, boxes at the theatre, and invitations. The Emperor of Russia would be very glad to give fifty thousand francs a year for such a marvellously groomed and carefully curled Constitutional poodle; it is such a good guard; such an amiable, sweet-tempered, docile animal; so fond and—faithful! But, alas! the private secretary is not to be grown, found, discovered, or developed anywhere save in the hotbeds of a representative government. Under an absolute monarch you can only have courtiers and servitors; whereas with a Charter, free men will serve you, and flatter you, and fawn upon you. Wherefore ministers in France are more fortunate than women or crowned kings; they have somebody to understand them. Perhaps, at the same time, private secretaries are as much to be pitied as women or white paper—they must take all that is put upon them. Like a virtuous wife, a private secretary is bound to display his talents in private only, and for his minister. If he exhibits his abilities in public, he is ruined. Therefore a private secretary is a friend given by the Government. But to return to our Government offices.

Three office-messengers lived in harmony in La Billardière's division, to wit, one messenger for the two offices; another shared by the two chief clerks; and a third for the head of the division exclusively. All three were clothed and warmed at the public expense; all three wore the well-known livery—royal blue with a scarlet piping for an undress uniform, and a wide red-white-and-blue galoon for state occasions. La Billardière's man had been put into an usher's uniform. The secretary-general, willing to flatter the self-love of a minister's cousin, permitted an encroachment which reflected glory upon the administration. These three messengers were veritable pillars of the department, and experts in bureaucratic customs. They wanted for nothing; they were well warmed and clothed at the expense of the State; and well-to-do, because they were frugal. They probed every man in the department to the quick; for the one interest in their lives consisted in watching the clerks and studying their hobbies. Wherefore they knew exactly how far it was safe to go in the matter of loans, performing their commissions with the utmost discretion, undertaking errands to the pawnbroker, buying pawn-tickets, lending money without interest. No one, however, borrowed any sum however trifling without giving a gratuity; and as the loans were usually very small, the practice was equivalent to the payment of a usurious interest.

The three masterless servants had a salary of nine hundred francs; New Year's tips and perquisites raised the income to twelve hundred; and they were in a position to make almost as much again out of the clerks, for all the breakfasts of those who breakfasted passed through their hands. In some Government offices the doorkeeper actually provides the breakfasts. The doorkeeper's place in the finance department had been worth something like four thousand francs to fat old Thuillier senior, whose son was now a clerk in La Billardière's division. Sometimes attendants feel a five-franc piece slipped into the palm of their right hands if a petitioner is in a hurry, an occurrence which they take with rare impassibility. The seniors only wear their uniform when on duty, and go out in plain clothes.

The messenger of the general office was the best off,

for he exploited the staff of clerks.   He was a thick-set
corpulent man of sixty, with bristling white hair, an
apoplectic neck, a common pimpled countenance, grey
eyes, and a mouth like a stove-door ; here you have a
sketch of Antoine, the oldest messenger in the department.
ment.   Antoine had sent for his nephews from Échelles
in Savoy, and found places for them ; Laurent with the
chief clerks, Gabriel with the head of the division.
The two Savoyards were dressed like their uncle, in
broadcloth.   As to appearance, they were simply ordinary
servants in uniform.   At night they took checks at a
subsidised theatre (La Billardière had obtained the
places for them).   Both had married skilled lace-cleaners,
who also undertook fine darning and repairs of cashmere
shawls.   As the uncle was a bachelor, the whole family
lived together, and lived very much more comfortably
than most chief clerks.   Gabriel and Laurent, having
only been a matter of ten years in the service, had not
yet learned to look down upon the government costume ;
they went abroad in uniform, proud as dramatic authors
after a success from a pecuniary point of view.   The
uncle, whom they took for a very acute person, and served
with blind devotion, gradually initiated them into the
mysteries of the craft.

The three had just opened the offices.   Between
seven and eight they used to sweep out the offices, read
the newspapers, or discuss the politics of the division
with other porters, after the manner of their kind, with
due exchange of information.   Modern domestic servants
are perfectly acquainted with the affairs of the family ;
and the servants of the department, like spiders in the
middle of a web, could feel the slightest disturbance in
any part of it.

It was a Thursday morning, the day after the Minister's
reception and Mme. Rabourdin's At Home.   Uncle
Antoine, with the assistance of his nephews, was shaving
in the antechamber on the second floor, when the

arrival of ône of the clerks took them all by surprise.

'That is M. Dutocq,' remarked Antoine; 'I know him by the way he comes sneaking in. He always goes about as if he were skating, he does. He drops down upon you before you can tell which way he came. Yesterday, he was the last to leave the office, a thing that hasn't happened three times since he has been here.'

A man of thirty-eight, with a long visage of a bilious hue, and close-cropped woolly grey hair; a low forehead, thick eyebrows that met in the middle, a crooked nose, compressed lips, light green eyes that never looked you in the face; a tall figure, one shoulder slightly larger than the other; a brown coat, black waistcoat, a silk handkerchief round the throat, buff trousers, black woollen stockings, and shoes with mud-bedraggled laces, —here you have M. Dutocq, senior clerk in Rabourdin's office. Dutocq was incompetent and indolent. He detested his chief. Nothing could be more natural. Rabourdin had no weakness to flatter, no vice to which Dutocq could pander. The chief was far too high-minded to injure a subordinate; but, at the same time, he was too clearsighted to be duped by appearances. Dutocq only remained on sufferance, through Rabourdin's generosity; there was no prospect of advancement unless there was a change of chief. Dutocq was well aware that he himself was not fit to fill a higher post, but he knew enough of Government offices to understand that incompetence does not prevent a man from affixing his signature to the work of others. He would get out of the difficulty by finding a Rabourdin among the draughting clerks, for La Billardière's promotion had been a striking and disastrous object lesson to the department. Spite when combined with self-interest is a very fair substitute for intelligence; and Dutocq was very spiteful, and very much bent on his own interests. Wherefore he had set himself to consolidate his position by taking the office of spy upon himself. After 1816 he became a bigot of the deepest dye; he foresaw that persons then indiscriminately labelled 'Jesuits,' by fools that knew no better, would shortly be in favour. He belonged to the Congrégation, though he was not admitted to its inner circles. He went from office to office, sounded consciences with coarse jokes, and returned to paraphrase his 'reports' for des Lupeaulx's benefit. Des Lupeaulx was kept informed in this way of everything that went on; and, indeed, the secretary-general's profound knowledge of the ins and outs of affairs often astonished the Minister. Dutocq in good earnest was the Bonneau of a political Bonneau; he was intriguing for the honour of taking des Lupeaulx's secret messages, and des Lupeaulx tolerated the unclean creature, thinking that he might sometime make him useful, were it only to get himself or some great person out of a scrape by some shameful marriage. On some such good fortune indeed Dutocq was reckoning, for he remained a bachelor. The pair understood one another. Dutocq had succeeded M. Poiret senior, who retired to a boarding-house, and was put on a pension in 1814, at which time there had been a grand general reform of the staff. Dutocq lived on a fifth floor, in a house with a passage entry in the Rue Saint Louis Saint Honoré. As an enthusiastic amateur of old prints, it was his ambition to possess complete collections of the works of Rembrandt, Charlet, Sylvestre, Audran, Callot, Albrecht Dürer, and others; and, like most collectors who live by themselves, he aspired to pick these things up cheaply. Dutocq took his meals in a boarding-house in the Rue de Beaune, and spent his evenings at the Palais Royal. Sometimes he went to the play, thanks to du Bruel, who would give him an author's ticket every week. A word as to du Bruel.

Du Bruel came to the office simply for the sake of drawing his salary and believing and saying that he was

the chief clerk's assistant; but Sébastien did his work, as
has been seen, and received a very inadequate return for
it.   Du Bruel did the minor theatres for a ministerial
paper, for which he also wrote articles to order.   His
position was known, defined, and unassailable.   Nor did
he fail in any of the little diplomatic shifts that gain a
man the goodwill of his fellow creatures.   He always
offered Mme. Rabourdin a box on a first night, for
instance, and called for her and took her back in a
carriage, an attention of which she was very sensible.
Rabourdin was very easy with his subordinates, very
little given to tormenting them; so he allowed du Bruel
to attend rehearsals and to come and go and work at
his vaudevilles pretty much as he pleased.   M. le Duc
de Chaulieu was aware that du Bruel was writing a novel,
and meant to dedicate the book to him.   Du Bruel
accordingly dressed as carelessly as a vaudevilliste; in
the morning he appeared in footed trousers and thin-
soled shoes, a superannuated waistcoat, a greenish black
greatcoat and a black cravat, but at night he was
fashionably arrayed, for he aimed at being a gentleman.
    Du Bruel lived, for sufficient reasons, with Florine,
the actress for whom he wrote parts; and Florine at that
time lodged with Tullia, a dancer more remarkable for
beauty than for talent.   This arrangement permitted
him to see a good deal of the Duc de Rhétoré, oldest
son of the Duc de Chaulieu, a favourite with the King.
The Duc de Chaulieu had obtained the Cross of the
Legion of Honour for du Bruel after his eleventh play on
a topic of the hour.   Du Bruel—or de Cursy, if you
prefer it—was at work at the moment on a drama in
five acts for the Français.   Sébastien had a strong liking
for the assistant, who sometimes gave him an order for
the pit.   Du Bruel used to point out any doubtful
passages beforehand, and Sébastien, with the sincerity of
youth, would applaud with all his might; he regarded
du Bruel as a great man of letters.   Once it happened

that a vaudeville written, as usual, with two collaborators
had been hissed in several places.

'The public find out the parts written in collaboration,' du Bruel remarked next day to Sébastien.

'Why don't you write it all yourself?' Sébastien
answered in the simplicity of his heart.

There were excellent reasons why du Bruel should
not write the whole himself. He was the third part of
a dramatic author. Few people are aware that a dramatic
author is a composite being. First, there is the Man
of Ideas; it is his duty to find the subject and con-
struct the framework or scenario of the vaudeville;
the Plodder works out the dialogue, while the Man of
Details sets the couplets to music, arranges the choruses
and the accompaniments, and grafts the songs into the
plot. The same personage also looks after the practical
aspects of the play; he sees after the drawing up of the
placards, and never leaves the manager until he has
definitely secured the representation of a piece written
by the three partners for the following day.

Du Bruel, a born plodder, was in the habit of reading
new books at the office, and picking out the clever bits;
he made a note of these, and embroidered his dialogues
with them. Cursy (that was his *nom de guerre*) was held
in esteem by his collaborators on account of his impeccable accuracy; the Man of Ideas could feel sure
that Cursy would comprehend him, and might fold his
arms. His popularity among the clerks was sufficient
to bring them out in a body to applaud his pieces, for he
had the reputation of a 'good fellow,' and he deserved
it. He was free-handed; it was never very difficult to
screw a bowl of punch or ices out of him, and he would
lend fifty francs and never ask for the money. Du Bruel
was a man of regular habits; he had a house in the
country at Aulnay, and found investments for his money.
Besides his salary of four thousand five hundred francs,
he had a pension of twelve hundred from the civil list,

and eight hundred francs out of the hundred thousand crowns voted by the Chamber for the encouragement of the arts. Add to these various sources of income some nine thousand francs brought in by the 'thirds,' 'fourths,' and 'halves' of vaudevilles at three different theatres, and you will understand at once that du Bruel was broad, rotund, and fat, and looked like a man of substance. As to his morals, he was Tullia's lover; and, as usual, believed that he was preferred to her protector, the brilliant Duc de Rhétoré.

Dutocq beheld, not without dismay, the *liaison* (as he called it) between des Lupeaulx and Mme. Rabourdin. His smothered fury was increased. What was more, his prying eyes could not fail to detect that Rabourdin was throwing himself into some great work outside his official duties, and he despaired of finding out anything about it, whereas little Sébastien was either wholly or partly in the secret. Dutocq had tried successfully to make an ally of M. Godard, Baudoyer's assistant, du Bruel's colleague; the high esteem in which Dutocq held Baudoyer had led to an acquaintance. Not that Dutocq was sincere; but by crying up Baudoyer and saying nothing of Rabourdin, he satisfied his spleen, after the fashion of petty minds.

Joseph Godard was Mitral's cousin by the mother's side. His relationship to Baudoyer, therefore, was distant enough, but he had founded hopes upon it; he meant to marry Mlle. Baudoyer, and consequently Isidore was a brilliant genius in his eyes. He professed a high respect for Elizabeth and Mme. Saillard, failing to perceive that Mme. Baudoyer was 'simmering' Falleix for her daughter; and he used to bring little presents for Mlle. Baudoyer—artificial flowers, sugar-plums on New Year's Day, and pretty boxes on her birthday. Godard was a man of six-and-twenty, a dull plodder, well-conducted as a young lady, hum-drum and apathetic. Cafés, cigars, and horse exercise

L

he held in abhorrence; he went to bed regularly
at ten, and rose at seven. His various social talents
brought him into high favour with the Saillards and
Baudoyers; he could play dance music on the flageolet;
and in the National Guard he took a fife in the band to
avoid night-duty. Natural history was Godard's special
hobby. He collected minerals and shells; he could stuff
birds; his rooms were warehouses of curiosities picked
up for small sums; he had landscape-stones, models of
palaces in cork, various petrified objects from the springs
of Saint Allyre at Clermont (Auvergne), and the like.
Godard used to buy up scent-bottles to hold his specimens of baryta, his sulphates, salts, magnesia, coral, and
the like. He kept collections of butterflies in frames;
he covered the walls with dried fish-skins and Chinese
umbrellas.

Godard lived with his sister, a flower-maker in the
Rue de Richelieu. But though this model young man
was much admired by mothers of daughters, it is a
fact that he was held in much contempt by his sister's
work-girls, and more particularly by the young lady at
the desk, who had long hoped to entangle him. He was
thin and slim, and of average height; there were dark
circles about his eyes; his beard was scanty; his breath
was bad (according to Bixiou). Joseph Godard took
little pains with himself; his clothes did not fit him, his
trousers were large and baggy; he wore white stockings
all the year round, a narrow-rimmed hat, and laced
shoes. At the office he sat in a cane chair with the seat
broken through, and a round leather cushion on the top
of it. He complained a good deal of indigestion. His
principal failing was a tendency to propose picnics and
Sunday excursions in the summer to Montmorency, or a
walk to a dairy on the Boulevard Mont Parnasse.

After the acquaintance between Dutocq and Godard
had lasted for some six months, Dutocq began to go now
and again to Mlle. Godard's, hoping to do a piece of

business in the house, or to discover some feminine treasure.

And so it came to pass that in Dutocq and Godard Baudoyer had two men to sing his praises in the office. M. Saillard was incapable of discovering Dutocq's real character; sometimes he would drop in to speak to him at his desk. Young La Billardière, one of Baudoyer's supernumeraries, belonged to this set. Cleverer men laughed not a little at the alliance of Godard, Dutocq, and Baudoyer. Bixiou dubbed it *la Trinité sans Esprit*, and christened little La Billardière 'the Paschal Lamb.'

'You are up early,' said Antoine, with a laugh, as Dutocq came in.

'And as for you, Antoine,' returned Dutocq, 'it is plain that the newspapers sometimes come before you give them out to us.'

'It happens so to-day,' said Antoine, not a whit disconcerted; 'they never come in at the same time for two days together.'

The nephews looked furtively at one another, as if to say admiringly, 'What a cool hand!'

'He brings me in two sous on his breakfasts,' muttered Antoine as Dutocq shut the door, 'but I would as soon be without it to have him out of the department.'

'Ah! you are not the first to-day, M. Sébastien,' he remarked, a quarter of an hour afterwards.

'Who ever can have come?' the poor boy asked, and his face turned white.

'M. Dutocq,' said Laurent.

Virgin natures possess an unusual degree of that inexplicable power of second sight which perhaps depends upon an unjaded nervous system, upon the sensibility of an organisation that may be called new. Sébastien had guessed that Dutocq hated the venerated Rabourdin. So Laurent had scarcely pronounced the name before an ugly presentiment flashed upon the supernumerary.

'I suspected as much,' he exclaimed, and he was off like an arrow down the corridor.

'There will be a row in the offices,' remarked Antoine, shaking his white head as he put on his uniform. 'It is easy to see that M. le Baron is going to his last account. Yes, Mme. Gruget, his nurse, told me that he would not live the day out. What a stir there will be here, to be sure! Go and see if the stoves are burning up, some of you. *Sabre de bois!* all of them will come tumbling in upon us in a minute.'

'The poor little youngster was in a fine taking when he heard that that Jesuit of a M. Dutocq was in before him, and that's a fact,' commented Laurent.

'Well, I for one have told him (for, after all, one can't do less than tell a good clerk the truth, and what I call a good clerk is a clerk like this youngster, that pays up his ten francs sharp on New Year's Day), I have told him, I say, "The more you do, the more they will want you to do, and they will leave you where you are!" But it is no good. He will not listen to me. He kills himself with stopping till five o'clock, an hour after everybody else' (Antoine shrugged his shoulders). 'All nonsense; that's not the way to get on! And here's proof of it—nothing has been said yet of taking on the poor boy as an established clerk, and an excellent one he would make. After two years too! It sets your back up, upon my word!'

'M. Rabourdin has a liking for M. Sébastien,' said Laurent.

'But M. Rabourdin is not a minister,' retorted Antoine. 'It will be a hot day when he is a minister; the fowls will cut their teeth. He is much too—never mind what! When I think that I take round the muster-roll of salaries, to be receipted by humbugs that stop away and do what they please, while little La Roche is working himself to death, I wonder whether God gives a thought to Government offices. And as for these pets of M. le Maréchal and M. le Duc; what do they give you?—They *thank* you' (Antoine made a patronising nod). '"Thanks, my dear Antoine."— A pack of do-nothings; let them work, or they will bring on another Revolution! You should have seen whether they came it over us like this in M. Robert Lindet's time; for, such as you see me, I came to this shop under M. Robert Lindet. The clerks used to work when he was here! You ought to have seen those quilldrivers scratching away till midnight, all the stoves gone out, and nobody so much as noticing it; but for one thing, the guillotine was there too; and no need to say, it was a very different thing from simply taking down their names as we do now when they come late.'

'Daddy Antoine,' began Gabriel, 'since you are in a talking humour this morning, what do you make out that a clerk is?'

'A clerk!' Antoine returned gravely. 'A clerk is a man that sits in an office and writes.—What am I saying? Where should we be without clerks? Just go and look after your stoves and never say a word against the clerks. The stove in the large room draws like fury, Gabriel; you must shut off some of the draught.'

Antoine took up his position at the stairhead, so that he could see all the clerks as they came in under the arched gateway. He knew everybody in every office in the department, and used to watch their ways and notice the differences in their dress. And here, before entering upon the drama, it is necessary to give portraits in outline of the principal actors in La Billardière's division; for not merely will the reader make the acquaintance of the various types of the *genus* clerk, but he will find in them the justification of Rabourdin's observations, and likewise of the title of this essentially Parisian Study.

And on this head, let there be no misapprehensions:

from the point of view of poverty and eccentricity there are clerks and clerks, just as there are faggots and faggots. In the first place, you must distinguish between the clerk in Paris and his provincial brother. The provincial clerk is well off. He is spaciously housed; he has a garden; he is comfortable as a rule in his office. Sound wine is not dear; he does not dine off horse-steaks; he is acquainted with the luxury of dessert. People may not know precisely what he eats, but every one will tell you that he does not 'eat up his salary.' So far from running into debt, he positively saves on his income. If he is a bachelor, mothers of daughters greet him as he passes; if he is married, he and his wife go to balls at the receiver-general's, at the prefecture, at the sub-prefecture. People take an interest in his character; he makes conquests; he has a reputation for intelligence; his loss would probably be felt; the whole town knows him, and takes an interest in his wife and family. He gives evening parties; he may become a deputy if he has private means, and his father-in-law is in easy circumstances. His wife is always under the minute and inquisitive spy system of a small town; if he is unfortunate in his married life, he knows it, whereas a clerk at Paris is not bound to hear of his misfortune. Lastly, the provincial clerk is 'somebody,' while the Parisian is almost 'nobody.'

The next comer was a draughting-clerk, Phellion by name, a respectable father of a family. He was in Rabourdin's office. His chief's influence had obtained education for each of his two boys at half-cost at the Collége Henri IV., a well-timed favour; for Phellion had a third child, a girl, who was being educated free of expense in a boarding-school where her mother gave music lessons, and her father taught history and geography of an evening. Phellion was a man of forty-five, and a sergeant-major in the National Guard. He was very ready to give sympathy; but he never had a farthing to spare. He lived, not very far from the Sourds-Muets, in the Rue du Faubourg Saint-Jacques, on a floor of a house, with a garden attached. 'His place,' to use his own expression, only cost four hundred francs. The draughting-clerk was proud of his position, and rejoiced in his lot; he worked industriously for the Government, believed that he was serving his country, and boasted of his indifference to party-politics; he looked at nothing but AUTHORITY. Sometimes, to his delight, M. Rabourdin would ask him to stay for half an hour to finish some piece of work. Then Phellion would go to the boarding-school in the Rue Notre Dame des Champs, where his wife taught music, and say to the Demoiselles La Grave with whom he dined—

'Affairs compelled me to stay late at the office, mesdemoiselles. When a man is in the service of the Government, he is not his own master.'

Phellion had compiled various school-books in the form of question and answer for the use of ladies' schools. These 'small but condensed treatises,' as he called them, were on sale at the University bookseller's under the name of 'Historical and Geographical Catechisms.' He felt it incumbent upon him to present Mme. Rabourdin with each of these works as they came out, taking a copy printed on hand-made paper and bound in crimson morocco. On these occasions he appeared in the Rue Duphot in full dress: silk small clothes, silk stockings, shoes with gold buckles, and so forth. M. Phellion gave beer and patty soirees on Thursday evenings after the boarders had gone to bed. They played bouillotte, with five sous in the pool; and in spite of the slenderness of the stakes, it once fell out that M. Laudigeois, a registrar's clerk, lost ten francs in an evening by reckless gambling.

The walls of the sitting-room were covered with a green American paper with a red border, and adorned with portraits of the Royal family. The visitor might behold His Majesty the King, the Dauphiness, and Madame; with a pair of framed engravings, to wit, *Mazeppa*, after Horace Vernet, and *The Pauper's Funeral*, after Vigneron. This last-named work of art, according to Phellion, was 'sublime in its conception. It ought to console the lower classes by reminding them that they had more devoted friends than men, friends whose affections go beyond the grave.' From those words you can guess that Phellion was the sort of man to take his children to the Cimetière de l'Ouest on All Souls' Day, and point out the twenty square yards of earth (purchased 'in perpetuity') where his father and his mother-in-law lay buried. 'We shall come here some day,' he used to say, to familiarise his offspring with the idea of death.

It was one of Phellion's great amusements to explore Paris. He had treated himself to a map. Antony, Arcueil, Bièvre, Fontenay-aux-Roses, and Aulnay, all of them famous as the abode of more than one great writer, he knew already by heart, and he hoped in time to know all the suburbs on the west side. His eldest son he destined for the service of the Government; the second was to go to the École polytechnique. He often used to say to his eldest, 'When you have the honour to be employed by the Government!' but, at the same time, he suspected the boy of a turn for the exact sciences, and strove to repress the tendency, holding in reserve the extreme course of leaving him to shift for himself if he persisted in his ways.

Phellion had never ventured to ask M. Rabourdin to dine with him, though he would have regarded such a day as one of the greatest in his life. He used to say that if he could leave one of his sons to walk in the footsteps of M. Rabourdin, he should die the happiest father in the world. He dinned the praises of the worthy and much-respected chief into the ears of the Demoiselles La Grave, till those ladies longed to see M. Rabourdin, as a lad might crave a glimpse of M. de Chateaubriand. They would have been very glad, they said, to be intrusted with the education of his 'young lady.' If the Minister's carriage chanced to come in or out, Phellion took off his hat very respectfully whether there was anybody in it or not, and said that it would be well for France if everybody held authority in sufficient honour to revere it even in its insignia. When Rabourdin sent for him 'downstairs' to explain his work, Phellion summoned up all his intelligence, and listened to his chief's lightest words as a dilettante listens to an air at the Italiens. He sat silent in the office, his feet perched aloft on his wooden foot-rest; he never stirred from his place; he conscientiously gave his mind to his work. In administrative correspondence he expressed himself with solemnity; he took everything seriously; he emphasised the Minister's orders by translating them into pompous phraseology. Yet, great as he was upon propriety, a disastrous thing had happened once in his career—a disaster indeed. In spite of the minute care with which he drafted his letters, he once allowed a phrase thus conceived to escape him, 'You will therefore repair to the closet with the necessary papers.' The copying-clerks, delighted at the chance of a laugh at the expense of the harmless creature, went to consult Rabourdin behind Phellion's back. Rabourdin, knowing his draughting-clerk's character, could not help smiling as he indorsed the margin with a note, 'You will appear at the private office with the documents indicated.' The alteration was shown to Phellion; he studied it, pondered, and weighed the difference between the expressions, and candidly admitted that it would have taken him a couple of hours to find the equivalents. 'M. Rabourdin is a man of genius!' he cried. He always thought that his colleagues had shown a want of consideration for him by referring the matter so promptly to the chief; but he had too much respect for the established order of things

not to admit that they had acted within their right, and
so much the more so since he, Phellion, was absent at
the time. Still, in their place, he himself would have
waited—there was no pressing need for the circular.
This affair cost him several nights' rest. If any one
wished to make him angry, they had only to remind
him of the accursed phrase by asking as he went out,
' Have you the necessary papers?' At which question the
worthy draughting-clerk would turn and give the clerks
a withering glance. ' It seems to me, gentlemen, that
your remark is extremely unbecoming.' One day, however, he waxed so wroth that Rabourdin was obliged to
interfere, and the clerks were forbidden to allude to the
affair.

M. Phellion looked rather like a meditative ram.
His face was somewhat colourless, and marked with
smallpox; his lips were thick and underhung, his
eyes were pale blue, and in figure he was rather above
average height. Neat in his person he was bound to be,
as a master of history and geography in a ladies' school;
he wore good linen, a pleated shirt-front, an open black
kerseymere waistcoat that afforded glimpses of the braces
which his daughter embroidered for him, a diamond
pin, a black coat, and blue trousers. In winter he
adopted a nut-brown box-coat with three capes, and
it was his wont to carry a loaded cane—'a precaution
rendered necessary by the extreme loneliness of some
parts of the neighbourhood.' He had given up the
habit of taking snuff, a reform which he was wont
to cite as a striking instance of the command that a man
may gain over himself. Having what he called a 'fat
chest,' it was his wont to ascend staircases slowly for
fear of contracting an asthma.

He saluted Antoine with dignity.

A copying-clerk, an odd contrast to this exemplary
worthy, immediately followed. Vimeux was a young
fellow of five-and-twenty, with a salary of fifteen hundred

francs. He was well made and slim-waisted; his eyes,
eyebrows, and beard were as black as jet; he had good
teeth and sweetly pretty hands, while his moustache was
so luxuriant and well cared for that its cultivation might
have been his principal occupation in life. Vimeux's
aptitude for his work was so great that he had always
finished it long before anybody else.

'He is a gifted young man!' Phellion would exclaim,
as he saw Vimeux cross his legs, at a loss to know what
to do with the rest of his time. 'And look!' he would
say to du Bruel, 'how exquisitely neat it is!'

Vimeux breakfasted off a roll of bread and a glass of
water, dined at Katcomb's for twenty sous, and lived in
furnished lodgings at twelve francs a month. Dress was
his one joy and pleasure in life. He ruined himself
with wonderful waistcoats, tight-fitting or semi-fitting
trousers, thin boots, carefully-cut coats that outlined his
figure, bewitching collars, fresh gloves, and hats. His
hand was adorned by a signet-ring, which he wore outside
his glove; he carried an elegant walking-cane, and did
his best to look and behave like a wealthy young man.
Toothpick in hand, he would repair to the main alley
in the Tuileries Gardens, and stroll about, looking for
all the world like a millionaire just arisen from table.
He had studied the art of twirling a cane and ogling
with an eye to business, *à l'américaine*, as Bixiou said;
for Vimeux lived in the hope that some widow, Englishwoman or foreign lady, might be smitten with his charms;
he used to laugh to show his fine set of teeth; he went
without socks to have his hair curled every day. Vimeux
laid it down as a fixed principle that an eligible hunch-
backed girl must have six thousand livres a year; he
would take a woman of five-and-forty with an income
of eight thousand, or an Englishwoman with a thousand
crowns. Phellion took compassion on the young man.
He was so much pleased with Vimeux's penmanship that
he lectured him, and tried to persuade him to turn writing-

master; it was, he said, a respectable profession which might ameliorate his existence and even render it agreeable. He promised him the school kept by the Demoiselles La Grave. But Vimeux's belief in his star was not to be shaken—it was too firmly fixed in his head. He continued, therefore, to exhibit himself like one of Chevet's sturgeons; albeit his luxuriant moustache had been displayed in vain for three years. Vimeux lowered his eyes every time that he passed Antoine; he owed the porter thirty francs for his breakfasts, and yet towards noon he always asked him to bring him a roll.

Rabourdin had tried several times to put a little sound sense into the young fellow's foolish head, but he gave up at last. Vimeux's father was a clerk to a justice of the peace in the department of the Nord. Adolphe Vimeux had given up dinners at Katcomb's lately, and lived entirely on bread. He was saving up to buy a pair of spurs and a riding-switch. In the office they jeered at his matrimonial calculations, calling him the Villiaume pigeon; but any scoff at this vacuous Amadis could only be attributed to the mocking spirit that creates the vaudeville, for Vimeux was a friendly creature, and nobody's enemy but his own. The great joke in both offices was to bet that he wore stays.

Vimeux began his career under Baudoyer, and intrigued to be transferred to Rabourdin, because Baudoyer was inexorable on the matter of 'Englishmen,' for so the clerks called duns. The 'Englishmen's' day is the day on which the public are admitted; and creditors, being sure of finding their debtors, flock thither to worry them, asking when they will be paid, threatening to attack their salaries. Baudoyer the inexorable compelled his clerks to face it out. 'It was their affair,' he said, 'not to get into debt'; and he regarded his severity as a thing necessary for the public welfare. Rabourdin, on the other hand, stood between his clerks and their creditors; duns were put out at the

door. 'Government offices,' he said, 'were not meant
for the transaction of private business.' Loud was the
scoffing when Vimeux clanked up the stairs and along
the corridors with spurs on his boots. Bixiou, practical
joker to the department, drew a caricature of Vimeux
mounted on a pasteboard hobby horse, and sent the
drawing circulating through Clergeot's and La Billardière's divisions. A subscription list was attached. M.
Baudoyer's name was put down for a hundredweight of
hay from the stock supplied for his own private consumption, and all the clerks cut gibes at their neighbours' expense. Vimeux himself, like the good-natured
fellow that he was, subscribed under the name of 'Miss
Fairfax.'

The handsome clerk of Vimeux's stamp has his post
for a living and his face for his fortune. He is a faithful
supporter of masked balls at carnival-tide, though sometimes even there he fails in his quest. A good many of
his kind give up the search, and end by marrying
milliners or old women ; sometimes some young lady
is charmed with his fine person, and with her he spins
out a clandestine romance that ends in marriage, a love
story diversified by tedious letters, which, however, produce their effect. Occasionally one here and there waxes
bolder. He sees a woman drive past in the Champs-
Élysées, procures her address, hurls impassioned letters
at her, finds a bargain which, unfortunately, encourages
ignoble speculation of this kind.

The Bixiou (pronounced Bisiou) mentioned above
was a caricaturist ; Dutocq and Rabourdin, whom he
dubbed *La vertueuse Rabourdin*, were alike fair game
to him ; Baudoyer he called *La Place-Baudoyer*, by way
of summing up his chief's commonplace character ; du
Bruel was christened *Flonflon*. Bixiou was beyond
question the wittiest and cleverest man in the division,
or, indeed, in the department ; but his was a monkey's
cleverness, desultory and aimless. Baudoyer and Godard

protected him in spite of his malicious ways, because he was extremely useful to them; he did their work for them out of hand. He wanted du Bruel's or Godard's place, but he stood in his own light. Sometimes—this was when he had done some good stroke of business, such as the portraits in the Fualdès case (which he drew out of his own head), or pictures of the Castaing trial— he turned the service to ridicule. Sometimes he would be very industrious in a sudden fit of desire to get on; and then again he would neglect the work for a vaudeville, which he never by any chance finished. He was, moreover, selfish, close-fisted, and yet extravagant; or, in other words, he lavished money only upon himself; he was fractious, aggressive, and indiscreet, making mischief for pure love of mischief.

Bixiou was especially given to attacking the weak; he respected nothing and no one; he believed neither in France, nor God, nor Art, in neither Greek nor Turk, nor Champ-d'Asile, nor in the Monarchy; and he made a point of jeering at everything which he did not understand. He was the very first to put a black priest's cap on Charles x.'s head on five-franc pieces. He took off Dr. Gall at his lectures till the most closely-buttoned diplomate must have choked with laughter. It was a standing joke with this formidable wag to heat the office stoves so hot that if any one imprudently ventured out of the sudatorium he was pretty certain to catch cold; while Bixiou enjoyed the further satisfaction of wasting the fuel supplied by the Government. Bixiou was not an ordinary man in his hoaxes; he varied them with so much ingenuity that somebody was invariably taken in. He guessed every one's wishes; this was the secret of his success in this line; he knew the way to every castle in Spain; and a man is easy to hoax through his day-dreams, because he is a willing accomplice. Bixiou would draw you out for hours together. And yet, though Bixiou was a profound observer, though he displayed extraordinary tact for purposes of quizzing, he could not apply his aptitude to the purpose of making other men useful to him, nor to the art of getting on in life. He liked best of all to torment La Billardière junior, his pet aversion and nightmare; but nevertheless he coaxed and flattered the young fellow the better to quiz him. He used to send him love letters-signed 'Comtesse de M——' or 'Marquise de B——', making an appointment under the clock in the *foyer* of the Opéra at Shrovetide, and then after making a public exhibition of the young man he would let loose a grisette upon him. He made common cause with Dutocq (whom he regarded as a serious hoaxer); he made it a labour of love to support him in his detestation of Rabourdin and his praises of Baudoyer.

Jean Jacques Bixiou was the grandson of a Paris grocer. His father died as a cólonel in the army, leaving the boy to the care of his grandmother, who had lost her husband and married one Descoings, her shopman. Descoings died in 1822. When Bixiou left school and looked about for some means of earning a livelihood, he tried Art for a while; but in spite of his friendship for Joseph Bridau, a friend of childhood, he gave up painting for caricatures, and vignettes, and the kind of work known twenty years afterwards as book illustration. The influence of the Ducs de Maufrigneuse and de Rhétoré (whose acquaintance he made through opera-dancers) procured him his place in 1819. He was on the best of terms with des Lupeaulx, whom he met in society as an equal; he talked familiarly to du Bruel; he was a living proof of Rabourdin's observations on the continual process of destruction at work in the administrative hierarchy of Paris, when a man acquired personal importance outside the office. Short but well made, small of feature, remarkable for a vague resemblance to Napoleon; a young man of twenty-seven, with thin lips, a flat, perpendicular chin, fair hair, auburn whiskers, sparkling eyes, and a caustic voice—here you have Bixiou. All senses and intellect, he spoiled his career by an unbridled love of pleasure, which plunged him into continual dissipation. He was an intrepid man of pleasure; he ran about after grisettes, smoked, dined, and supped, and told good stories, everywhere adapting himself to his company, and shining behind the scenes, at a grisettes' ball, or the Allée des Veuves. At table or as one of a pleasure party Bixiou was equally astonishing; he was equally alert and in spirits at midnight in the street, or at his first waking in the morning; but, like most great comic actors, he was gloomy and depressed when by himself. Launched forth into a world of actors, actresses, writers, artists, and a certain kind of woman whose riches are apt to take wings, he lived well, he went to the theatre without payment, he played at Frascati's, and often won. He was, in truth, profoundly an artist, but only by flashes; life for him was a sort of swing on which he swayed to and fro without troubling himself about the moment when the cord would break. Among people accustomed to a brilliant display of intellect, Bixiou was in great request for the sake of his liveliness and prodigality of ideas; but none of his friends liked him. He could not resist the temptation of an epigram; he sacrificed his neighbour on either hand at dinner before the first course was over. In spite of his superficial gaiety, a certain secret discontent with his social position crept into his conversation; he aspired to something better, and the fatal lurking imp in his character would not permit him to assume the gravity which makes so much impression on fools. He lived in chambers in the Rue de Ponthieu; it was a regular bivouac; the three rooms were given up to the disorder of a bachelor establishment. Often he would talk of leaving France to try a violent assault on fortune in America. No fortune-teller could have predicted his future, for all his talents were incomplete; he could not work hard and steadily; he was always intoxicated with pleasure, always behaving as if the world were to come to an end on the morrow.

As to dress, his claim was that he was not ridiculous on that score; and, perhaps, he was the one man in the department of whom it would not be said, ' There goes a Government clerk! ' He wore elegant boots, black trousers with straps to them, a fancy waistcoat, a cravat (the eternal gift of the grisette), a hat from Bandoni's, and dark kid gloves. His bearing was not ungraceful, being both easy and unaffected. So it came to pass that when summoned to hear a reprimand from des Lupeaulx, after carrying his insolence towards the Baron de la Billardière a little too far, he was content to rejoin, ' You would take me on again for the sake of my clothes.' And des Lupeaulx could not help laughing.

The most pleasing hoax ever perpetrated by Bixiou in the offices was devised for Godard's benefit. To him Bixiou presented a Chinese butterfly, which the senior clerk put in his collection, and exhibits to this day; he has not yet found out that it is a piece of painted paper. Bixiou had the patience to elaborate a masterpiece for the sake of playing a trick upon the chief clerk's assistant.

The devil always provides a Bixiou with a victim. Baudoyer's office accordingly contained a butt, a poor copying-clerk, aged two-and-twenty. Auguste-Jean-François Minard, for that was his name, was in receipt of a salary of fifteen hundred francs. He had married for love. His wife was a doorkeeper's daughter, an artificial-flower maker, who worked at home for Mlle. Godard. Minard had seen the girl in the shop in the Rue de Richelieu. Zélie Lorain, in the days before her marriage, had many dreams of changing her station in life. She had been trained at the Conservatoire as dancer, singer, and actress by turns; and often she had

thought of doing as many other girls did, but the fear
that things might turn out badly for her, and she might
sink to unspeakable depths, had kept Zélie in the paths
of virtue.   She was revolving all kinds of hazy projects
in her mind when Minard came forward with his offer
of marriage and gave them a definite shape.   Zélie was
earning five hundred francs a year ; Minard had fifteen
hundred.   In the belief that two persons can live on
two thousand francs, they were married without settle-
ments and in the most economical fashion.   The pair
of turtle-doves found a nest on a third floor near the
Barrière de Courcelles, at a rent of a hundred crowns.
There was a very neat little kitchen, with a cheap plaid
paper at fifteen sous the piece upon the walls, a brick
floor assiduously beeswaxed and polished, walnut-wood
furniture, and white cotton curtains in the windows ;
there was a room in which Zélie made her flowers ;
a parlour beyond, with a round table in the middle, a
looking-glass on the wall, a clock representing a revolving crystal fountain, dark haircloth chairs, and gilt
candlesticks in gauze covers ; and a blue-and-white bedroom, with a mahogany bedstead, a bureau, a bit of
striped carpet at the bed-foot, half a dozen easy-chairs
and four chairs, and a little cherry-wood cot in the
corner where the little ones, a boy and girl, used to
sleep.   Zélie nursed her children herself, did the cook-
ing and the work of the house, and made her flowers.
There was something touching in their happy, hard-
working, unpretending comfort.   As soon as Zélie
felt that Minard loved her, she loved him with all her
heart.   Love draws love; it is the 'deep calling unto
deep' of the Bible.
   Minard, poor fellow, used to leave his wife asleep in
bed in the morning and do her marketing for her.   He
took the finished flowers to the shop on his way to the
office of a morning, and bought the materials as he
came home in the afternoon.   Then, as he waited for

dinner, he cut or stamped out the petals, made the stalks, and mixed the colours for her. The little, thin, slight, nervous man, with the curled chestnut hair, clear hazel eyes, and dazzlingly fair but freckled complexion, possessed a quiet and unboasting courage below the surface. He could write as well as Vimeux. At the office he kept himself to himself, did his work, and maintained the reserve of a thoughtful man whose life is hard. Bixiou, the pitiless, nicknamed him 'the white rabbit,' on account of his white eyelashes and scanty eyebrows. Minard was a Rabourdin on a lower level. He was burning with a desire to put his Zélie in a good position; he wanted to make a fortune quickly, and to this end he was trying to hit upon an idea, a discovery, or an improvement in the ocean of Parisian industries and cravings for new luxury. Minard's seeming stupidity was the result of mental tension; he went from the *Double Pâte des Sultanes* to *Cephalic Oil*; from phosphorus boxes to portable gas; from hinged clogs to hydrostatic lamps, making the entire round of the infinitesimally small details of material civilisation. He bore Bixiou's jests as a busy man bears with the buzzing of a fly; he never even lost his temper. And Bixiou, quickwitted though he was, never suspected the depth of contempt that Minard felt for him. Minard regarded a quarrel with Bixiou as a waste of time, and so at length he had tired out his persecutor.

Minard was very plainly dressed at the office; he wore trousers of drill till October, shoes and gaiters, a mohair waistcoat, a beaver-cloth coat in winter and twill in summer, and a straw or silk hat according to the season, for Zélie was his pride. He would have gone without food to buy a new dress·for her. He breakfasted at home with his wife, and ate nothing till he returned. Once a month he took Zélie to the theatre with a ticket given by du Bruel or Bixiou; for Bixiou did all sorts of things, even a kindness now and again.

On these occasions Zélie's mother left her porter's room to look after the baby. Minard had succeeded to Vimeux's place in Baudoyer's office.

Mme. and M. Minard paid their calls in person on New Year's Day. People used to wonder how the wife of a poor clerk on fifteen hundred francs a year could manage to keep her husband in a suit of black, and afford to drive in a cab, and to wear embroidered muslin dresses and silk petticoats, a Tuscan straw bonnet with flowers in it, prunella shoes, magnificent fichus, and a Chinese parasol, and yet be virtuous; while Mme. Colleville or such and such a 'lady' could scarcely make both ends meet on two thousand four hundred francs.

Two of the clerks were friends to a ridiculous degree, for anything is matter for a joke in a Government office. One of these was the senior draughting-clerk in Baudoyer's office; he had been chief clerk's assistant, and even chief clerk, for some considerable time during the Restoration. Colleville, for that was his name, had in Mme. Colleville a wife as much above the ordinary level in her way as Mme. Rabourdin in another. Colleville, the son of a first violin at the Opéra, had been smitten with the daughter of a well-known opera-dancer. Some clever and charming Parisiennes can make their husbands happy without losing their liberty; Mme. Colleville was one of these. She made Colleville's house a meeting-place for orators of the Chamber and the best artists of the day. People were apt to forget how humble a place Colleville occupied in his own house. Flavie was a little too prolific; her conduct offered such a handle to gossip that Mme. Rabourdin had refused all her invitations.

Colleville's friend, one Thuillier, was senior draughting-clerk in Rabourdin's office; and while he occupied precisely the same position, his career in the service had been cut short for the same reasons. If any one knew

Colleville, he knew Thuillier, and *vice versâ*. It had so
fallen out that they both entered the office at the same
time, and their friendship arose out of this coincidence.
Pretty Mme. Colleville (so it was said among the clerks)
had not repulsed Thuillier's assiduities. Thuillier's
wife had brought him no children. Thuillier, otherwise 'Beau Thuillier,' had been a lady-killer in his
youth, and now was as idle as Colleville was industrious.
Colleville not only played the first clarionet at the
Opéra-Comique—he kept tradesmen's books in the
morning before he went to the office, and worked very
hard to bring up his family although he did not lack
influence. Others regarded him as a very shrewd
individual, and so much the more so because he hid
his ambitions under a semblance of indifference. To
all appearance he was satisfied with his lot; he liked
work; he found everybody, even to the chiefs themselves, inclined to aid so brave a struggle for a livelihood.
Only recently, within the last few days in fact, Mme.
Colleville had reformed her ways, and seemed to be
tending towards religion; whereupon a rumour went
abroad through the offices that the lady meant to
betake herself to the Congrégation in search of some
more certain support than the famous orator François
Keller, for his influence hitherto had failed to procure a
good place for Colleville. Flavie had previously addressed
herself (it was one of the mistakes of her life) to des
Lupeaulx.

Colleville had a mania for reading the fortunes of
famous men in anagrams made by their names. He
would spend whole months in arranging and rearranging
the letters to discover some significance in them. In
Révolution française, he discovered *Un Corse la finira*;
—*Vierge de son mari* in Marie de Vigneros, Cardinal de
Richelieu's niece;—*Henrici mei casta dea* in Catharina
de Medicis;—*Eh! c'est large nez* in Charles Genest,
the Abbé whose big nose amused the Duc de Bour-

gogne so much at the Court of Louis xiv. All anagrams known to history had set Colleville wondering.
He raised the play on words into a science; a man's
fate (according to him) was written in a phrase composed of the letters of his name, style, and titles. Ever
since Charles x. came to the throne he had been busy
with that monarch's anagram. Thuillier maintained
that an anagram was a pun in letters; but Thuillier
was rather given to puns. Colleville, a man of generous
nature, was bound by a well-nigh indissoluble friendship
to Thuillier, a pattern of an egoist! It was an insoluble
problem, though many of the clerks explained it by the
observation that 'Thuillier is well to do, and Colleville's
family is a heavy burden!' And, truth to say, Thuillier
was supposed to supplement his salary by lending money
out at interest. Men in business often sent to ask to
speak with him, and Thuillier would go down for a few
minutes' talk with them in the courtyard; but these
interviews were undertaken on account of his sister,
Mlle. Thuillier. The friendship thus consolidated by
time was based upon events and attachments that came
about naturally enough; but the story has been given
elsewhere,[1] and critics might complain of the tedious
length of it if it were repeated. Still, it is perhaps
worth while to point out that while a great deal
was known in the offices as to Mme. Colleville, the
clerks scarcely knew that there was a Mme. Thuillier.
Colleville, the active man with a burdensome family of
children, was fat, flourishing, and jolly; while Thuillier,
the 'buck of the Empire,' with his idle ways and no
apparent cares, was slender in figure, haggard, and
almost melancholy to behold.

'We do not know whether our friendships spring
from our unlikeness or likeness to each other,' Rabourdin
would say, in allusion to the pair.

Chazelle and Paulmier, in direct contrast to the

---

[1] In *Les Petits Bourgeois.*

Siamese twins, were always at war with each other. One of them smoked, the other took snuff, and the pair quarrelled incessantly as to the best way of using tobacco. One failing common to both made them equally tiresome to their fellow-clerks—they were perpetually squabbling over the cost of commodities, the price of green peas or mackerel, the amounts paid by their colleagues for hats, boots, coats, umbrellas, ties, and gloves. Each bragged of his new discoveries, and always kept them to himself. Chazelle collected booksellers' prospectuses and pictorial placards and designs ; but he never subscribed to anything. Paulmier, Chazelle's fellow-chatterbox, went once to the great Dauriat to congratulate him on bringing out books printed on hot-pressed paper with printed covers, and bade him persevere in the path of improvements—and Paulmier had not a book in his possession ! Chazelle, being henpecked at home, tried to give himself independent airs abroad, and supplied Paulmier with endless gibes ; while Paulmier, a bachelor, fasted as frequently as Vimeux himself, and his threadbare clothes and thinly disguised poverty furnished Chazelle with an inexhaustible text. Chazelle and Paulmier were both visibly increasing in waist girth ; Chazelle's small, rotund, pointed stomach had the impudence, according to Bixiou, to be always first, Paulmier's fluctuated from right to left ; Bixiou had them measured once or so in a quarter. Both were between thirty and forty, and both were sufficiently vapid ; they did nothing after hours. They were specimens of your thoroughbred Government clerk—their brains had been addled with scribbling and long continuance in the service. Chazelle used to doze over his work, while the pen which he still held in his hand marked his breathings with little dots on the paper. Then Paulmier would say that Chazelle's wife gave him no rest at night. And Chazelle would retort that Paulmier had taken drugs for four months

out of the twelve, and prophesy that a grisette would
be the death of him.   Whereupon Paulmier would
demonstrate that Chazelle was in the habit of marking
the almanac when Mme. Chazelle showed herself com-
plaisant.   By dint of washing their dirty linen in public,
and flinging particulars of their domestic life at one
another, the pair had won a fairly-merited and general
contempt. 'Do you take me for a Chazelle?' was a
remark that put an end to a wearisome discussion.

M. Poiret junior was so called to distinguish him
from an elder brother who had left the service.   Poiret
senior had retired to the Maison Vauquer, at which
boarding-house Poiret junior occasionally dined, meaning likewise to retire thither some day for good.   Poiret
junior had been thirty years in the department.   Every
action in the poor creature's life was part of a routine;
Nature herself is more variable in her revolutions.   He
always put his things in the same place, laid his pen on
the same mark in the grain of the wood, sat down in his
place at the same hour, and went to warm himself at the
stove at the same minute; for his one vanity consisted in
wearing an infallible watch, though he always set it daily
by the clock of the Hôtel de Ville, which he passed on
his way from the Rue du Martroi.

Between six and eight o'clock in the morning Poiret
made up the books of a large draper's shop in the Rue
Saint-Antoine; from six to eight in the evening he
again acted as bookkeeper to the firm of Camusot in the
Rue des Bourdonnais.   In this way he made an income
of a thousand crowns a year, including his salary.   By
this time he was within a few months of his retirement
upon a pension, and therefore treated office intrigues
with much indifference.   Retirement had already dealt
Poiret senior his deathblow; and probably when Poiret
junior should no longer be obliged to walk daily from
the Rue du Martroi to the office, to sit on his chair at
a table and copy out documents daily, he too would age

very quickly. Poiret junior collected back numbers of the *Moniteur* and of the newspaper to which the clerks subscribed. He achieved this with a collector's enthusiasm. If a number was mislaid, or if one of the clerks took away a copy and forgot to bring it back again, Poiret junior went forthwith to the newspaper office to ask for another copy, and returned delighted with the cashier's politeness. He always came in contact with a charming young fellow; journalists, according to him, were pleasant and little known people. Poiret junior was a man of average height, with dull eyes, a feeble, colourless expression, a tanned skin puckered into grey wrinkles with small bluish spots scattered over them, a snub nose, and a sunken mouth, in which one or two bad teeth still lingered on. Thuillier used to say that it was useless for Poiret to look in the mirror, because he had lost his eye-teeth.[1] His long, thin arms terminated in big hands without any pretension to whiteness; his grey hair, flattened down on his head by the pressure of his hat, gave him something of a clerical appearance; a resemblance the less welcome to him, because though he was not able to give an account of his religious opinions, he hated priests and ecclesiastics of every sort and description. This antipathy, however, did not prevent him from feeling an extreme attachment for the Government, whatever it might happen to be. Even in the very coldest weather, Poiret never buttoned his old-fashioned greatcoat, or wore any but laced shoes or black trousers. He had gone to the same shops for thirty years. When his tailor died, he asked for leave to go to the funeral, shook hands at the graveside with the man's son, and assured him of his custom. Poiret was on friendly terms with all his tradesmen; he took an interest in their affairs, chatted with them, listened to

[1] *Parce qu'il ne se voyait pas dedans (de dents).* Here, as in many other instances, it is only possible to suggest in the English version that a pun has been made in the French.—*Tr.*

the tale of their grievances, and paid promptly. If he
had occasion to write to make a change in an order, he
observed the utmost ceremony, dating the letter, and
beginning with 'Monsieur' on a separate line; then he
took a rough copy, and kept it in a pasteboard case,
labelled 'My Correspondence.'

No life could be more methodical. Poiret kept every
receipted bill, however small the amount; and all his
private account books, year by year, since he came into
the office, were put away in paper covers. He dined for
a fixed sum per month at the same eating-house (the
sign of the *Sucking Calf*, in the Place du Châtelet), and at
the same table (the waiters used to keep his place for him);
and as he never gave *The Golden Cocoon*, the famous silk-
mercer's establishment, so much as five minutes more
than the due time, he always reached the Café David, the
most famous café in the Quarter, at half-past eight, and
stayed there till eleven o'clock. He had frequented that
café likewise for thirty years, and punctually took his
bavaroise at half-past ten; listening to political discussions
with his arms crossed on his walking-stick, and his chin
on his right hand, but he never took part in them. The
lady at the desk was the one woman with whom he liked to
converse; to her ears he confided all the little events of
his daily existence, for he sat at a table close beside her.
Sometimes he would play at dominoes, the one game
that he had managed to learn; but if his partners failed
to appear, Poiret was occasionally seen to doze, with his
back against the panels, while the newspaper frame in
his hand sank down on the slab before him.

Poiret took an interest in all that went on in Paris.
He spent Sunday in looking round at buildings in course
of construction; he would talk to the pensioner who
sees that no one goes inside the hoardings, and fret
over the delays, the lack of money or of building
materials, and other obstacles in the way of the archi-
tect. He was heard to say, 'I have seen the Louvre

rise from its ruins; I saw the first beginnings of the Place du Châtelet, the Quai aux Fleurs, and the Markets.' He and his brother were born at Troyes; their father, a clerk of a farmer of taxes, had sent them both to Paris to learn their business in a Government office. Their mother brought a notorious life to a disastrous close; for the brothers learned to their sorrow that she died in the hospital at Troyes, in spite of frequent remittances. And not merely did they vow then and there never to marry, but they held children in abhorrence; they could not feel at ease with them; they feared them much as others might fear lunatics, and scrutinised them with haggard eyes. Drudgery had crushed all the life out of them both in Robert Lindet's time. The Government had not treated them justly, but they thought themselves lucky to keep their heads on their shoulders, and only grumbled between themselves at the ingratitude of the administration—for they had 'organised' the 'Maximum'! When the before-mentioned trick was played upon Phellion, and his famous sentence was taken to Rabourdin for correction, Poiret took the draughting-clerk aside into the corridor to say, ' You may be sure, sir, that I opposed it with all my might.'

Poiret had never been outside Paris since he came into the city. He began from the first to keep a diary, in which he set out the principal events of the day. Du Bruel told him that Byron had done the same; the comparison overwhelmed Poiret with joy, and induced him to buy a copy of Chastopalli's translation of Byron's works, of which he understood not a word. At the office he was often seen in a melancholy attitude; he looked as if he were meditating deeply, but his mind was a blank. He did not know a single one of his fellow-lodgers; he went about with the key of his room in his pockets. On New Year's Day he left a card himself on every clerk in the division, and paid no visits.

Once, it was in the dog-days, Bixiou took it into his head to grease the inside of Poiret's hat with lard. Poiret junior (he was then fifty-two years of age) had worn the hat for nine whole years; Bixiou had never seen him in any other. Bixiou had dreamed of the hat of nights; it was before his eyes while he ate; and in the interests of his digestion, he made up his mind to rid the office of the unclean thing. Poiret junior went out towards four o'clock. He went his way through the streets of Paris, in a tropical heat, for the sun's rays were reflected back again from the walls and the pavement. Suddenly he felt that his head was streaming with perspiration; and he seldom perspired. Deeming that he was ill, or on the verge of an illness, he went home instead of repairing to the *Sucking Calf*, took out his diary, and made the following entry :—

'This day, July 3rd, 1823, surprised by an un-accountable perspiration, possibly a symptom of the sweating sickness, a malady peculiar to Champagne. Incline to consult Dr. Haudry. First felt the attack by the Quai d'École.'

Suddenly, as he wrote bareheaded, it struck him that the supposed sweat arose from some external cause. He wiped his countenance and examined his hat; but he did not venture to undo the lining, and could make nothing of it. Subsequently he made another entry in the diary :—

'Took the hat to the Sieur Tournan, hatter in the Rue Saint-Martin; seeing that I suspect that something else caused the sweat, which in that case would not be a sweat at all, but simply the effect of an addition of some kind, more or less recently made.'

M. Tournan immediately detected the presence of a

fatty substance obtained by distillation from a hog or
sow, and pointed it out to his customer. Poiret departed in a hat lent by M. Tournan till the new one
should be ready for him; but before he went to bed he
added another sentence to his diary :—

'It has been ascertained that my hat contained lard,
otherwise hog's fat.'

The inexplicable fact occupied Poiret's mind for a
fortnight; he never could understand how the phenomenon had been brought about. There was talk at
the office of showers of frogs and other canicular
portents; a portrait of Napoleon had been found in an
elm-tree root; all kinds of grotesque freaks of natural
history cropped up. Vimeux told him one day that
he, Vimeux, had had his face dyed black by his hat,
and added that hatters sold terrible trash. Poiret went
several times after that to Sieur Tournan's to reassure
his mind as to the processes of manufacture.

There was yet another clerk in Rabourdin's office.
This personage avowedly had the courage of his opinions,
professed the politics of the Left Centre, and worked
himself into indignation over the unlucky white slaves
in Baudoyer's office, and against that gentleman's
tyranny. Fleury openly took in an Opposition sheet,
wore a wide-brimmed grey felt hat, blue trousers with
red stripes, a blue waistcoat adorned with gilt buttons,
and a double-breasted overcoat that made him look like
a quartermaster in the gendarmerie. His principles
remained unshaken, and the administration nevertheless
continued to employ him. Yet he prophesied evil of
the Government if it persisted in mixing politics and
religion. He made no secret of his predilection for
Napoleon, especially since the great man's death made
a dead letter of the law against all partisans of the
'usurper.' Fleury, ex-captain of a regiment of the line

under the Emperor, a tall, fine, dark-haired fellow, was
a money-taker at the Cirque-Olympique. Bixiou had
never indulged in a caricature of him; for the rough
trooper was not only a very good shot and a first-rate
swordsman, but he appeared capable of going to brutal
extremities upon occasion. Fleury was a zealous sub-
scriber to *Victoires et Conquêtes*; but he declined to pay,
and kept the issues as they appeared, basing his refusal
upon the fact that the number stated in the prospectus
had been exceeded.

He worshipped M. Rabourdin, for M. Rabourdin had
interfered to save him from dismissal. A remark once
escaped the ex-warrior, to the effect that if anything
should come to M. Rabourdin through anybody else, he,
Fleury, would kill that some one else; and Dutocq
ever since went in such fear of Fleury, that he fawned
upon him.

Fleury was overburdened with debts. He played his
creditors all kinds of tricks. Being expert in the law,
he never by any chance put his name to a bill; and as
he himself had attached his salary in the names of
fictitious creditors, he drew pretty nearly the whole of
it. He had formed a very intimate connection with a
super at the Porte Saint-Martin, and his furniture was
removed to her house. So he played écarté joyously,
and charmed social gatherings with his talents; he could
drink off a glass of champagne at a draught without
moistening his lips, and he knew all Béranger's songs
by heart. His voice was still fine and sonorous; he
allowed it to be seen that he was proud of it. His
three great men were Napoleon, Bolivar, and Béranger.
Foy, Laffitte, and Casimir Delavigne only enjoyed his
esteem. Fleury, as you guess, was a man of the South;
he was pretty sure to end as the responsible editor of
some Liberal paper.

Desroys was the mysterious man of the division. He
rubbed shoulders with no one, talked little, and hid his

life so successfully that no one knew where he lived, nor how he lived, nor who his protectors were. Seeking a reason for this silence, some held that Desroys was one of the Carbonari, and some that he was an Orleanist; some said that he was a spy, others that he was a deep individual. But Desroys was simply the son of a member of the Convention who had not voted for the king's death. Reserved and cold by temperament, he had formed his own conclusions of the world, and looked to no one but himself. As a Republican in secret, an admirer of Paul Louis Courier, and a friend of Michel Chrestien's, he was waiting till time and the common-sense of the majority should bring about the triumph of his political opinions in Europe. Wherefore his dreams were of Young Germany and Young Italy. His heart swelled high with that unintelligent collective affection for the species, which must be called 'humanitarianism,' eldest child of a defunct philosophy, an affection which is to the divine charity of the Catholic religion as system is to art, as reasoning is to effort. This conscientious political Puritan, this apostle of an impossible Equality, regretted that penury forced him into the service of the Government; he was trying to get employment in some coach office. Lean and lank, prosy and serious, as a man may be expected to be if he feels that he may be called upon some day to give his head for the great object of his life, Desroys lived on a page of Volney, studied St. Just, and was engaged upon a rehabilitation of Robespierre, considered as a continuer of the work of Jesus Christ.

One more among these personages deserves a stroke or two of the pencil. This is little La Billardière. For his misfortune he had lost his mother. He had interest with the minister; he was exempt from the rough and ready treatment that he should have received from ' la Place-Baudoyer'; and all the ministerial salons were open to him. Everybody detested the youth for his

insolence and conceit. Heads of departments were civil
to him, but the clerks had put him beyond the pale of
good fellowship with a grotesque politeness invented
for his benefit. Little La Billardière was a tall, slim,
wizened youth of two-and-twenty, with the manners of
an Englishman; his dandy's airs were an affront to the
office; he came to it scented and curled with impeccable
collars and primrose-coloured gloves, and a constantly
renewed hat lining; he carried an eyeglass; he breakfasted at the Palais Royal. A veneer of manner which
did not seem altogether to belong to him covered his
natural stupidity. Benjamin de la Billardière had an
excellent opinion of himself; he had every aristocratic
defect, and no corresponding graces. He felt quite sure
of being 'somebody,' and had thoughts of writing a
book; he would gain the Cross as an author and set it
down to his administrative talents. So he cajoled Bixiou
with a view to exploiting him, but as yet he had not
ventured to broach the subject. This noble heart was
waiting impatiently for the death of the father who had
but lately been made a baron. 'The Chevalier de la
Billardière' (so his name appeared on his cards) had his
armorial bearings framed and hung up at the office, to
wit, *sable*, two swords saltire-wise, on a chief *azure*, three
stars, and the motto: A TOUJOURS FIDÈLE. He had a
craze for talking of heraldry. Once he asked the young
Vicomte de Portenduère why his arms were blazoned
thus, and drew down upon himself the neat reply, 'It
was none of my doing.' Little La Billardière talked
much of his devotion to the Monarchy, and of the
Dauphiness's graciousness to him. He was on very
good terms with des Lupeaulx, often breakfasted with
him, and believed that des Lupeaulx was his friend.
Bixiou, posing as his mentor, had hopes of ridding
the division, and France likewise, of the young coxcomb by plunging him into dissipation; and he
made no secret of his intentions.

Such were the principal figures in La Billardière's division. Some others there were besides which more or less approached these types in habits of life or appearance. Baudoyer's office boasted various examples of the genus clerk in diverse bald-fronted, chilly mortals, with frames well wadded round with flannel. These individuals carried thorn-sticks, wore threadbare clothes, and never were seen without an umbrella. They perched, as a rule, on fifth floors, and cultivated flowers at that height. Clerks of this type rank halfway between the prosperous porter and the needy artisan; they are too far from the administrative centre to hope for any promotion whatsoever; they are pawns upon the bureaucratic chessboard. When their turn comes to go on guard, they rejoice to get a day away from the office. There is nothing that they will not do for extras. How they exist at all their very employers would be puzzled to say; their lives are an indictment against the State that assuredly causes the misery by accepting such a condition of things.

At sight of their strange faces it is hard to decide whether these quill-bearing mammals become cretinous at their task, or whether, on the other hand, they would never have undertaken it if they had not been, to some extent, cretins from birth. Perhaps Nature and the Government may divide the responsibility between them. 'Villagers,' according to an unknown writer, 'are submitted to the influences of atmospheric conditions and surrounding circumstances. They do not seek to explain the fact to themselves. They are in a manner identified with their natural surroundings. Slowly and imperceptibly the ideas and ways of feeling awakened by those surroundings will permeate their being, and come to the surface of their lives, in their personal appearance and in their actions, with variations for each individual organisation and temperament. And thus, if any student feels attracted to the little known and fruitful field of

N

physiological inquiry, which includes the effects produced by external natural agents upon human character,
for him the villager becomes a most interesting and
trustworthy book.' But for the employé, Nature is
replaced by the office; his horizon is bounded upon all
sides by green pasteboard cases. For him atmospheric
influences mean the air of the corridors, the stuffy
atmosphere of unventilated rooms where men are
crowded together; and the odour of paper and quills.
A floor of bare bricks or parquetry, bestrewn with strange
litter, and besprinkled from the messenger's watering-
can, is the scene of his labours; his sky is the ceiling,
to which his yawns are addressed; his element is dust.
The above remarks on the villager might have been
meant for the clerk; he too is 'identified' with his
surroundings. The sun scarcely shines into the horrid
dens known as public offices; the thinking powers of
their occupants are strictly confined to a monotonous
round. Their prototype, the mill-horse, yawns hideously
over such work, and cannot stand it for long. And
since several learned doctors see reason to dread the
effects of such half-barbarous, half-civilised surroundings upon the mental constitution of human beings
pent up among them, Rabourdin surely was profoundly
right when he proposed to cut down the number of the
staff, and asked for heavy salaries and hard work for
them. Men are not bored when they have great things
to do.

As government offices are at present constituted,
four hours out of the nine which the clerks are supposed
to give to the State are wasted, as will presently be
seen, over talk, anecdotes, and squabbles, and, more than
all, over office intrigues. You do not know, unless you
frequent government offices, how much the clerk's little
world resembles the world of school; the similarity
strikes you wherever men live together; and in the
army or the law-courts you find the school again on

a rather larger scale. The body of clerks, thus pent up for eight hours at a stretch, looked upon the offices as classrooms in which a certain amount of lessons must be done. The master on duty was called the head of the division; extra pay took the place of good conduct prizes, and always fell to favourites. They teased and disliked each other, and yet there was a sort of good-fellowship among them—though, even so, it was cooler than the same feeling in a regiment; and in the regiment, again, it is not so strong as it is among school-boys. As a man advances in life, egoism develops with his growth and slackens the secondary ties of affection. What is an office, in short, but a world in miniature? —a world with its unaccountable freaks, its friendships and hatreds, its envy and greed, its continual movement to the front? There, too, is the light talk that makes many a wound, and espionage that never ceases.

At this particular moment the whole division, headed by M. le Baron de la Billardière, was shaken by an extraordinary commotion; and, indeed, coming events fully justified the excitement, for heads of divisions do not die every day; and no tontine insurance association can calculate the probabilities of life and death with more sagacity than a government office. In government clerks, as in children, self-interest leaves no room for pity; but the clerk has hypocrisy in addition.

Towards eight o'clock Baudoyer's staff were taking their places, whereas Rabourdin's clerks had scarcely begun to put in an appearance at nine; and yet the work was done much more quickly in the latter office. Dutocq had weighty reasons of his own for arriving early. He had stolen into the private office the night before, and detected Sébastien in the act of copying out papers for Rabourdin. He had hidden himself, and watched Sébastien go out without the papers; and then, feeling sure of finding a tolerably bulky rough draft and the fair copy, he had hunted through one

pasteboard case after another, till at last he found the
terrible list.   Hurrying away to a lithographer's establishment, he had two impressions of the sheet taken off
with a copying-press, and in this way became possessed
of Rabourdin's own handwriting.   Then, to prevent
suspicion, he went to the office the first thing in the
morning and put the rough draft back in the case.
Sébastien had stayed till midnight in the Rue Duphot.
In spite of his diligence, hatred was beforehand with
him.   Hatred dwelt in the Rue Saint Louis Saint
Honoré, whereas devotion lived in the Rue du Roi
Doré in the Marais.   Rabourdin was to feel the effect
of that trivial delay through the rest of his life.   Sébastien
hurried to open the case, found all in order, and locked
up the rough draft and unfinished copy in his chief's
desk.

On a morning towards the end of December the
light is usually dim ; in our offices, indeed, they often
work by lamplight until ten o'clock.   So Sébastien did
not notice the mark of the stone on the paper ; but at
half-past nine, when Rabourdin looked closely at his
draft, he saw that it had been submitted to some copying
process ; he was the more likely to see the traces of the
slab, because of late he had been much interested in
experiments in lithography, for he thought that a press
might do the work of a copying-clerk.

Rabourdin seated himself in his chair.   So deeply
was he absorbed in his reflections, that he took the
tongs and began to build up the fire.   Then, curious to
know into what hands his secret had fallen, he sent for
Sébastien.

'Did any one come to the office before you ?'

'Yes ; M. Dutocq.'

'Good.   He is punctual.   Send Antoine to me.'

Rabourdin was too magnanimous to cause Sébastien
needless distress by reproaching him now that the
mischief was done.   He said no more about it.   Antoine

came. Rabourdin asked if any of the clerks had stayed after four o'clock on the previous day. Antoine said that M. Dutocq had stayed even later than M. de la Roche. Rabourdin nodded, and resumed the course of his reflections.

'Twice I have prevented his dismissal,' he said to himself, 'and this is my reward!'

For Rabourdin that morning was to be the solemn crisis when great captains decide upon a battle after weighing all possible consequences. No one better knew the temper of the offices; he was perfectly aware that anything resembling espionage or tale-telling is no more pardoned by clerks than by school-boys. The man that can tell tales of his comrades is disgraced, ruined, and traduced; ministers in such a case will drop their instrument. Any man in the service, under these circumstances, sends in his resig-nation—no other course is open to him; upon his honour there lies a stain that can never be wiped out. Explanations are useless—nobody wants them, nobody will listen to them. A cabinet minister in the like case is a great man; it is his business to choose men; but a mere subordinate is taken for a spy, no matter what his motives may be. Even while Rabourdin measured the emptiness of this folly, he saw the depths of it—saw, too, that he must sink. He was not so much overwhelmed as taken by surprise; so he sat pondering his best course of action ih the matter, and knew nothing of the commotion caused in the offices by the news of the death of M. de la Billardière till he heard of it through young de la Brière, who could appreciate the immense value of the chief clerk.

Meanwhile in the Baudoyers' office (for the clerks were respectively known as the Baudoyers and the Rabourdins) Bixiou was giving the details of La Billardière's last moments for the benefit of Minard, Desroys, M. Godard (whom he had fetched out of his sanctum), and Dutocq. A double motive had sent the last-named individual hurrying over to the Baudoyers.

BIXIOU (*standing before the stove, holding first one boot and then the other to the fire to dry the soles*). 'This morning at half-past seven I went to inquire after our worthy and revered director, Chevalier of Christ, et cætera. Et cætera? My goodness, I should think so, gentlemen; only yesterday the Baron was a score of *et cæteras*, and now to-day he is nothing, not even a government clerk. I asked what sort of a night he had had. His nurse, who does not die, but surrenders, told me that towards five o'clock this morning he had felt uneasy about the Royal Family. He got somebody to read over the names of those that had sent to make inquiries. Then he said, "Fill my snuff-box, give me the newspaper, bring me my glasses, and change my ribbon of the Legion of Honour, for it is getting very dirty." (He wears his orders in bed, you know.) So he was fully conscious, you see, quite in the possession of all his faculties and habitual ideas. But, pooh! ten minutes afterwards the water had gone up, up, up; up to his heart and into his lungs. He knew he was dying when he felt the cysts break. At that supreme moment he showed what he was—how strong his character, his intellect how vast! Ah! some of us did not appreciate him. We used to laugh at him; we took him for a dunce; for the veriest dunce, did we not, M. Godard?'

GODARD. 'For my own part, nobody could have a higher opinion of M. de la Billardière's talents than I.'

BIXIOU. 'You understood each other.'

GODARD. 'After all, 'twas not a spiteful man. He never did anybody harm.'

BIXIOU. 'A man must do something if he is to do harm, and he never did anything. Then if it was not you that thought him hopelessly inept, it must have been Minard.'

MINARD (*shrugging his shoulders*). 'I?'

BIXIOU. 'Well, then, it was you, Dutocq. (*As Dutocq makes signs of vehement protest.*) What? you none of you thought so? Good! Everybody here, it seems, took him for an intellectual Hercules? Very well, you were right; he made an end like a man of talent, an intelligent man, a great man, as he was, in fact.'

DESROYS (*growing impatient*). 'Gracious me! what has he done that is so extraordinary? Did he make confession?'

BIXIOU. 'Yes, sir, and expressed a wish to receive the sacraments. But do you know how he received them? He had himself put into a court suit as Gentleman in Ordinary, he had all his orders, he even had his hair powdered; they tied up his queue (poor queue) with a new riband (and it is only a man of some character, I can tell you, that can mind his p's and queues when he lies a-dying; there are eight of us here, and not a single one of us could do it). And that is not all; you know that celebrated men always make a last "speech"—that is the English word for a parliamentary gag—well, he said—what did he say now?—ah! yes; he said, "I ought surely to put on my best to receive the King of Heaven, when I have so many times dressed within an inch of my life to pay my respects to an earthly sovereign!" Thus ended M. de la Billardière; he might have done it on purpose to justify the saying of Pythagoras that "we never know men until. they are dead."'

COLLEVILLE (*coming in*). 'At last, gentlemen, I have a famous piece of news for you——'

OMNES. 'We know it.'

COLLEVILLE. 'I defy you to guess it! I have been at this ever since His Majesty's accession to the thrones of France and Navarre; and I finished it last night. It bothered me so much that Mme. Colleville wanted to know what it was that worried me so much.'

DUTOCQ. 'Do you suppose that anybody has time to

think of your anagrams when the highly-respected M. de la Billardière has just died?'

COLLEVILLE. 'I recognise Bixiou's hand. I have only just been to M. de la Billardière's; he was still alive, but he is not expected to last long.' (*Godard discovers that he has been hoaxed, and goes back in disgust to his sanctum.*) 'But, gentlemen, you would never guess the events that lie in that sacramental phrase' (*holds out a paper*), '*Charles Dix, par la grâce de Dieu, roi de France et de Navarre.*'

GODARD (*coming back*). 'Out with it at once, and do not waste their time.'

COLLEVILLE (*triumphantly, displaying the folded end of the sheet*).

> *A. H. V. il cedera*
> *De S. C. l. d. partira*
> *En nauf errera*
> *Decede à Gorix.*

'All the letters are there: "To H. V." (Henri v.) "he will yield" (his crown, that is); "From S. C. l. d." (Saint Cloud) "he will set forth; On a bark" (that means a boat, skiff, vessel, whatever you like, it is an old French word), " on a bark he will wander abroad——"'

DUTOCQ. 'What a tissue of absurdities! How do you make it out that the King will resign his crown to Henri v., who, on your showing, would be his grandson, when there is His Highness the Dauphin in between? You are prophesying the Dauphin's death anyhow.'

BIXIOU. 'What is Gorix? A cat's name?'

COLLEVILLE (*nettled*). 'It is a lapidary's abbreviation of the name of a town, my dear friend; I looked it up in Malte-Brun. Gorix, the Latin *Gorixia*, is situated somewhere in Bohemia or Hungary; it is in Austria any way——'

BIXIOU (*interrupting*). 'Tyrol, Basque provinces, or South America. You ought to have looked out an air at the same time so as to play it on the clarionet.'

GODARD (*shrugging his shoulders as he goes*). 'What rubbish!'

COLLEVILLE. 'Rubbish! rubbish! I should be very glad if you would take the trouble to study fatalism, the religion of the Emperor Napoleon.'

GODARD (*nettled by Colleville's tone*). 'M. Colleville, Bonaparte may be styled "Emperor" by historians, but in a Government office he ought not to be recognised in that character.'

BIXIOU (*smiling*). 'Find an anagram in that, my good friend. There! as for anagrams, I like your wife better. (*sotto voce*) She is easier to turn round.—Flavie really ought to make you chief clerk at some odd moment when she has time to spare, if it were only to put you out of reach of a Godard's stupidity——'

DUTOCQ (*coming to Godard's support*). 'If it wasn't all rubbish, you might lose your place, for the things you prophesy are not exactly pleasant for the King; every good Royalist is bound to assume that when he has been twice in exile he has seen enough of foreign parts.'

COLLEVILLE. 'If they took away my post, François Keller would walk into your Minister' (*deep silence*). 'Know, Master Dutocq, that every known anagram has been fulfilled. Look here, don't you marry, there is *coqu* in your name!'

BIXIOU. 'And D T left over for "detestable."'

DUTOCQ (*not apparently put out*). 'I would rather it went no further than my name.'

PAULMIER (*aside to Desroys*). 'Had you there, Master Colleville!'

DUTOCQ (*to Colleville*). 'Have you done, *Xavier Rabourdin, chef de bureau*——'

COLLEVILLE. 'Egad I have.'

BIXIOU (*cutting a pen*). 'And what did you make out?'

COLLEVILLE. 'It makes this: *D'abord rêva bureaux, E. U.*—Do you take it?—*Et il eut fin riche.* Which means that after beginning in the civil service he chucked it over to make his fortune somewhere else.'

DUTOCQ. 'It is funny, anyhow.'

BIXIOU. 'And *Isidore Baudoyer* ?'

COLLEVILLE (*mysteriously*). 'I would rather not tell anybody but Thuillier.'

BIXIOU. 'Bet you a breakfast I will tell you what it is !'

COLLEVILLE. 'I will pay if you find out.'

BIXIOU. 'Then you are going to stand treat; but don't be vexed, two artists such as you and I will die of laughing. *Isidore Baudoyer* gives *Ris d'aboyeur d'oie*, he laughs at the fellow that barks at a goose.'

COLLEVILLE (*thunderstruck*). 'You stole it !'

BIXIOU (*stiffly*). 'M. Colleville, do me the honour to believe that I am so rich in folly that I have no need to steal from my neighbours.'

BAUDOYER (*a letter-file in his hand*). 'Talk just a little louder, gentlemen, I beg; you will bring the office into good odour. The estimable M. Clergeot, who did me the honour to come to ask for some information, has had the benefit of your conversation' (*goes to Godard's office*).

DUTOCQ (*aside to Bixiou*). 'I have something to say to you.'

BIXIOU (*fingering Dutocq's waistcoat*). 'You are wearing a neat waistcoat which cost you next to nothing, no doubt. Is that the secret ?'

DUTOCQ. 'What ? Next to nothing ? I never gave so much for a waistcoat before. The stuff costs six francs a yard at the big shop in the Rue de la Paix; it is a fine dull silk, just the thing for deep mourning.'

BIXIOU. 'You understand prints, but you do not know the rules of etiquette. One cannot know everything. Silk is not the proper thing to wear in deep mourning. That is why I only wear wool myself. M. Rabourdin, M. Clergeot, and the Minister are all-wool; the Faubourg Saint-Germain is all-wool. Every one goes about in wool except Minard; he is afraid that people will take him for a sheep, styled *laniger* in rustical Latin; and on that pretext he dispensed with mourning for King Louis XVIII., a great legislator, a witty man, the author of the Charter, a king that will hold his own in history, as he held it everywhere else; for—do you know the finest touch of character in his life? No?— Well, then, when he received all the allied sovereigns at his second entry, he walked out first to table.'

PAULMIER (*looking at Dutocq*). 'I do not see——'

DUTOCQ (*looking at Paulmier*). 'No more do I.'

BIXIOU. 'You do not understand? Well, then; he did not regard himself as at home in his own house. It was ingenious, great, epigrammatic! The allied sovereigns understood it no more than you do, even when they put their heads together to make it out. It is true that they were pretty nearly all of them strangers——'

BAUDOYER (*in his assistant clerk's sanctum, where he has been conversing in an undertone beside the fire, while the talk went on outside*). 'Yes, our worthy chief is breathing his last. Both Ministers are there to receive his latest sigh; my father-in-law has just been informed of the event. If you wish to do me a signal service, take a cabriolet and go to Mme. Baudoyer with the news; M. Saillard cannot leave his desk, and I dare not leave the office to look after itself. Put yourself at Mme. Baudoyer's disposal; she has her own views, I believe, and might possibly wish to take several steps simultaneously' (*they go out together*).

GODARD. 'M. Bixiou, I am leaving the office for the day, so will you take my place?'

BAUDOYER (*looking benignly at Bixiou*). 'You might consult me should occasion require it.'

BIXIOU. 'This time, La Billardière is really dead!'

DUTOCQ (*whispers to Bixiou*). 'Look here! Now is the time for coming to an understanding about getting on.

Suppose that you are chief clerk and I assistant; what do you say?'

BIXIOU (*shrugging his shoulders*). 'Come, no nonsense!'

DUTOCQ. 'If Baudoyer gets the appointment, Rabourdin will not stay on; he will send in his resignation. Between ourselves, Baudoyer is so incompetent that if you and du Bruel will not help him he will be cashiered in two months' time. If I can put two and two together, we have three vacant places ahead of us.'

BIXIOU. 'Three places that will be given away under our noses; they will go to swag-bellied toadies, flunkeys, spies, and men of the "Congrégation"; to Colleville here, whose wife has gone the way of all pretty women, to—a devout ending.'

DUTOCQ. 'It will go to you, my dear fellow, if for once in your life you care to employ your wits *consistently*' (*stopping short to note the effect of the adverb upon his listener*). 'Let us be open and aboveboard.'

BIXIOU (*imperturbably*). 'What is your game?'

DUTOCQ. 'For my own part, I want to be chief clerk's assistant and nothing else. I know myself; I know that I have not the ability to be chief, and that you have. Du Bruel may get La Billardière's place, and then you would be chief clerk under him. He will leave you his berth when he has feathered his nest; and as for me, with you to protect me, I shall potter along till I get my pension.'

BIXIOU. 'Sly dog. But how do you mean to bring this through? It is a matter of forcing a Minister's hand and spitting out a man of talent. Between ourselves, Rabourdin is the only man that is fit to take the division—the department, who knows? And you propose to put that square block of stupidity, that cube of incompetence, *La Place-Baudoyer*, in his stead?'

DUTOCQ (*bridling up*). 'My dear fellow, I can set the whole place against Rabourdin? You know how Fleury loves him? Well and good, Fleury shall look down upon him.'

BIXIOU. 'To be despised by Fleury!'

DUTOCQ. 'Nobody will stand by him. The clerks will go in a body to the Minister to complain of·him; and not our division only, but Clergeot's division and the Bois-Levants, all the departments in a mass.',

BIXIOU. 'Just so; cavalry, infantry, artillery, and horse marines, all to the front! You are off your head, my dear fellow! And what have I, for one, to do in this?'

DUTOCQ. 'Draw a cutting caricature, a thing that a man cannot get over.'

BIXIOU. 'Are you going to pay for it?'

DUTOCQ. 'A hundred francs.'

BIXIOU (*to himself*). 'There is something in it, then.'

DUTOCQ. 'Rabourdin might be dressed as a butcher; but the likeness must be unmistakable. Find out points of resemblance between an office and a kitchen; put a larding-knife in Rabourdin's hand; draw a lot of poultry, give them the heads of the principal clerks in the department, and put them in a huge coop with "Dispatch Department" written over it, and Rabourdin must be supposed to be cutting their throats one after another. There should be geese, you know, and ducks with faces like ours; just a sort of a likeness, you understand! Rabourdin ought to have a fowl in his hand—Baudoyer, for example, got up as a turkey.'

BIXIOU. '"Laughs at those that bark at a goose"' (*stares a long while at Dutocq*). 'Did you think of this yourself?'

DUTOCQ. 'Yes.'

BIXIOU (*to himself*). 'Violent hatred and talent, it seems, reach the same end!' (*To Dutocq*) 'My dear fellow, I will do it' (*Dutocq starts with joy in spite of himself*) 'if'—(*pause*)—'if I know whom I can look to to back me up; for if you do not succeed, I shall lose my berth, and I must live. And what is more, your good-nature is somewhat singular, my dear colleague.'

DUTOCQ. 'Well, do not make the drawing until success is plain to you——'

BIXIOU. 'Why not make a clean breast of it at once?'

DUTOCQ. 'I must scent out how things are in the offices first. We will talk of this again afterwards' (*goes*).

BIXIOU (*left standing by himself in the corridor*). 'That stock-fish (for he is more like a fish than a man), that Dutocq has got hold of a good idea, I do not know where he found it. It would be funny if *La Place-Baudoyer* got La Billardière's place; it would be better than funny; we should get something by it.' (*Goes back to the office.*) 'Gentlemen, some famous changes will be seen here directly; Daddy La Billardière is really dead this time. No humbug! Word of honour! There goes Godard post-haste on an errand for our revered chief Baudoyer, heir-presumptive to the late lamented!' (*Minard, Desroys, and Colleville raise their heads and drop their pens in astonishment; Colleville blows his nose.*) 'Some of us will get a step! Colleville is going to be assistant clerk at least; Minard, perhaps, will be first draughting-clerk; why not? He is every bit as great a fool as I am. If you were raised to two thousand five hundred francs—hey, Minard!—your little wife would be finely pleased, and you might buy yourself a pair of boots.'

COLLEVILLE. 'But *you* have not two thousand five hundred francs yet.'

BIXIOU. 'M. Dutocq gets as much as that in the Rabourdins'. Why should not I within the year? So had M. Baudoyer——'

COLLEVILLE. 'That was through M. Saillard's influence. Not a single draughting-clerk gets so much in Clergeot's division.'

PAULMIER. 'By the way! M. Cochin, may be, has not three thousand? He succeeded M. Vavasseur, and M.

Vavasseur was here for ten years under the Empire on four thousand, he was cut down to three thousand on the first return of the Bourbons, and died on two thousand five hundred. But M. Cochin's brother's influence raised it, and so he gets three.'

COLLEVILLE. 'M. Cochin signs himself E. L. L. E. Cochin; his name is Emile Louis Lucien Emmanuel, and his anagram gives *Cochenille*. Well, and he became a partner in a drug business in the Rue des Lombards, and the firm of Matifat made money by speculating in that particular colonial product.'

BIXIOU. 'Matifat, poor man, he had a year of Florine.'

COLLEVILLE. 'Cochin sometimes comes to our parties, for he is a first-rate performer on the violin.' (*To Bixiou, who has not begun to work.*) 'You ought to come to our concert next Tuesday. They will play a quartette by Reicha.'

BIXIOU. 'Thanks, I would rather look at the score.'

COLLEVILLE. 'Do you say that for a joke? For an artist of your attainments ought surely to be fond of music.'

BIXIOU. 'I am going, but it is for madame's sake.'

BAUDOYER (*returning*). 'M. Chazelle not here yet? Give him my compliments, gentlemen.'

BIXIOU (*who had put a hat on Chazelle's place as soon as he heard Baudoyer's footstep*). 'Begging your pardon, sir, he has gone to make an inquiry of the Rabourdin's for you.'

CHAZELLE (*coming in with his hat on his head, misses Baudoyer*). 'Old La Billardière has gone out, gentlemen! Rabourdin is head of the division, and Master of Requests! He has fairly earned his step, he has!——'

BAUDOYER (*to Chazelle*). 'You found the appointment in your second hat, sir, did you not?' (*pointing to the hat on Chazelle's desk.*) 'This is the third time this month that you have come in after nine o'clock; if you keep it up, you will get on, but in what sense remains to be seen.' (*To Bixiou, who is reading the newspaper.*) My dear M. Bixiou, for pity's sake, leave the paper to these gentlemen (they are just going to take their breakfasts), and come and set about to-day's business. I do not know what M. Rabourdin does with Gabriel; he keeps him for his own private use, I suppose, for I have rung three times' (*disappears with Bixiou into Godard's office*).

CHAZELLE. 'Cursed luck!'

PAULMIER (*delighted to tease Chazelle*). 'So they did not tell you downstairs that he had gone up? Anyhow, could you not use you eyes when you came in, and see the hat on your desk, and that elephant——'

COLLEVILLE (*laughing*) '——in the menagerie.'

PAULMIER. 'You ought to have seen him—he is big enough.'

CHAZELLE (*desperately*). 'Egad! even if the Government pays us four francs seventy-five centimes per day, I do not see that we are slaves in consequence.'

FLEURY (*coming in at the door*). 'Down with Baudoyer! Long live Rabourdin! That is the cry all through the division.'

CHAZELLE (*lashing himself into fury*). 'Baudoyer is welcome to cashier me if he has a mind; I shall be no worse off than before. There are a thousand ways of earning five francs a day in Paris; you can make *that* at the Palais by copying for the lawyers——'

PAULMIER. 'So you say, but a berth is a berth; and Colleville, that courageous fellow who works like a galley-slave after hours, and might make more than his salary if he lost his post by giving music lessons—he will keep his berth. Hang it all, a man does not throw up his chances.'

CHAZELLE (*continuing his philippic*). 'He may, not I. We haven't any chance to lose. Confound it! There was a time when nothing was more tempting than a career in the civil service; there were so many men in the army that they were wanted in the administration. The maimed and the halt, toothless old men, unhealthy fellows like Paulmier, and short-sighted people got on rapidly. The lycées swarmed with boys, and families were dazzled with the brilliant prospect. A young fellow in spectacles wore a blue coat, and a red ribbon blazing at his button-hole, and drew a thousand or so of francs every month for spending a few hours every day at some office looking after something or other. He went late and came away early; he had hours of leisure like Lord Byron, and wrote novels; he strolled in the Tuileries Gardens with a bit of a swagger; he was on exhibition at balls and theatres and everywhere else; he was admitted into the best society; he spent his salary, returning to France all that France gave him, and even doing something in return. In those days, in fact, employés (like Thuillier) were petted by pretty women; they were supposed to be intelligent, and by no means overworked themselves at the office. Empresses, queens, and princesses had their fancies in those happy days. All those noble ladies had the passion of noble natures—they loved to play the protector. So there was a chance of filling a high position in twenty-five years or so; you might be auditor to the Council of State; or a Master of Requests, and draw up reports for the Emperor, while you amused yourself with his august family. People used to work and play at the same time. Everything was done quickly. But nowadays, since the Chamber bethought itself of entering the expenditure under separate items, and the heading 'Staff,' we are not even like private soldiers. It is a thousand to one if you get the smallest appointment, for there are a thousand sovereigns——'

BIXIOU (returning). 'Chazelle must be crazy. Where does he discover a thousand sovereigns? Are they by any chance in his pocket?——'

CHAZELLE. 'Let us reckon them up! Four hundred

at the further end of the Pont de la Concorde (so called because it leads to perpetual discord between the Right and the Left in the Chamber); three hundred more at the top of the Rue de Tournon. So the Court, which ought to count for three hundred, is obliged to have seven hundred times the Emperor's strength of will, if it means to give any place whatsoever by patronage——'

FLEURY. 'Which all means that, if a clerk has no interest and no one to help him but himself in a country where there are three centres of power, the betting is a thousand to one that he will never get any further.'

BIXIOU (*looking from Fleury to Chazelle*). 'Aha! my children, you have yet to learn that to be in the service of the State is to be in the worst state of all——'

FLEURY. 'Because there is a constitutional Government.'

COLLEVILLE. 'Gentlemen! let us not talk politics.'

BIXIOU. 'Fleury is right. If you serve the State in these days, gentlemen, you do not serve a prince who rewards and punishes. The State is Anybody and Everybody. Now, Everybody cares for Nobody. If you serve Everybody, you serve Nobody; and Nobody cares about Anybody. A civil servant lives between these two negatives. The world is pitiless, heartless, brainless, and thoughtless; Everybody is selfish, Everybody forgets the services of yesterday. You are (like M. Baudoyer) an administrative genius from a most tender age; you are the Chateaubriand of reports, the Bossuet of circulars, the Canalis of memorials, the 'sublime child' of the dispatch—in vain! There is a disheartening law against administrative genius; the law of advancement on the average.

'That fatal average is worked out from the tables of the law of promotion and the tables of mortality. It is certain that if you enter any department whatsoever at the age of eighteen, you will not have a salary of eighteen hundred francs till you are thirty years old; if you are to get six thousand by the time you are fifty, Colleville's career proves that though you have a genius for a wife, and the support of various peers of France, and of diverse influential deputies to boot, it profiteth you nothing. Let a young man have studied the humanities, let him be vaccinated, exempt from military service, and in full possession of his wits; well, there is no free and independent career in which, without a transcendent intellect, such a man could not put by a capital of forty-five thousand francs of centimes in the time. That sum would bring in a yearly interest equal to our salary, and it would be a perpetual income; whereas our salaries are by their nature transitory, we have not even our berths, such as they are, for life. In the same time, a tradesman would have money put out to interest, and an independent income of ten thousand francs; he would have filed his schedule, or he would be a president of the commercial court. A painter would have covered a square mile of canvas with paint; he would either wear the Cross of the Legion of Honour, or set up for a neglected genius. A man of letters would be a professor of something or other; or a journalist, paid at the rate of a hundred francs for a thousand lines; or he is a *feuilletonniste*, or some fine day he is landed in Saint-Pélagie for writing a luminous pamphlet which displeased the Jesuits; his value incontinently goes up tremendously, and the pamphlet makes a political personage of him. Indeed, your idler that never did anything in his life (for there are idlers that do something, and idlers that do nothing), your idler has made debts and found a widow to pay them. A priest has had time to become a bishop *in partibus*. A vaude-villiste is a landed proprietor, even if, like du Bruel, he never wrote a whole vaudeville by himself. If a steady, intelligent young fellow starts in the money-lending line with a very small capital (like Mlle. Thuillier, for instance), he can buy a fourth of a stockbroker's connection in twelve years. Let us go lower down! A petty clerk becomes a notary; the ragpicker has a thousand crowns of independent income; the working man at worst has managed to set up for himself; whereas, in the midst of the rotatory movement of that civilisation which takes infinite subdivision for progress, a Chazelle has been existing on twenty-two sous per head. He argues with his tailor and shoemaker, he is in debt; that's nothing—he is *cretinised*!—Come, gentlemen, one glorious movement; let us send in our resignations in a body, hey? Fleury and Chazelle, make a plunge into a new line, and become great men in it!——'

CHAZELLE (*calming down under Bixiou's discourse*). 'Thanks' (*general laughter*).

BIXIOU. 'You are wrong. In your position I would be beforehand with the Secretary-General.'

CHAZELLE (*uneasily*). 'Why, what has he to say to me?'

BIXIOU. 'Odry would tell you, Chazelle, with more charm in the manner of the telling than des Lupeaulx will put into the observation, that the one place open to you is the Place de la Concorde.'

PAULMIER (*clasping the stove-pipe*). 'Egad! Baudoyer will not have pity on you, that is certain!'

FLEURY. 'Another thing to put up with from Baudoyer. Now, there's a queer fish for you! Talk of M. Rabourdin—there is a man! The work he put on my table to-day would take three days in this office, but he will have it by four o'clock this afternoon. But *he* is not always at my heels to stop my chat with friends.'

BAUDOYER (*returning*). 'Gentlemen, if anybody has a right to find fault with the parliamentary system or the proceedings of the administration, you must admit that this is not the proper place for such talk.' (*To Fleury*) 'Why are you here, sir?'

FLEURY (*insolently*). 'To advise these gentlemen of a general move! The Secretary-General has sent for du Bruel; Dutocq has gone too. Everybody is wondering about the appointment.'

BAUDOYER (*returning*). 'That, sir, is no business of yours. Go back to your office, and do not upset mine.'

FLEURY (*from the doorway*). 'It would be tremendously unfair if Rabourdin were to be done out of it. My word! I would leave the service.' (*Comes back.*) 'Did you make out your anagram, Daddy Colleville?'

COLLEVILLE. 'Yes, here it is.'

FLEURY (*leaning over Colleville's desk*). 'Famous! famous! It will be sure to happen if the Government keeps to its hypocritical line.' (*Gives warning to the others that Baudoyer is listening.*) 'If the Government openly stated its intentions without an afterthought, then the Liberals would see what they would have to do. But when a Government sets its best friends against it, and sends such men as Chateaubriand and Royer-Collard and the *Débats* into opposition, it makes you sorry to see it.'

COLLEVILLE (*after a look round at his fellow-clerks*). 'Look here, Fleury, you are a good fellow, but you must not talk politics here. You do us more harm than you know.'

FLEURY (*drily*). 'Good day, gentlemen. I will go to my copying.' (*Comes back and speaks to Bixiou in an undertone.*) 'They say that Mme. Colleville is making allies among the Congrégation.'

BIXIOU. 'In what way?——'

FLEURY (*breaking into a laugh*). 'You are never to be caught napping!'

COLLEVILLE (*uneasily*). 'What are you saying?'

FLEURY. 'Our theatre took a thousand crowns yesterday with the new piece, though this is the fortieth representation. You ought to come and see it. The scenery is something superb.'

Meanwhile, des Lupeaulx was giving du Bruel audience in the secretary's rooms; and Dutocq had followed
du Bruel. Des Lupeaulx's man brought the news of
M. de la Billardière's death, and the Secretary-General
intended to please both Ministers by inserting an obituary
notice in that evening's paper.

'Good day, my dear du Bruel,' was the semi-minister's
greeting, as he saw the clerk enter, and left him
to stand. 'You know the news? La Billardière is
dead; the two Ministers were present when he took
the sacrament. The old man strongly recommended
Rabourdin; said that he could not die easy unless he
knew that his successor was to be the man who had
filled his place all along. It would seem that the death-
agony is like the "question," and everything comes out.
. . . The Minister is so much the more pledged to
this course because it is his intention, and the intention
of the Board likewise, to reward M. Rabourdin's
numerous services' (wagging his head)—'the Council
of State desires the benefit of his lights. They say that
M. de la Billardière is to be transferred to the Seals,
which is as good as if the King had made him a present
of a hundred thousand francs—the place is like a notary's
connection, and may be sold. That piece of news will
be received with joy in your division, for they might
imagine that Benjamin would be put in there.—Du
Bruel, some one ought to knock off ten or a dozen
lines about the old boy, by way of a news item. It will
come under the notice of their Excellencies.' 'Do
you know all about old La Billardière?' he added,
taking up the papers.

Du Bruel made a gesture to signify that he knew
nothing.

'No?' returned des Lupeaulx. 'Oh, well, he was
mixed up in the La Vendée business; he was in the
late King's confidence. Like M. le Comte de la
Fontaine, he never would come to terms with the

First Consul. He did a little in Chouannerie. He was born in Brittany of a parliamentary family; but their dignities were so recent that he was ennobled by Louis XVIII. See—how old was he now? Never mind. Just put it properly something this way: "A loyalty that never swerved, an enlightened piety "— (the poor old boy had a craze for never setting foot in a church). Give him out for a pious servant of the Crown. Lead up nicely to the remark that he might have sung the Song of Simeon over the accession of Charles X.—The Comte d'Artois had a great esteem for him, for La Billardière unfortunately co-operated with him in the Quiberon affair, and took all the blame upon himself; you know, of course. . . . La Billardière justified the King in a pamphlet which he wrote to refute an impertinent History of the Revolution got up by some journalist. So you can lay stress on the devotion. Finally, weigh your words well, so that the other papers may not laugh at us, and bring me the article. Were you at Rabourdin's yesterday?'

'Yes, my lord,' said du Bruel, 'that is—I beg pardon——'

'There is no harm done,' des Lupeaulx answered, laughing.

'His wife is delightfully pretty,' continued du Bruel. 'There are not two such women in Paris. There are women as clever, but they are not so charming in their cleverness; and there may be a woman as handsome as Célestine, but scarcely one so various in her beauty. Mme. Rabourdin is far superior to Mme. Colleville!' added du Bruel, for he remembered an old story about des Lupeaulx. 'Flavie is what she is, thanks to her intercourse with men, while Mme. Rabourdin owes everything to herself; she knows everything; you could not tell a secret in Latin before her. I should think that nothing was beyond my reach if I had such a wife.'

'You have more brains than an author's allowance,' returned des Lupeaulx in a thrill of gratified vanity. And turning his head, he saw Dutocq.

'Oh! good day, Dutocq. I sent to ask if you would lend me your Charlet, if it is complete. The Countess knows nothing of Charlet.'

Du Bruel withdrew.

'Why do you come when you are not called?' des Lupeaulx asked in a hard voice, when they were alone. 'Why do you come to me at ten o'clock, just as I am about to breakfast with His Excellency? Is the Government in danger?'

'Perhaps, sir. If I had had the honour of an interview with you this morning, you certainly would not have pronounced the Sieur Rabourdin's panegyric after you had read what he has written of you.'

Dutocq unbuttoned his greatcoat, and took out a quire of paper, with an impression on the side of the sheets. He laid them down on des Lupeaulx's desk and pointed to a paragraph. Then he bolted the door, as though he feared an explosion. This was what the Secretary-General read against his name :—

'M. DES LUPEAULX.—A Government lowers itself by employing such a man openly. His proper place is in the diplomatic police. Such a person may be pitted with success against the political buccaneers of other cabinets. It would be a pity to put him into the ordinary police. . . . He stands above the level of the common spy; he can grasp a scheme, he could carry out a necessary bit of dirty work successfully, and cover his retreat with skill,' and so forth and so forth. Des Lupeaulx's character was succinctly analysed in five or six sentences. Rabourdin gave the gist of the biographical sketch at the beginning of this history.

At the first words the Secretary-General knew that he had been weighed and found wanting by an abler man ; but he determined to reserve himself for a further examination into a piece of work which went both high and far, without admitting such a man as Dutocq into his confidence. The Secretary-General, like barristers, magistrates, diplomates, and others, was obliged to explore the human heart; like them too, he was astonished at nothing. He was accustomed to treachery, to the snares set by hate, to traps of all kinds. He could receive a stab in the back without a change of countenance. So it was a calm and grave countenance that des Lupeaulx turned upon the office spy.

'How did you get hold of this document?' he asked.

Dutocq gave the history of his good luck; but des Lupeaulx's face showed no sign of approval while he listened. Consequently the story begun in high triumph was ended in fear and trembling.

'You have put your finger between the tree and the bark, Dutocq,' was the Secretary-General's dry comment. 'Observe the utmost secrecy as to this affair, unless you want to make very powerful enemies; it is a work of the greatest importance, and I have cognisance of it.'

And des Lupeaulx dismissed Dutocq with a glance of a kind which speaks more than words.

Dutocq was dismayed to find a rival in his chief. 'Aha!' he said to himself, 'so that scoundrel of a Rabourdin is in it too. He is a staff-officer, while I am a private soldier. I would not have believed it.'

So to all his previous motives for detesting Rabourdin, was added another and most cogent reason for hate —the jealousy that one workman feels of another in the same trade.

When des Lupeaulx was left alone his meditations took a singular turn. Rabourdin was an instrument in the hands of some power; what power was it? Should he profit by this surprising document to ruin the man? Or should he use it the better to succeed with the man's wife? The mystery was perfectly obscure. Des

Lupeaulx turned the pages in dismay. The men whom he knew were summed up with unheard-of sagacity. He admired Rabourdin, while he felt the stab to the heart. He was still reading when breakfast was announced.

'You will keep His Excellency waiting if you do not go down at once,' the Minister's footman came to say.

The Minister breakfasted with his wife and children and des Lupeaulx. There were no servants in the room. The morning meal is the one moment of home life that a statesman can snatch from the all-absorbing demands of public business; but in spite of the barriers raised with ingenious care, so that one hour may be given up entirely to the family and the affections, many intruders, great and small, find ways of breaking in upon it. Public business, as at this moment, often comes athwart their enjoyment.

'I thought Rabourdin was above the ordinary level of clerks; and lo and behold! ten minutes after La Billardière's death, he takes it into his head to send me a regular stage billet through La Brière,' said the Minister, and he held out the sheet of paper which he was twisting in his fingers.

Rabourdin had written the note before he heard of M. de la Billardière's death through La Brière; he was too noble-minded to think of the base construction that might be put upon it, and allowed La Brière to retain and deliver the missive. Des Lupeaulx read as follows:—

'MONSEIGNEUR,—If twenty-three years of irreproachable service may merit a favour, I entreat Your Excellency to grant me an audience this very day. It is a matter in which my honour is involved,' and the note ended with the usual respectful formulas.

'Poor man!' said des Lupeaulx, in a pitying tone, which left the Minister still under a misapprehension;

' we are by ourselves, let him come. You go to the Council after the House rises, and Your Excellency is bound to give an answer to the Opposition to-day; this is the only time that you can give him——'

Des Lupeaulx rose, sent for the usher, said a word to him, and came back to the table.

' I am adjourning him to the dessert,' said he.

His Excellency, like most other ministers under the Restoration, was past his youth. The Charter granted by Louis xviii., unluckily, tied the King's hands; he was forced to give the destinies of the country over to quadragenarians of the Chamber of Deputies and peers of seventy. A king had not power to look wheresoever he would for an able political leader, and to put him forward in spite of his youth or poverty. Napoleon, and Napoleon alone, might employ young men if he chose; no considerations led him to pause. And so it fell out that since the fall of that mighty Will, energy had deserted authority. And in France, of all countries in the world, the contrast between slackness and vigour is a dangerous one. As a rule, the minister who comes into power late in life, is a mediocrity; while young ministers have been the glory of European kingdoms and Republics. The world is ringing yet with the contest between Pitt and Napoleon; and they, like Henri iv., like Richelieu, Mazarin, Colbert, Louvois, the Prince of Orange, the Duc de Guise, Francesco della Rovere, and Machiavelli, like all great statesmen, in short, whether they come of low origin or are born to a throne, began to govern at an early age. The Convention, that model of energy, was in great part composed of young heads; and no sovereign can afford to forget that the Convention brought fourteen armies into the field against Europe; the policy that brought about such disastrous results for absolute power (as it is called) was none the less dictated by true monarchical principles, and the Convention bore itself as a great king.

After ten or twelve years of parliamentary strife, after going again and again over the same ground till he grew jaded, this particular minister had been, in truth, put in office by a party which regarded him as its man of business. Fortunately for him, he was nearer sixty than fifty years old; if he had shown any signs of youthful energy, he would have come promptly to grief. But being accustomed to give way, to beat a retreat, and return to the charge, he could stand against the blows dealt him by all and sundry, by the Opposition or by his own side, by the Court or the clergy; opposing to it all the *vis inertiæ* of a soft but unyielding substance. In short, he enjoyed the advantages of his misfortune. Like some old barrister that has pleaded every conceivable cause, he had passed through the fire on countless questions of Government, till his mind no longer retained the keen edge preserved by the solitary thinker; and he lacked that faculty of making prompt decisions, which is acquired early in a life of action, and more especially in a military career. How should he have been other than he was? All his life long he had juggled with questions instead of using his own judgment upon them; he had criticised effects without going into the causes; and besides, and above all this, his head was full of the endless reforms which a party thrusts upon its leader; he was burdened with pro- grammes designed to gain the private ends of various personages; for if an orator has a future before him, he is sure to be embarrassed with all kinds of impracticable schemes and unpractical advice. So far from starting fresh, the minister was jaded and tired with marches and counter-marches. And when at last he reached the long-desired heights, he found his paths beset with thorns on every side, and a thousand contrary dispositions to be reconciled. If the statesmen of the Restoration could but have followed out their own ideas, their capacities would no doubt be less exposed to criticism;

but while their wills were overruled, their age was the salvation of them; they were physically incapable of contending, as younger men would have done, with low intrigue in high places, intrigues which sometimes proved too much even for the strength of a Richelieu. To such knavery in a lower sphere Rabourdin was about to fall a victim. To the throes of early struggles succeeded the throes of office, for men not so much old as aged before the time. And so, just as they needed the keen sight of the eagle, their eyes were growing dim; and their faculties were exhausted when their work called for redoubled vigour.

The Minister to whom Rabourdin meant to confide his scheme was accustomed to hear the most ingenious theories propounded to him daily by men of unquestioned ability; schemes more or less applicable, or inapplicable, to public business in France were brought continually before his eyes. Their promoters had not the remotest conception of the difficulties of general policy; they used to waylay the Minister on his return from a pitched battle in the House, or a struggle with folly behind the scenes at Court; they assailed him on the eve of a wrestling-bout with public opinion, or on the morrow of some diplomatic question on which the Cabinet had split in three. A statesman thus situated naturally has a gag ready to apply at the first hint of an improvement in the established order of things. Daring speculators and men from behind the scenes in politics or finance were not wont to meet round a dinner-table in those days to sum up the opinions of the Stock Exchange and the Money Market, together with some utterance let fall by Diplomacy, in one profound saying. The Minister had, however, a sort of privy council in his private secretary and secretary-general; they chewed the cud of reflection, and controlled and analysed the interests that spoke through so many insinuating voices.

It was the Minister's unfortunate habit (the invariable

habit of sexagenarian ministers) to shuffle out of difficulties. No question was fairly faced ; the Government
was quietly trying to gag journalism instead of striking
openly ; it was evading the financial question ; tem-
porising with the clergy as with the National Property
difficulty, with Liberalism as with the control of the
Chamber. Now as the Minister in seven years had out-
flanked the powers that be, he considered that he could
come round every question in the same way. It was
natural that a man should try to keep his position by
continuing to use the methods by which he rose ; so
natural, that nobody ventured to criticise a system
devised by mediocrity to please mediocrity. The
Restoration (like the Revolution in Poland) clearly
showed how much a great man is worth to a nation,
and what happens if he is not forthcoming. The last
and greatest defect of the Restoration statesmen was
their honesty, for their opponents availed themselves of
slander and lies and all the resources of political rascality,
until, by the most subversive methods, they let loose the
unintelligent masses ; and the large body of the people
are quick to grasp but one idea—the idea of riot.

All this Rabourdin had told himself. Still, he had
decided to hazard all to win all, much as a jaded game-
ster agrees with himself to try but one more throw ; and
fate, meanwhile, sent him a trickster for his opponent in
the shape of des Lupeaulx. And yet, however sagacious
Rabourdin might be, he was better skilled in administrative work than in parliamentary perspective. He did
not imagine the whole truth ; it had not occurred to
him that the great practical work of his life was about
to become a theory for the Minister, or that a statesman
would inevitably class him with after-dinner innovators
and armchair reformers.

His Excellency had just risen from table. He was
thinking not of Rabourdin, but of François Keller. His
wife detained him by offering him a bunch of grapes,

when the chief clerk was announced. Des Lupeaulx had
reckoned upon this preoccupied mood; he knew that His
Excellency's mind would be taken up by his 'extem-
pore' speeches; so, seeing that the Minister was engaged
in a discussion with his wife, the Secretary-General came
forward. Rabourdin was thunderstruck by the first
words.

'We, His Excellency and I, have been informed of
the work in which you are engaged,' said des Lupeaulx,
lowering his voice; 'you have nothing to fear from
Dutocq, or from any one whatever,' he added, speaking
the last few words aloud.

'Do not worry yourself in any way, Rabourdin,' His
Excellency said kindly, but he made as though he
would retreat.

Rabourdin came forward respectfully, and the Minister
could not choose but remain.

'Will Your Excellency condescend to permit me to
say a few words in private?' said Rabourdin, with a
significant glance.

The Minister looked at the clock, then he went
towards a window, and Rabourdin followed him.

'When may I have the honour of submitting the
affair to Your Excellency, so that I may explain the
scheme of administration to which that paper relates?
It is sure to be used to sully——'

'A scheme of administration,' the Minister broke in,
knitting his brows as he spoke. 'If you have anything
of the kind to lay before me, wait till the day when we
work together. I have to attend the Council to-day, and
I must make a reply to a question raised by the Opposition
yesterday just before the House rose. Next Friday is
your day; we did no work yesterday, for I had no time
to attend to the business of the department. Political
affairs stood in the way of purely administrative
business.'

'I leave my honour with confidence in Your Excellency's hands,' Rabourdin answered gravely, 'and I beg of you to remember that I was not permitted to offer an explanation of the missing document at once——'

'Why, you need fear nothing,' broke in des Lupeaulx, as he came between them; 'you are sure of your nomination in a week's time——'

The Minister began to laugh; he remembered des Lupeaulx's enthusiasm over Mme. Rabourdin, and looked slyly at his wife. The Countess smiled. This by-play surprised Rabourdin; he wondered what it meant; for a moment he ceased to hold the Minister with his eye, and His Excellency took the opportunity of escape.

'We will have a chat together over all this,' said des Lupeaulx, when Rabourdin, not without bewilderment, found himself alone with the Secretary-General. 'But do not bear malice against Dutocq; I will answer for him.'

'Mme. Rabourdin is a charming woman,' put in the Countess, for the sake of saying something.

The children gazed curiously at the visitor. Rabourdin had been prepared for a great ordeal; now he felt as if he were a big fish taken in the toils of a fine net. He struggled with himself.

'Mme. la Comtesse is very kind,' he said.

'May I not have the pleasure of seeing you on one of my Fridays?' continued the lady; 'bring your wife to us, you will do me a favour——'

'That is Mme. Rabourdin's night,' put in des Lupeaulx, knowing what official Fridays were like; 'but since you are so good, you are giving a small evening party soon, I believe——'

The Minister's wife seemed annoyed.

'You are the master of the ceremonies,' she said, addressing des Lupeaulx as she rose.

In those ambiguous words she expressed her vexation; des Lupeaulx was intruding guests upon one of her small parties, to which none but a select few were admitted. Then, with a bow to Rabourdin, she went, and des Lupeaulx and the chief clerk were left alone in the little breakfast-room. Des Lupeaulx was crumpling a bit of paper between his fingers; Rabourdin recognised his own confidential note.

' You do not really know me,' the Secretary-General began with a smile. ' On Friday evening we will come to a thorough understanding. I am bound to give audience now; the Minister is putting everything on my shoulders to-day, for he is preparing for the Chamber. But, Rabourdin, you have nothing to fear, I repeat.'

Slowly Rabourdin made his way downstairs. He was bewildered by the unexpected turn that things were taking. He believed that Dutocq had denounced him; he was not mistaken; the list in which des Lupeaulx was so severely criticised was now in the hands of that worthy, and yet des Lupeaulx was flattering his judge. It was hopelessly bewildering. Straightforward people find it hard to see their way through a maze of intrigue, and Rabourdin lost himself in a labyrinth of conjecture, but failed to understand the Secretary-General's game.

' Either he has not read the article upon himself, or he is in love with my wife!'

These were the thoughts that brought him to a stand as he crossed the courtyard; and the glance exchanged between Célestine and des Lupeaulx, and intercepted last night, flashed like lightning upon his memory.

During Rabourdin's absence his office had, of course, suffered from a sudden accession of vehement excitement; the relations between the upper powers and subordinates are very much laid down by rule; and great, therefore, was the comment when an usher appeared from His Excellency to ask for the chief clerk, especially as he came at an hour when ministers are invisible. As this extraordinary communication coincided, moreover, with the death of M. de la Billardière,

P

it seemed peculiarly significant to M. Saillard when he heard of it through M. Clergeot. He went to confer with his son-in-law. Bixiou happened to be working with his chief at the time; he left Baudoyer with his relative and betook himself to the Rabourdins. Work was suspended.

BIXIOU (*coming in*). 'You are taking things coolly here, gentlemen! You don't know what is going on downstairs. *La Vertueuse Rabourdin* is in for it; yes, cashiered! A painful scene with the Minister.'

DUTOCQ (*looking at Bixiou*). 'Is that a fact?'

BIXIOU. 'Who will be any the worse? Not you for one; du Bruel will be chief clerk, and you his assistant. M. Baudoyer will be head of the division.'

FLEURY. 'I'll bet a hundred francs that Baudoyer will never be head of the division.'

VIMEUX. 'Will you join us, M. Poiret, and take the bet?'

POIRET. 'I get my pension on the 1st of January.'

BIXIOU. 'What, shall we never more behold your shoe-laces! What will the department do without you? Who will take my bet?——'

DUTOCQ. 'Not I; I should be betting on a certainty. M. Rabourdin is nominated. M. de la Billardière, on his deathbed, recommended him to the two ministers, and said that he had drawn the pay while Rabourdin did all the work. He had scruples of conscience; so, subject to orders from above, they promised to nominate Rabourdin to ease his mind.'

BIXIOU. 'Gentlemen, all of you take my wager; there are seven of you, for you will be one, M. Phellion. I bet you a dinner of five hundred francs at the *Rocher de Cancale* that Rabourdin will not get La Billardière's place. It won't cost you a hundred francs apiece, whereas I risk five hundred. I'll take you single-handed, in short. Does that suit? Will you go in, du Bruel?'

PHELLION (*laying down his pen*). 'On what, Môsieur, does your contingent proposition depend? for contingent it is; but I err in using the word "proposition," I mean to say "contract." A wager constitutes a contract.'

FLEURY. 'No, you can't call it a contract, the Code does not recognise a wager; you can't take action to enforce it.'

DUTOCQ. 'The Code recognises it if it makes provision against it.'

BIXIOU. 'Well put, Dutocq, my boy.'

POIRET. 'Indeed!'

FLEURY. 'That is right. It is as if you refuse to pay your debts, you admit them.'

THUILLIER. 'Famous jurisconsults you would make!'

POIRET. 'I am as curious as M. Phellion to know what M. Bixiou's bet is about——'

BIXIOU (*shouts across the office*). 'Du Bruel! are you going in?'

DU BRUEL (*showing himself*). 'Fiddle-de-dee! gentlemen, I have something difficult to do; I have to draw up the announcement of M. de la Billardière's death. For mercy's sake, a little quiet; you had better laugh and bet afterwards.'

THUILLIER. 'Better bet! you are infringing on my puns.'

BIXIOU (*going into du Bruel's office*). 'The old boy's panegyric is a very hard thing to write, du Bruel, and that is a fact; I would sooner have made a caricature of him.'

DU BRUEL. 'Do help me, Bixiou.'

BIXIOU. 'I am quite willing, though this sort of thing is easier to do after dinner.'

DU BRUEL. 'We will dine together.' (*Reads.*) '"Every day Religion and the Monarchy lose some one of those who fought for them in the time of the Revolution——"'

BIXIOU. 'Bad. I should put—"Death is particularly

busy among the oldest champions of the Monarchy and
the most faithful servants of a King, whose heart bleeds
at each fresh blow."' (*Du Bruel writes hastily.*) '"M.
le Baron Flamet de la Billardière died this morning of
dropsy on the chest, brought on by heart complaint . . ."
You see, it is of some consequence to prove that a man
in a government office has a heart; you might slip in a
little padding about the emotions of Royalists during
the Terror, eh? It would not be amiss. Yet—no.
The minor newspapers would be saying that the emotions struck not the heart, but regions lower down.
We won't mention it.—What have you put?'

Du Bruel (*reads*). '"A scion of an old parliamentary
stock——"'

Bixiou. 'Very good! That is poetical, and *stock* is
profoundly true.'

Du Bruel (*continues*). '"—in whom devotion to the
throne, no less than attachment to the faith of our
fathers, was handed down from generation to generation; M. de la Billardière——"'

Bixiou. 'I should put "M. le Baron."'

Du Bruel. 'But he wasn't a baron in 1793.'

Bixiou. 'It is all one. Don't you know that Fouché,
in the time of the Empire, was once telling an anec-
dote of the Convention and Robespierre; and in the
course of it he said, "Robespierre said to me, '*Duc
d'Otrante*, go to the Hôtel de Ville!'"—so there is a
precedent.'

Du Bruel. 'Just let me jot that down! But we
must not put "the Baron" here; I am keeping all the
favours the King showered upon him for the end.'

Bixiou. 'Ah! right—it is the dramatic effect, the
curtain picture of the article.'

Du Bruel. 'It comes here, do you see?—"By
raising M. de la Billardière to the rank of Baron, by
appointing him Gentleman in Ordinary——"'

Bixiou (*aside*). 'Very ordinary.'

Du Bruel. '"—of the Bedchamber, etc., His Majesty rewarded the services of the provost who tempered a rigorous performance of his duty with the habitual mildness of the Bourbons, and the courage of a Vendean who did not bow the knee to the Imperial idol. M. de la Billardière leaves a son who inherits his devotion and his talents," and so on and so on.'

Bixiou. 'Aren't you coming it rather too strong? Isn't the colouring too rich? There is that poetical flight "the Imperial idol" and "bowing the knee"; I should tone it down a bit. Hang it all! Vaudevilles spoil your hand, till you cannot write pedestrian prose. *I* should put—"He belonged to the small number of those who," etc. Simplify; you have a simpleton to deal with.'

Du Bruel. 'There is another joke for a vaudeville! You would make your fortune at writing for the stage, Bixiou!'

Bixiou. 'What have you put about Quiberon?' (*Reads.*) 'That is not the thing! This is how I should draft it—"In a work recently published, he took all the responsibility of the misfortunes of the Quiberon expedition upon himself, thus giving the measure of a devotion which shrank from no sacrifice."—That is neat and ingenious, and you save La Billardière's character.'

Du Bruel. 'But at the expense of whom?'

Bixiou (*serious as a priest in a pulpit*). 'Of Hoche and Tallien, of course. Why, don't you know your history?'

Du Bruel. 'No. I have subscribed to the Baudoins' collection, but I have not had time to look into it: there are no subjects for vaudevilles.'

Phellion (*in the doorway*). 'M. Bixiou, we should all like to know what it is that can induce you to believe that M. Rabourdin will not be nominated as head of the division, when the virtuous and worthy M. Rabourdin has taken the responsibility of the division for nine months, and stands first in order of seniority in the department;

and the Minister no sooner comes back from M. de la Billardière's than he sends the usher to fetch him.'

Bixiou. 'Daddy Phellion, do you know geography?'

Phellion (*swelling visibly*). 'So I flatter myself, sir.'

Bixiou. 'History?'

Phellion (*modestly*). 'Perhaps.'

Bixiou (*looking at him*). 'Your diamond is not properly set; it will drop out directly.—Well, you know nothing of human nature; you have gone no further in that study than in your explorations of the suburbs of Paris.'

Poiret (*in a low voice to Vimeux*). 'Suburbs of Paris! I thought that we were talking about M. Rabourdin.'

Bixiou. 'Does Rabourdin's office in a body take my bet?'

Omnes. 'Yes.'

Bixiou. 'Du Bruel, are you going in?'

Du Bruel. 'I should think so! It is to our interest that our chief clerk should be head of the division, for all the rest of us go up a step.'

Thuillier. 'We all go *a-head!*' (*Aside to Phellion.*) 'That was neat.'

Bixiou. 'I bet he won't; and for this reason. You will hardly understand it; but I will tell you why, all the same. It is right and fair that M. Rabourdin should get the appointment (*looks at Dutocq*); for seniority, ability, and probity are recognised, appreciated, and rewarded in his person. Besides, it is, of course, to the interest of the administration to appoint him.' (*Phellion, Poiret, and Thuillier, listening without comprehending a word, look as though they were trying to see through darkness.*) 'Well, because the appointment is deserved and so suitable in all these ways, I (knowing all the while how wise and just the measure is) will bet that it will not be taken. No; it will end in failure, like the Boulogne and Russian expeditions, though genius had left nothing undone to ensure success. I am playing the devil's game.'

Du Bruel. 'But whom else can they appoint?'

Bixiou. 'The more I think of Baudoyer, the more plainly it appears that in the matter of qualifications for the post he is the exact opposite of Rabourdin. Consequently, *he* will be head of the division.'

Dutocq (*driven to extremities*). 'But M. des Lupeaulx sent for me this morning to ask for my Charlet; and he told me that M. Rabourdin had just been nominated, and young La Billardière was to be transferred to the Audit Office.'

Bixiou. 'Appointed! appointed! The nomination will not be so much as signed for ten days to come. They will make the appointment for New Year's Day. There, look at your chief down there in the courtyard, and tell me if *La Vertueuse Rabourdin* looks like a man in favour! Any one would think he had been cashiered.' (*Fleury rushes to the window.*) 'Good day, gentlemen. I am just going to announce the nomination to M. Baudoyer; it will infuriate him, at any rate, the holy man! And then I will tell him about our bet, to hearten him up again. That is what we call a *peripateia* on the stage, is it not, du Bruel?—What does it matter to me? If I win, he will take me for assistant clerk?' (*goes out.*)

Poiret. 'Everybody says that that gentleman is clever; well, for my own part, I never can make anything out of his talk' (*writing as he speaks*). 'I listen and listen, I hear words, and cannot grasp any sense in them. He brings in the suburbs of Paris when he is talking about human nature; then he begins with the Boulogne and Russian expeditions, and says that he is playing the Devil's game.' (*Lays down his pen and goes to the stove.*) 'First of all, you must assume that the Devil gambles, then find out what game he plays! First of all, there is the game of dominoes——' (*blows his nose.*)

Fleury (*interrupting him*). 'Old Poiret is blowing his nose; it is eleven o'clock.'

Du Bruel. 'So it is!—Already! I am off to the secretary's office.'

Poiret. 'Where was I?'

Thuillier. '*Domino,* which is "to the lord"; for you were talking of the Devil, and the Devil is a suzerain without a charter. But this is not so much a pun as a play on words. Anyhow, I see no difference between a play on words and——' (*Sébastien comes in to collect circulars to be checked and signed.*)

Vimeux. 'Here you are, my fine fellow! Your time of trial is over; you will be established! M. Rabourdin will get the appointment. You were at Mme. Rabourdin's party yesterday. How lucky you are to go to that house! They say that very handsome women go there.'

Sébastien. 'I do not know.'

Fleury. 'Are you blind?'

Sébastien. 'I am not at all fond of looking at things when I cannot have them!'

Phellion (*delighted*). 'Well said, young man.'

Vimeux. 'You surely look at Mme. Rabourdin. Why, hang it all! a charming woman.'

Fleury. 'Pooh! a thin figure. I have seen her at the Tuileries Gardens. Percilliée, Ballet's mistress and Castaing's victim, is much more to my taste.'

Phellion. 'But what has an actress to do with a chief clerk's wife?'

Dutocq. 'Both are playing a comedy.'

Fleury (*looking askance at Dutocq*). 'The physical has nothing to do with the moral; and if by that you understand——'

Dutocq. 'For my own part, I understand nothing.'

Fleury. 'Which of us will be chief clerk? who wants to know?'

Omnes. 'Tell us!'

Fleury. 'It will be Colleville.'

Thuillier. 'Why?'

FLEURY. 'Mme. Colleville has finally taken the shortest way—through the sacristy.'

THUILLIER (*drily*). 'I am too much M. Colleville's friend, M. Fleury, not to beg of you to refrain from speaking lightly of his wife.'

PHELLION. 'Women, who have no way of defending themselves, should never be the subject of our conversations——'

VIMEUX. 'And so much the less, since pretty Mme. Colleville would not ask Fleury to her house; so he blackens her character by way of revenge.'

FLEURY. 'She would not receive me on the same footing as Thuillier, but I went——'

THUILLIER. 'When? Where? Under her windows?'

Fleury's swagger made him so formidable a person in the office, that every one was surprised when he took Thuillier's last word. His resignation had its source in a bill for two hundred francs with a tolerably doubtful signature, which document Thuillier was to present to his sister. A deep silence succeeded to the skirmish. Everybody worked from one o'clock till three. Du Bruel did not come back.

Towards half-past three preparations for departure were made—brushing of hats and changing of coats went on simultaneously all through the department. The cherished half-hour thus spent on small domestic cares shortened the working day by precisely thirty minutes. The temperature of overheated rooms fell several degrees; the odour peculiar to offices evaporated; silence settled down once more; and by four o'clock none were left but the real workers, the clerks who took their duties in earnest. A Minister may know the men that do the work of the department by making a round thereof punctually at four o'clock; but such great and serious persons never by any chance indulge in espionage of this kind.

At that hour diverse chief clerks met each other in the courtyard and exchanged their ideas on the day's events. Generally speaking, as they walked off by twos and threes, the opinion was in favour of Rabourdin ; but a few old stagers, such as M. Clergeot, would shake their heads with a '*Habent sua sidera lites.*' Saillard and Baudoyer were courteously avoided. Nobody knew quite what to say to them about Billardière's death, and everybody felt that Baudoyer might want the berth though he had no right to it.

When the last-named pair had left the buildings some distance behind, Saillard broke silence with, 'This is not going well for you, my poor Baudoyer.'

'I fail to understand what Elizabeth is thinking about,' returned his son-in-law. 'She sent Godard post-haste for a passport for Falleix. Godard said that, acting on Uncle Mitral's advice, she hired a post-chaise, and Falleix is on the way back to his own country at this moment.'

'Something connected with the business, no doubt,' said Saillard.

'The most urgent business for us just now is to find a way of getting M. de La Billardière's place.'

They had come along the Rue Saint-Honoré, till by this time they had reached the Palais Royal. Dutocq came up and raised his hat.

'If I can be of any use to you, sir, under the circumstances, pray command me,' he said, addressing Baudoyer. 'I am not less devoted than M. Godard to your interests.'

'Such an overture is, at any rate, a consolation,' returned Baudoyer; 'one has the esteem of honest people.'

'If you will condescend to use your influence to procure the place of assistant-clerk under you, and the chief clerk's place for M. Bixiou, you will make the fortunes of two men, and both of them are capable of doing anything to secure your elevation.'

'Are you laughing at us, sir ? ' asked Saillard, opening wide foolish eyes.

'Far be the thought from me,' said Dutocq. 'I have just been to take the obituary notice of M. de la Billardière to the newspaper office; M. des Lupeaulx sent me. I have the highest respect for your talents after reading the article in the paper. When the time comes for making an end of Rabourdin, it is in my power to strike the final blow ; condescend to recollect that.'

Dutocq disappeared.

'I'll be hanged if I understand a word of this,' said Saillard, as he stared at Baudoyer, whose little eyes expressed no common degree of bewilderment. 'We must send out for the paper this evening.'

When the pair entered the sitting-room on the ground floor, they found Mme. Saillard, Elizabeth, M. Gaudron, and the vicar of St. Paul's all seated by a large fire. The vicar turned as they came in ; and Elizabeth, look- ing at her husband, made a sign of intelligence, but to little purpose.

'Sir,' the curé was saying, 'I was unwilling to delay my thanks for the magnificent gift with which you have adorned my poor church ; I could not venture into debt to buy that splendid monstrance. It is fit for a cathedral. As one of the most regular and pious of our parishioners, you must have been particularly impressed by the bareness of the high altar. I am just going to see M. le Coadjuteur ; he will shortly express his satisfaction.'

'I have done nothing as yet——' began Baudoyer, but his wife broke in upon him.

'M. le Curé,' said she, 'I may betray the whole of his secret now. M. Baudoyer counts upon completing what he has begun by giving you a canopy against Corpus Domini. But the purchase depends, to some extent, upon the state of our finances, and our finances depend upon our advancement.'

'God rewards those who honour Him,' said M. Gaudron, as he followed the curé.

'Why do you not do us the honour to take pot-luck with us?' asked Saillard.

'Don't go, my dear Gaudron,' said the curé. 'I have an invitation to dine with the curé of Saint-Roch, you know; he will take M. de la Billardière's funeral service to-morrow.'

'M. le Curé de Saint-Roch might say a word for us, perhaps?' began Baudoyer, but his wife gave a sharp tug at his coat-tails.

'Do be quiet, Baudoyer!' she whispered, as she drew him into a corner. 'You have given a monstrance worth five thousand francs to our parish church. I will explain it all by and by.'

Baudoyer, the close-fisted, made a hideous grimace, and appeared pensive throughout dinner.

'What ever made you take so much trouble to get a passport for Falleix? What is this that you are meddling in?' he asked at length.

'It seems to me that Falleix's business is, to some extent, ours,' Elizabeth answered drily, warning her husband with a glance not to speak before M. Gaudron.

'Certainly it is,' said old Saillard, thinking of the partnership.

'You reached the newspaper office in time, I hope,' continued Elizabeth, addressing M. Gaudron, as she handed him a plate of soup.

'Yes, my dear madam,' the curé replied. 'The editor made not the slightest difficulty when he read the few words from the Grand Almoner's secretary. Through his good offices the little paragraph was put in the most suitable position. I should never have thought of that, but the young man at the newspaper office was very wide awake. The champions of religion may now combat infidelity with equal forces, for there is much talent shown in the Royalist newspapers. I have every reason to believe that success will crown your hopes. But you must remember, my dear Baudoyer, to use your influence for M. Colleville. It is in him that His Eminence is interested, and I received an injunction to mention M. Colleville to you.'

'If I am head of the division, he shall be one of my chief clerks if they like,' said Baudoyer.

The clue to the riddle was discovered after dinner when the porter came in with the ministerial paper. The two following paragraphs (called *entre-filets* in journalistic language) appeared therein among the items of news :—

'M. LE BARON DE LA BILLARDIÈRE died this morning after a long and painful illness. In him the King loses a devoted servant, and the Church one of the most pious among her children. M. de la Billardière's end was a worthy crown of a great career, a fitting termination of a life that was wholly devoted to perilous missions in perilous times, and subsequently to the fulfilment of very difficult duties. As grand provost of a department, M. de la Billardière's force of character triumphed over all obstacles raised by rebellion; and later, when he accepted an arduous post as the head of a department, his insight was not less useful than his Frenchman's urbanity in the conduct of the weighty affairs transacted in his province. No rewards were ever better deserved than those by which His Majesty was pleased to crown a loyalty that never wavered under the usurper.—The ancient family will live again in a younger scion, who inherits the talent and devotion of the excellent man whose loss is mourned by so many friends. His Majesty, with a gracious word, has already given out that M. Benjamin de la Billardière is to be one of the Gentlemen in Ordinary of the Bedchamber.

'Any of the late M. de la Billardière's numerous friends who have not yet received cards, and may not receive them in time, are informed that the funeral will take place to-morrow at Saint-Roch at four o'clock. The funeral sermon will be preached by M. l'Abbé Fontanon.'

'M. ISIDORE BAUDOYER, representative of one of the oldest burgher families in Paris, and chief clerk in the La Billardière division, has just revived memories of the old traditions of piety which distinguished the great burgher houses of olden times, when citizens were so jealous of the pomp of Religion, and such lovers of her monuments. The Church of St. Paul, a basilica which we owe to the Society of Jesus, lacked a monstrance in keeping with its architectural splendours. Neither the vestry nor the incumbent could afford to give such an adornment to the altar. M. Baudoyer has just presented the parish with the monstrance that many persons have admired at the establishment of M. Gohier, the King's goldsmith; and, thanks to piety that did not shrink from so large a sum, the Church of St. Paul now possesses a masterpiece of the goldsmith's craft, executed from M. de Sommervieux's designs. We are glad to give publicity to a fact which shows the absurdity of Liberal bombast as to the state of feeling among the Parisian bourgeoisie. The upper middle classes have been Royalist through all time, and always will prove themselves Royalists at need.'

'The price was five thousand francs,' said the Abbé Gaudron, 'but for ready money the Court goldsmith lowered his demands.'

'Representative of one of the oldest burgher families in Paris!' repeated Saillard. 'There it is in print, and in the official paper too!'

'Dear M. Gaudron, do help my father to think of something to slip into the Countess's ear when he takes her the monthly allowance—just a few words that say everything. I will leave you now. I must go out with Uncle Mitral. Would you believe it?—I could not find Uncle Bidault. What dog-hole can he be living in! M. Mitral, knowing his ways, said that all his business is done between eight o'clock and noon; after that hour he is only to be found at a place called the Café Thémis—a queer-sounding name——'

'Do they do justice there?' the Abbé asked, laughing.

'How does he get to a café at the corner of the Quai des Augustins and the Rue Dauphine? He plays a game of dominoes there with his friend M. Gobseck every night, they say. I don't want to go all by myself, but uncle will take me and bring me back again.'

As she spoke, Mitral shoved his yellow countenance beneath a wig that might have been made of twitch-grass and plastered down on the top of his head. This worthy made a sign, which, being interpreted, meant that his niece had better come at once, without further waste of time which was paid at the rate of two francs an hour; and Mme. Baudoyer went accordingly, without a word of explanation to her father or husband.

When Elizabeth had gone, M. Gaudron turned to Baudoyer.

'Heaven,' observed he, 'has bestowed on you a treasure of prudence and virtue in your wife; she is a pattern of wisdom, a Christian woman with a divine gift of understanding. Religion alone can form a character so complete. To-morrow I will say the mass for the success of the good cause. In the interests of the Monarchy and Religion you must be appointed. M. Rabourdin is a Liberal; he subscribes to the *Journal des Débats*, a disastrous publication that levies war on M. le Comte de Villèle to serve the interests of M. de Chateaubriand. His Eminence is sure to see the paper this evening, if it is only on account of his poor friend M. de la

Billardière; and Monseigneur le Coadjuteur will be sure to mention you and Rabourdin. I know M. le Curé; if any one thinks of his dear Church, he does not forget them in his sermon; and now, at this moment, he has the honour to dine with the Coadjuteur at the house of M. le Curé de Saint-Roch.'

At these words it began to dawn upon Saillard and Baudoyer that Elizabeth had not been idle since Godard brought her the news.

'She is a sharp one, is Elizabeth!' cried Saillard. He could appreciate his daughter's quick, mole-like progress more fully than the Abbé could.

'She sent Godard to M. Rabourdin's to find out what newspaper he takes,' continued Gaudron, 'and I gave His Eminence's secretary a hint; for as things are at this moment, the Church and the Crown are bound to know their friends and their enemies.'

'These five days I have been trying to think of something to say to His Excellency's wife,' said Saillard.

Baudoyer could not take his eyes off the paper. 'All Paris is reading that,' he said.

'Your praise costs us four thousand eight hundred francs, sonny!' said Mme. Saillard.

'You have adorned the house of God,' put in the Abbé.

'We might have saved our souls without that though,' returned she. 'But the place, if Baudoyer gets it, is worth an extra eight thousand francs, so the sacrifice will not be great. And if he doesn't? Eh! *ma mère*?' she continued, as she looked at her husband. 'If he doesn't—what a drain on us!'

'Oh! well,' cried Saillard, in the enthusiasm of the moment, 'then we should make it up out of the business. Falleix is going to expand his business. He made his brother a stock-jobber on purpose to make him useful. Elizabeth might as well have told

us why Falleix had flown off.—But let us think of
something to say. This is what I thought of:
"Madame, if you would only say a word to His
Excellency——"'

'"Would only!"' broke in Gaudron. '"If you
would condescend" is more respectful. Besides, you
must first make sure that Madame la Dauphine will
use her influence for you, for in that case you might
insinuate the notion of falling in with Her Royal Highness's wishes.'

'The vacant post ought to be expressly named,' said
Baudoyer.

'"Madame la Comtesse,"' began Saillard, as he rose
to his feet, with an ingratiating smile directed at his
wife.

'Good gracious, Saillard, how funny you look! Do
take care, my boy, or you will make her laugh.'

'"Madame la Comtesse!" . . . (Is that better?)' he
asked of his wife.

'Yes, ducky,'

'"The late M. de la Billardière's place is vacant; my
son-in-law, M. Baudoyer——'

'"A man of talent and lofty piety,"' prompted
Gaudron.

'Put it down, Baudoyer,' cried old Saillard; 'put it
down!'

Baudoyer, in all simplicity, took up a pen and wrote
his own panegyric without a blush, precisely as Nathan
or Canalis might review one of his own books.

'"Madame la Comtesse,"' repeated Saillard, for the
third time, then he broke off; 'you see, mother, I am
making believe that you are the Minister's wife.'

'Do you take me for a fool?' retorted she. 'I see
that quite well.'

'"The late worthy M. de la Billardière's place is
vacant; my son-in-law, M. Baudoyer, a man of con-
summate talent and lofty piety——"'

He paused for a moment, looked at M. Gaudron, who seemed to be pondering something, and then added—

'"Would be very glad to get it." Ha! not bad; it is short, and says all we want to say.'

'But just wait a bit, Saillard! You surely can see that M. l'Abbé is turning things over in his mind,' exclaimed his wife, 'so don't disturb him.'

'——— "Would be very happy if you would deign to interest yourself on his behalf,"' resumed Gaudron; '"and by saying a few words to His Excellency you would be doing Mme. la Dauphine a particular pleasure, for it has been his good fortune to find a protectress in her."'

'Ah! M. Gaudron, that last remark was well worth the monstrance; I am not so sorry now about the four thousand eight hundred francs.—Besides, Baudoyer, I say, you are going to pay for it, my boy. Have you put that down?'

'I will hear you say that over, night and morning, *ma mère*,' said Mme. Saillard. 'Yes, it is very well hit off, is that speech. How fortunate you are to be so learned, M. Gaudron! That is what comes of studying in these seminaries; you are taught how to speak to God and the saints.'

'He is as kind as he is learned,' said Baudoyer, grasping the Abbé's hands as he spoke. 'Did you write that article?' he continued, pointing to the paper.

'No,' returned Gaudron. 'It was written by His Eminence's secretary, a young fellow who lies under great obligations to me, and takes an interest in M. Colleville. I paid for his education at the Seminary.'

'A good deed never loses its reward,' commented Baudoyer.

When these four personages sat themselves down to their game of boston, Elizabeth and Uncle Mitral had reached the *Café Thémis*, talking by the way of the business on hand. Elizabeth's tact had discovered the most powerful lever to force the Minister's hand. Uncle Mitral, a retired bailiff, was an expert in chicanery, in legal expedients, and precautions. He considered that the honour of the family was involved in his nephew's success. Avarice had led him to cast an eye into Gigonnet's strong box; he knew that all the money would go to his nephew Baudoyer; and therefore he wished to see Baudoyer in a position that befitted the fortunes of the Saillards and Gigonnet, for all would come some day to Elizabeth's little daughter. What may not a girl look for when she has more than a hundred thousand francs a year? Mitral had taken up his niece's ideas and grasped them thoroughly. So he had hastened Falleix's journey by explaining that you can travel quicker by post. Since then he had reflected, over his dinner, upon the proper curve to be given to a spring of Elizabeth's designing.

Arrived at the *Café Thémis*, he told his niece that he had better go in alone to arrange with Gigonnet, and left her outside in the cab till the time should come for her intervention. Elizabeth could see Gobseck and Bidault through the window-panes; their heads were thrown into relief by the bright yellow-painted panels of the old-fashioned coffee-house; they looked like two cameos; it seemed as if the cold, unchanging expression on their countenances had been caught and fixed there by the carver's art. The misers were surrounded by aged faces, each one furrowed with curving wrinkles that started from the nose and brought the glazed cheek-bones into prominence—wrinkles in which thirty per cent. discount seemed to be written. All the faces brightened up at sight of Mitral; a tigerish curiosity glittered in all eyes.

'Hey! hey! it is Daddy Mitral!' cried Chaboisseau, a little old bill-discounter, who did his business among publishers and booksellers.

'My word! so it is,' replied a paper merchant, by

name Métivier. 'Ah! 'tis an old monkey, you can't teach him any tricks!'

'And you are an old raven, a good judge of corpses.'

'Precisely so,' said the stern Gobseck.

'Why have you come here, my boy? To nab our friend Métivier?' asked Gigonnet, pointing out a man who looked like a retired porter.

'Your grandniece Elizabeth is outside, Daddy Gigonnet,' whispered Mitral.

'What? Anything wrong?' queried Bidault. The old man scowled as he spoke, and his air was about as tender as the expression of a headsman on a scaffold; but, in spite of his Roman manhood, he must have felt perturbed, for his deep carmine countenance lost a trifle of its colour.

'Well, and if something had gone wrong, wouldn't you help Saillard's child, a little thing that has knitted stockings for you these thirty years?' cried Mitral.

'If security is forthcoming, I do not say no,' returned Gigonnet. 'Falleix is in this. Your Falleix has set up his brother as a stockbroker; he does as much business as the Brézacs; with what? His brains, no doubt. After all, Saillard is not a baby.'

'He knows the value of money,' remarked Chaboisseau. And one and all the old men wagged their heads. A man of imagination would have shuddered if he had heard those words as they were uttered.'

'Besides, if anything happens to my kith or kin, it is no affair of mine,' began Bidault-Gigonnet. 'I make it a principle,' continued he, 'never to be let in with my friends or relatives; for you only get your death through your weakest spot. Ask Gobseck; he is soft.'

All the bill-discounters applauded this doctrine, nodding their metallic heads, till you might have listened for the creaking of ill-greased machinery.

'Oh, come now, Gigonnet,' put in Chaboisseau, 'a

little tenderness, when your stockings have been knitted for you for thirty years.'

'Ah! that counts for something,' commented Gobseck.

'There are no outsiders here,' pursued Mitral, who had been taking a look round, 'so we can speak freely. I have come here with a good bit of business——'

'If it is good, what makes you come to us?' Gigonnet interrupted sourly.

'A chap that was a Gentleman of the Bedchamber, an old Chouan, what's his name—La Billardière—is dead.'

'Really?' asked Gobseck.

'And here is my nephew giving monstrances to churches!' said Gigonnet.

'He is not such a fool as to give, he is selling them, Daddy,' Mitral retorted proudly. 'It is a question of getting M. de la Billardière's place; and to reach it, one must seize——'

'Seize! Always a bailiff!' cried Métivier, clapping Mitral on the shoulder. 'I like that, I do!'

—— 'Seizing the Sieur Chardin des Lupeaulx between our claws,' continued Mitral. 'Now, Elizabeth has found out how to do it, and it is——'

'Elizabeth!' Gigonnet broke in again. 'Dear little creature! She takes after her grandfather, my poor brother. Bidault had not his like. Ah! if you had only seen him at old furniture sales. Such an instinct! Up to everything!—What does she want?'

'Oh, come now! Daddy Gigonnet, you find your family affections very quickly. There must be some cause for this phenomenon.'

'You child!' said Gobseck, addressing Gigonnet, 'always too impetuous.'

'Come, my masters, Gobseck and Gigonnet both, you need des Lupeaulx; you recollect how you plucked him, and you are afraid that he may ask for a little of his down again,' said Mitral.

'Can we talk of this business with him?' Gobseck asked, indicating Mitral.

'Mitral is one of us; he would not play a trick on old customers,' returned Gigonnet. 'Very well, Mitral. Between ourselves,' he continued, lowering his voice for the retired bailiff's ear, 'we three have just been buying up certain debts, and the admission of them lies with the Committee of Liquidation.'

'What can you concede?' asked Mitral.

'Nothing,' said Gobseck.

'Our names don't appear in it,' added Gigonnet. 'Samanon is acting as our fence.'

'Look here, Gigonnet,' began Mitral. 'It is cold, and your grandniece is waiting. I'll put the whole thing in a word or two, and you will understand. You two between you must lend Falleix two hundred and fifty thousand francs, without interest. At this present moment he is tearing along the road thirty leagues away from Paris, with a courier riding ahead.'

'Is it possible?' asked Gobseck.

'Where is he going?' cried Gigonnet.

'Why, he is going down to des Lupeaulx's fine estate in the country. He knows the neighbourhood; and with the aforesaid two hundred and fifty thousand francs he is going to buy up some of the excellent land round about the Secretary-General's hovel. The land will always fetch what was given for it. And a deed signed in the presence of a notary need not be registered for nine days—bear that in mind! With these trifling additions, des Lupeaulx's "estate" will pay a thousand francs per annum in taxes. *Ergo*, des Lupeaulx will be an elector of the "*grand collége*," qualified for election, a Count and anything that he likes. Do you know the deputy that backed out of it?'

The two usurers nodded.

'Des Lupeaulx would cut off a leg to be a deputy,' continued Mitral. 'But when we show him the con-

tracts, he will be for having them made out in his name;
our loan to be charged, of course, as a mortgage on the
land, reserving the right to sell. (Aha! do you take
me?) First of all, we want the place for Baudoyer;
afterwards we hand over des Lupeaulx to you. Falleix
is stopping down there, getting ready for the election;
so through Falleix you will have a pistol held to des
Lupeaulx's head all through the election, for Falleix's
friends are in the majority. Do you see Falleix's hand
in this, Daddy Gigonnet?'

'I see Mitral's too,' remarked Métivier. 'The trick
is neatly done.'

'It is a bargain,' said Gigonnet. 'That is so, isn't it,
Gobseck? Falleix must sign counter-deeds for us, and
have the mortgage made out in his own name; and we
will pay des Lupeaulx a visit in the nick of time.'

'And *we* are being robbed,' put in Gobseck.

'Ah! I should very much like to know the man
that robs you, Daddy,' retorted Mitral.

'Why, no one can rob us but ourselves,' returned
Gigonnet. 'We thought we were doing a good thing
when we bought up all des Lupeaulx's debts at a
discount of sixty per cent.'

'You can add them to the mortgage on his place, and
have yet another hold on him through the interest,'
returned Mitral.

'That is possible,' said Gobseck.

Bidault, *alias* Gigonnet, exchanged a quick glance
with Gobseck, and went to the door.

'Go ahead, Elizabeth!' he said, addressing his niece.
'We have your man fast, but look after details. You
have made a good beginning, sly girl! Go through
with it, you have your uncle's esteem——' and he struck
his hand playfully in hers.

'But Métivier and Chaboisseau may try a sudden
stroke,' said Mitral; 'they might go to-night to some
Opposition paper, catch the ball at a rebound, and pay

us back for the Ministerialist article. Go back by yourself, child; I will not let those two cormorants go out of
sight.'

And he returned to the Café.

'To-morrow the money shall go to its destination
through a word to the receiver-general. We will raise a
hundred thousand crowns' worth of his paper *among friends*,'
said Gigonnet, when Mitral came to speak to him.

Next day the readers of a Liberal paper in wide
circulation beheld the following paragraph among the
items of news. It had been inserted by command of
MM. Chaboisseau and Métivier, to whom no editor
could refuse anything; for were they not shareholders
in two newspapers, and did they not also discount the
bills of publishers, printers, and paper-merchants?

'Yesterday,' so ran the paragraph, 'a Ministerialist
paper evidently pointed out M. le Baron de la Billardière's successor. M. Baudoyer is one of the most
eligible citizens of a thickly populated district, where
his beneficence is not less known than the piety upon
which the Ministerialist sheet lays so much stress. But
mention might have been made of M. Baudoyer's
abilities. Did our contemporary remember that even in
vaunting the antiquity of M. Baudoyer's burgher descent
(and an ancient burgher ancestry is as much a noblesse
as any other), in the matter of that very burgher
descent she touched upon the reason of the probable
exclusion of her candidate? Gratuitous treachery!
The good lady, according to her wont, flatters those
whom she destroys. M. Baudoyer's appointment would
be a tribute to the virtue and capacity of the middle
classes, and of the middle class we shall always be the
advocates, though we may see that often we are only
defending a lost cause. It would be a piece of good
policy and an act of justice to nominate M. Baudoyer to
the vacant post; so the Ministry will not permit it.

The Religious sheet for once showed more sense than its masters; it will get into trouble.'

The next day was Friday, the day of Mme. Rabourdin's dinner-party. At midnight on Thursday des Lupeaulx had left her on the staircase at the Bouffons, where she stood, in her radiant beauty, her hand on Mme. de Camps' arm (for Mme. Firmiani had recently married); and when the old libertine came to himself again, his ideas of revenge had calmed down, or rather they had grown cooler.—he could think of nothing but that last glance exchanged with Mme. Rabourdin.

'I will make sure of Rabourdin,' he thought, 'by forgiving him in the first instance; I will be even with him later on. At present, if he does not get his step, I must give up a woman who might be an invaluable aid to a great political success, for she understands everything; she shrinks back from no idea. What is more, in that case I should not find out this administrative scheme of Rabourdin's until it was laid before the Minister. Come, dear des Lupeaulx; it is a question of overcoming all obstacles for your Célestine. You may grimace, Mme. la Comtesse, but you are going to invite Mme. Rabourdin to your next small select party.'

Some men can put revenge into a corner of their hearts till they gratify their passions; des Lupeaulx was one of them. His mind was fully made up; he determined to carry Rabourdin's nomination.

'I am going to prove to you, dear chief clerk, that I deserve a high place in your diplomatic galleys,' he said to himself, as he took his seat in his private office and opened his newspapers.

He had known the contents of the Ministerial sheet only too well at five o'clock on the previous day, so he did not care to amuse himself by reading it through; but he opened it to glance at the obituary notice of La Billardière, thinking as he did so of the predicament in which du Bruel had put him, when he brought in the satirical performance composed under Bixiou's editorship. He could not help laughing as he perused the biography of the late Comte de la Fontaine, adapted and reprinted, after a few months' interval, for M. de la Billardière. Then, all of a sudden, his eyes were dazzled by the name of Baudoyer! With fury he read the specious article which compromised the department. He rang the bell vigorously and sent for Dutocq, meaning to send him to the newspaper office. But what was his astonishment when he read the reply in the Opposition paper, for it so happened that the Liberal sheet was the first to come to hand. The thing was getting serious. He knew the dodge; it seemed to him that the master hand was making a mess of his cards, and he took his opponent for a Greek of the first order. To dispose so adroitly of two papers of opposite politics, and that at once, and on the same evening; to begin the game, moreover, by guessing at the Minister's intentions! He fancied that he recognised the hand of an acquaintance, a Liberal editor, and vowed to question him that night at the Opéra. Dutocq appeared.

'Read that,' said des Lupeaulx, holding out the two papers while he ran his eyes over the rest of the batch to see whether Baudoyer had pulled other wires. Just go and find out who it was that took it into his head to compromise the department in this way.'

'It was not M. Baudoyer, anyhow,' replied Dutocq. 'He did not leave the office yesterday. There is no need to go to the office. When I took your article yesterday, I saw the Abbé there. He came provided with a letter from the Grand Almoner; you yourself would have given way if you had seen it.'

'Dutocq, you have some grudge against M. Rabourdin, and it is not right of you, for he prevented your dismissal twice. Still we cannot help our feelings; and one may happen to dislike a man who does one a

kindness. Only, bear in mind that if you permit yourself the smallest attempt at treachery against him until
I give the word, it will be your ruin; you can count
me as your enemy. As for my friend and his newspaper,
let the Grand Almonry subscribe for our number of
copies, if its columns are to be devoted to their exclusive
use. The year is almost at an end, the question of
subscriptions will be raised directly, and then we shall
see. As for La Billardière's post, there is one way of
putting a stop to this sort of thing, and that is, to make
the appointment this very day.'

Dutocq went back to the office.

'Gentlemen,' he remarked, 'I do not know whether
Bixiou has the gift of reading the future; but if you
have not seen the Ministerial paper, I recommend
the paragraph on Baudoyer to your careful attention;
and then as M. Fleury takes the Opposition paper, you
may see the double of it. Certainly, M. Rabourdin is a
clever man; but a man who, gives a monstrance worth
six thousand francs to a church, is deucedly clever too,
as times go.'

Bixiou (coming in). 'What do you say to the first
chapter of an epistle to the Corinthians in our religious
paper, and the epistle to the ministers in the Liberal
sheet?—How is M. Rabourdin, du Bruel?'

Du Bruel (coming in). 'I do not know.' (Draws
Bixiou into his sanctum and lowers his voice.) 'My dear
fellow, your way of helping a man is uncommonly like
the hangman's way, when he hoists you on his shoulders
the better to break your neck. You let me in for a
whipping from des Lupeaulx, and I deserved it for my
stupidity. A nice thing that article on La Billardière!
It is a trick that I shall not forget! The very first
sentence as good as told the King that it was time to
die. And the account of the Quiberon affair clearly
meant that His Majesty was a—— The whole thing
was ironical, in fact.'

BIXIOU (*bursting into a laugh*). 'Oh, come! are you getting cross? Cannot one have a joke?'

DU BRUEL. 'A joke! a joke! When you want to be chief clerk's assistant they will put you off with jokes, my dear fellow.

BIXIOU (*with a threat in his tones*). 'Are we getting cross?'

DU BRUEL. 'Yes.'

BIXIOU (*drily*). 'Very well, so much the worse for you.'

DU BRUEL (*reflecting uneasily*). 'Could you get over it yourself?'

BIXIOU (*insinuatingly*). 'From a friend? I should think I could.' (*Fleury's voice is heard in the office.*) 'There is Fleury cursing Baudoyer. It was a neat trick, hey? Baudoyer will get the step.' (*Confidentially.*) 'After all, so much the better. Follow up the consequences carefully, du Bruel. Rabourdin would show a poor spirit if he stopped on under Baudoyer; he will resign, and that will leave two vacant places. You will be chief clerk, and you will take me with you as assistant. We will write vaudevilles in collaboration, and I will fag for you at the office.'

DU BRUEL (*brightening*). 'I say, I did not think of that. Poor Rabourdin! Still, I should be sorry.'

BIXIOU. 'Ah! so that is how you love him!' (*Changing his tone.*) 'Oh, well, I do not pity him either. After all, he is well to do; his wife gives parties, and does not ask me, when I go everywhere! Come, good-bye, no malice, du Bruel; there is a good fellow!' (*Goes out into the general office.*) 'Good-day, gentlemen! Did I not tell you yesterday that if a man has nothing but principles and ability, he will always be very badly off, even with a pretty wife?'

FLEURY. 'You are rich yourself!'

BIXIOU. 'Not bad, dear Cincinnatus! But you are going to give me a dinner at the *Rocher de Cancale.*'

POIRET. 'I never know what to make of M. Bixiou!'

PHELLION (*ruefully*). 'M. Rabourdin so seldom reads the papers, that it may be worth while to take them in for him, and to do without them ourselves for a bit.' (*Fleury hands over his sheet; Vimeux passes the newspaper taken by the office; and Phellion goes out with them.*)

At that moment des Lupeaulx was going downstairs to breakfast with the Minister. As he went, he was wondering within himself whether prudence did not dictate that he should fathom the wife's heart before displaying the fine flower of scoundrelism for the husband, and make sure, first of all, that his devotion would be rewarded. He was feeling the little pulse that still throbbed in his heart, when he met his attorney on the staircase, and was greeted with, 'A word or two with you, my lord!' uttered with the smiling familiarity of a man who knows that he is indispensable.

'What, my dear Desroches!' exclaimed the politician. 'What has happened? These people lose their tempers; they cannot do as I do, and wait.'

'I came at once to give you warning that your bills are in the hands of Messrs. Gobseck and Gigonnet, under the name of one Samanon.'

'Men that I put in the way of making enormous amounts of money!'

'Look here!' continued Desroches in lowered tones; 'Gigonnet's name is Bidault; Saillard your cashier is his nephew; and Saillard is besides the father-in-law of a certain Baudoyer who thinks he has a right to the vacant post in your department. I had cause to give you warning, had I not?'

'Thanks,' said des Lupeaulx, with a nod of good-bye and a knowing glance.

'One stroke of the pen and you get a receipt in full,' said Desroches, as he went.

'That is the way with these immense sacrifices, you can't speak of them to a woman,' thought des Lupeaulx. 'Is Célestine worth the riddance of all my debts? I will go and see her this morning.'

And so, in a few hours' time, the fair Mme. Rabourdin was to be the arbiter of her husband's destinies; and no power on earth could warn her of the importance of her replies, no danger signal bid her compose her voice and manner. And, unluckily, she was confident of success; she did not know that the ground beneath Rabourdin was undermined in all directions with the burrowings of teredos.

'Well, my lord,' said des Lupeaulx, as he entered the breakfast-room, 'have you seen the paragraphs on Baudoyer?'

'For Heaven's sake, my dear fellow, let nominations alone for a minute,' returned the Minister. 'I had that monstrance flung at my head yesterday. To secure Rabourdin, the nomination must go before the board at once; I will not have my hand forced. It is enough to make one sick of public life. If we are to keep Rabourdin, we must promote one Colleville——'

'Will you leave me to manage this farce and think no more about it? I will amuse you every morning with an account of the moves in a game of chess with the Grand Almonry,' said des Lupeaulx.

'Very well,' replied the Minister, 'work with the chief of the staff. Don't you know that an argument in an Opposition paper is the most likely thing of all to strike the King's mind? A Minister overruled by a Baudoyer; just think of it!'

'A bigot and a driveller,' said des Lupeaulx; 'he is as incompetent as——'

'La Billardière,' put in His Excellency.

'La Billardière at least behaved like a Gentleman in Ordinary of the Bedchamber,' said des Lupeaulx.— 'Madame,' he continued, turning to the Countess, 'it will be absolutely necessary now to invite Mme. Rabourdin to your next small party. I must point out that Mme. de Camps is a friend of hers; they were at the Italiens together yesterday, and she has been to my knowledge at the Hôtel Firmiani; so you can see whether she is likely to commit any solecism in a salon.'

'Send an invitation to Mme. Rabourdin, dear, and let us change the subject,' said the Minister.

'So Célestine is in my clutches!' des Lupeaulx said to himself, as he went up to his rooms for a morning toilette.

Parisian households are eaten up with a desire to be in harmony with the luxury which surrounds them on all sides; those who are wise enough to live as their income prescribes are in a small minority. Perhaps this failing is akin to a very French patriotism, an effort to preserve supremacy in matters of costume for France. France lays down the law to all Europe in fashions, and everybody in the country regards it as a duty to preserve her commercial sceptre, for France rules the fashions if Britain rules the waves. The patriotic fervour which leads the Frenchman to sacrifice everything to 'seemliness' (as d'Aubigné said of Henri III.) causes an immense amount of hard work behind the scenes; work that absorbs a Parisienne's whole morning, especially if, like Mme. Rabourdin, she tries to live on an income of twelve thousand livres in a style which many wealthier people would not attempt on thirty thousand.

So, every Friday, the day of the weekly dinner-party, Mme. Rabourdin used to assist the housemaid who swept and dusted the rooms, for the cook was despatched to the Market at an early hour, and the man-servant was busy cleaning the silver, polishing the glasses, and arranging the table napkins. If any ill-advised caller had escaped the porter's vigilance and climbed the stairs to Mme. Rabourdin's abode, he would have found her in a most unpicturesque disorder. Arrayed in a loose morning-gown, with her feet thrust into an old pair of slippers, and her hair in a careless knot, she was engaged in trimming lamps or arranging flowers, or hastily preparing an unromantic breakfast. If the visitor had not been previously initiated into the mysteries of Paris life, he would certainly learn there and then that it is inexpedient to set foot behind the scenes thereof; before very long he would be held up as an example, he would be capable of the blackest deeds. A woman surprised in her morning mysteries will talk of his stupidity and indiscretion, till she ruins the intruder. Indulgent as the Parisienne may be to curiosity that turns to her profit, she is implacable to indiscretion which finds her at a disadvantage. Such a domiciliary visit is not so much an indecent assault, to use the language of the police-courts, as flat burglary, and theft of the dearest treasure of all, to wit, Credit. A woman may have no objection to be discovered half dressed with her hair about her shoulders; if all her hair is her own, she is a gainer by the incident; but no woman cares to be seen sweeping out her rooms, there is a loss of 'seemliness' in it.

Mme. Rabourdin was in the thick of her Friday preparations, and surrounded by provisions fished up from that ocean, the Great Market, when M. des Lupeaulx made his surreptitious call. Truly, the Secretary-General was the last person whom the fair Rabourdin expected to see; so hearing his boots creak on the stairs, she cried, 'The hairdresser already!' If the sound of the words struck unpleasantly in des Lupeaulx's ears, the sight of des Lupeaulx was not a whit more agreeable to the lady. She took refuge in her bedroom amid a terrible muddle, a perfect Shrovetide assemblage of motley furniture and heterogeneous elegance, which had been pent thither to be out of sight; but the negligent morning-dress proved so alluring, that the bold des Lupeaulx followed the frightened fair· one. A vague, indescribable something tantalised him; glimpses caught through a half-fastened slip seemed a thousand times more enticing than a full display of every graceful curve, from the line traced round the shoulders by a low velvet bodice to the vanishing point of the prettiest rounded swan-like throat that ever lover kissed before a ball. If your eyes rest on a splendidly developed bust set off by full dress, it suggests a comparison with the elaborate dessert of a great dinner; but the glance that steals under cambrics crumpled by slumber will find dainties there on which to feast, sweets to be relished like the stolen fruit that reddens among the leaves upon the trellis.

'Wait! wait!' cried the fair lady, bolting herself in with her disorder.

She rang for Thérèse, for the cook, for the man-servant, for her daughter, imploring a shawl. She longed for stage machinery to shift the scene at the manager's whistle. And the whistle was given and the transformation worked in a hand's turn after all. And behold a new phenomenon! The room took on a piquant air of morning which harmonised with an impromptu toilette, all devised for the greater glory of a woman who, in this instance, clearly rose superior to her sex.

'You!' she exclaimed, 'and at this hour! What ever can it be?'

'The most serious thing in the world,' returned des Lupeaulx. 'To-day we must arrive at a clear under-standing of each other.'

Célestine looked straight through the eyeglasses into the man's thoughts, and understood.

'It is my chief weakness,' said she, 'to be prodigiously fanciful; I do not mingle politics and affection, for

R

instance; let us talk of politics and business, and afterwards we shall see. And besides, this is not a mere
whim; it is one consequence of my artistic taste; I
cannot put discordant colours or incongruous things
together; I shun jarring contrasts. We women have
a policy of our own.'

Even as she spoke, her pretty ways and the tones of
her voice produced their effect; the Secretary-General's
brutality was giving place to sentimental courtesy.
She had recalled him to a sense of what was due from
him as a lover. A clever, pretty woman creates her
own atmosphere, as it were; nerves are relaxed and
sentiments softened in her presence.

'You do not know what is going on,' des Lupeaulx
returned abruptly, for he tried to persevere in his
brutality. 'Read that!'

Des Lupeaulx had previously marked the paragraphs
in red ink; he now held out the newspapers to the
graceful woman before him. As Célestine read, her
shawl slipped open; but she was either unconscious
of this, or successfully feigned unconsciousness. Des
Lupeaulx had reached the age when fancies are the
more potent because they pass so swiftly; but if he
found it difficult to keep self-control, Célestine was
equally hard put to it.

'What!' said she. 'Why, this is dreadful! Who
is this Baudoyer?'

'A jackass,' returned des Lupeaulx; 'but, as you see,
he carries the relics, and with a clever hand on the
bridle he will reach his goal.'

Mme. Rabourdin's debts rose up before her eyes and
dazzled her; she seemed to see one lightning flash after
another; the blood surged through her veins till her
ears rang with the heavy pulse beats; she sat in a stupor,
staring with unseeing eyes at a bracket on the wall.
Then she turned to des Lupeaulx.

'But you are true to us?' she said, with a glance

like a caress, a glance that was meant to bind him to herself.

'That depends,' he answered, returning her look with an inquisitive glance that brought the red into the poor woman's face.

'If you insist upon earnest-money, you will lose the full payment,' she said with a laugh. 'I imagined that you were greater than you are. And as for you, you think I am very small, a mere schoolgirl.'

'You did not understand,' he said meaningly. 'I meant that I cannot serve a man who is going against me, as l'Étourdi thwarts Mascarille.'

'What does this mean?'

'This will show you that I am great,' he said. And he gave her Dutocq's stolen list, pointing as he did so to her husband's shrewd analysis of his character.

'Read that!'

Célestine recognised the handwriting, read, and turned pale at this bludgeon blow.

'All the departments are in it,' added des Lupeaulx.

'But, fortunately, no one but you possesses a copy. I cannot explain it.'

'The thief that stole it is not so simple that he would not take a duplicate; he is too great a liar to confess to the copy, and too intelligent in his trade to give it up. I have not even asked him about it.'

'Who is he?'

'Your first draughting-clerk.'

'Dutocq. You are never punished except for doing a kindness.—But he is a dog that wants a bone,' she added.

'Do you know what a tentative offer has been held out to me, poor devil of a Secretary-General that I am?'

'What?'

'I owe a miserable thirty thousand odd francs. You will at once form a very poor opinion of me when you know that I am not more in debt; but, indeed, in this respect I am small! Well and good. Baudoyer's uncle has just bought up my debts, and is ready, no doubt, to give up my bills to me.'

'But all this is infernal.'

'Not a bit of it; it is monarchical and religious, for the Grand Almonry is mixed up in it——'

'What are you going to do?'

'What are your orders?' he asked, holding out a hand with an adorable charm of manner.

To Célestine he was no longer plain, nor old, nor frosted with powder, nor a secretary-general, nor anything unclean; but she did not give him her hand. In her drawing-room she would have allowed him to take it a hundred times in the course of an evening; but such a proceeding in the morning, when they were alone, was as good as a promise; it was rather too decisive—it might lead her further than she meant to go.

'And people say that statesmen have no hearts!' she cried, trying to soften the refusal with a gracious speech. 'That frightened me,' she added, with the most innocent air in the world.

'What a slander!' returned des Lupeaulx. 'One of the most impassive of diplomatists, a man that has kept power ever since he was born, has just married an actress's daughter, and imposed her upon the most rigorous of all Courts in the matter of quarterings.'

'And you will support us?'

'I work the nominations. But no trickery.'

She held out her hand for him to kiss, and gave him a light tap on the cheek.

'You are mine,' she said.

Des Lupeaulx admired that speech. (Indeed, the coxcomb told the story that evening at the Opéra, after his own fashion, as follows: 'A woman did not wish to tell a man that she was his, an admission that a well-

bred woman never makes, so she said, "You are mine!"
What do you think of the evasion?')

'But you must be my ally,' he began. 'Your husband said something to the Minister about a scheme of administration, and this list, in which I am handled so gently, is connected with it. Find out, and let me know this evening.'

'It shall be done,' said she. She saw no great importance in the matter that had brought des Lupeaulx to her house at such an early hour.

'The hairdresser, madame,' announced the housemaid.

'He has kept me waiting a very long time!' she said. 'I do not know how I should have come through if he had been any later,' she thought within herself.

'You do not know how far my devotion goes,' said des Lupeaulx, rising to his feet. 'You are going to be invited to the Countess's next special and intimate party——'

'Oh! you are an angel,' she said; 'and I see how much you love me. You love me intelligently.'

'This evening, dear child, I am going to the Opéra to find out who these journalists are that are conspiring for Baudoyer; and we will measure weapons.'

'Yes, but you will dine here, will you not? I have ordered the things you like.'

'All this is so much like love,' des Lupeaulx said to himself as he went downstairs, 'so much like love, that it would be pleasant to be deceived in such a way for a long while. But if she is laughing at me, I shall find it out. I have the most ingenious of snares ready for her, so that I may read her very heart before I sign. Ah! you kittens, we know you; for, after all, women are just as we are. Twenty-eight years old and virtuous, and here in the Rue Duphot! It is a rare piece of luck which is well worth the trouble of cultivation.'

And this eligible butterfly fluttered away down the staircase.

'Oh dear! that man yonder without his spectacles must look very funny in his dressing-gown when his hair is powdered!' Célestine was saying to herself meanwhile. 'He has the harpoon in his back; he is going to tow me at last to my goal—the Minister's house. He has played his part in my comedy.'

When Rabourdin came home at five o'clock to dress, his wife came into the room and brought him the list. It seemed like the slipper in the *Arabian Nights*—the unlucky man was fated to meet it everywhere.

'Who put that in your hands?' Rabourdin asked in amazement.

'M. des Lupeaulx.'

'Has he been here?' asked Rabourdin. A guilty woman would surely have turned pale beneath the look that he gave her, but his wife met it with marble brows and laughing eyes.

'Yes, and he is coming here again to dinner,' said she. 'Why do you look so horrified.'

'Dear,' said Rabourdin, 'I have given des Lupeaulx mortal offence. Men of that sort never forgive; and he is caressing me! Do you think that I cannot see why?'

'It seems to me that he has a very discriminating taste,' she said. 'I cannot blame him for it. After all, I know of nothing more flattering to a woman's vanity than the knowledge that she stimulates a jaded palate.'

'A truce to jesting, Célestine! Spare an overburdened man. I cannot speak with the Minister, and my honour is at stake.'

'Oh dear, no! Dutocq shall have the promise of a place, and you will be head of the division.'

'I see what you mean, darling,' said Rabourdin; 'but you are playing a game that is quite as dishonouring as if you meant it in earnest. A lie is a lie, and an honest woman——'

'Pray let me make use of the weapons that they turn against us.'

'Célestine, when that man sees how foolishly he has fallen into the snare, he will be all the more furious against me.'

'And how if I upset him?'

Rabourdin stared at his wife in amazement.

'I am only thinking of your advancement,' continued Célestine, 'and it is time I did so, my poor love.—But you are taking the sporting-dog for the game,' she added after a pause. 'In a few days' time des Lupeaulx will have fulfilled his mission very sufficiently. While you are trying to say a word to the Minister, and before you can so much as see him, *I* shall have had a talk with him. You have strained every nerve to bring out this scheme that you have kept from me; and in three months your wife will have done more than you have done in six years. Tell me about this great project of yours.'

So Rabourdin, as he shaved himself, began to explain his scheme, first obtaining a promise that his wife would not say a single word of his work; warning her, at the same time, that to give des Lupeaulx any idea of it would be to give the cream-jug to the cat. But at the fifth sentence Célestine interrupted him.

'Rabourdin, why did you not speak to me about it?' she said. 'Why, you would have saved yourself useless trouble. I can imagine that one may be blinded by an idea for a minute; but for six or seven years!—that I cannot conceive. You want to reduce the estimates? It is a commonplace, penny-wise economy! Rather we should aim at raising the income to two milliards. France would be twice as great. A new system would be this plan cried up by M. de Nucingen, a loan that would send an impulse through trade through the whole country. The poorest exchequer is the one that has most francs lying idle. It is the Finance

Minister's mission to fling money out of the windows, and it comes in at his cellars. And you would have him accumulate specie! Why, instead of reducing the number of posts under Government, you ought to increase them! Instead of paying off the national debt, you should increase the number of fund-holders. If the Bourbons mean to reign in peace, they ought to have fund-holders in every township; and, of all things, they should beware of raising foreign loans, for foreigners will be sure some day to require the repayment of the capital, whereas if none but Frenchmen have money invested in the funds, neither France nor national credit will perish. *That* saved England. This plan of yours is a little shopkeeper's scheme. An ambitious man should only present himself in the character of a second Law, without Law's ill-luck; he should explain the resources of credit; he should show that we ought not to sink money in extinguishing principal, but in payment of interest, as the English do——'

'Come, Célestine,' said Rabourdin, 'jumble up ideas together, make playthings of them, and contradict yourself! I am used to it. But do not criticise a piece of work before you know what it is.'

'Is there any need to know what it is, when the gist of the matter is to carry on the administration in France with six thousand officials instead of twenty thousand? Why, my dear, even if the scheme were invented by a man of genius, a King of France would lose his crown if he attempted to carry it into effect. You may subjugate an aristocracy by striking off a few heads, but you cannot quell a hydra with a thousand claws. No, no; insignificant folk cannot be crushed, they lie too flat beneath the foot.—And do you mean to move all these men through the ministers? Between ourselves, they are very poor creatures. You may shift men's interests, you cannot shift men; they make too much outcry, whereas the francs are dumb.'

'But, Célestine, if you talk all the time, and if you aim your wit wide of the mark, we shall never arrive at an understanding——'

'Ah! I see the drift of that analysis of men's administrative ability,' she went on, without listening to her husband. 'Goodness, you have been sharpening the axe for yourself. *Sainte Vierge!* why did you not consult me? I would at any rate have prevented you from putting a single line on paper; or at the worst, if you wished to have the memorandum, I would have copied it myself, and it should never have left this house. Oh! dear, why did you say nothing to me about it? Just like a man! A man can sleep beside his wife and keep a secret for seven years! He can hide himself from her, poor thing, for seven years and doubt her devotion.'

'But,' protested Rabourdin, 'whenever I have tried to discuss anything with you, for these eleven years, you have cut me short, and immediately brought out your own ideas instead. You know nothing of my work.'

'Nothing? I know all about it!'

'Then, pray, tell me about it,' cried Rabourdin, losing his temper for the first time since his marriage.

'There! it is half-past six; shave yourself and dress,' she retorted, answering him after the wont of women when pressed upon a point on which they are bound to be silent; 'I will finish dressing, and we will postpone the argument, for I do not want to be worried on my reception day.—Oh, dear me, poor man,' she said to herself as she went, 'to think that he should toil for seven years to bring about his own ruin! And put no trust in his wife.'

She turned back.

'If you had listened to me in time,' she said, 'you would not have interfered on behalf of your first clerk; he, no doubt, took the copies of that unlucky list. Good-bye, clever man!'

But seeing her husband's pain in his tragic attitude, she felt that she had gone too far; she sprang to him, and put her arms about him lovingly, all covered with soap as he was.

'Dear Xavier, do not be vexed,' she said, 'this evening we will go through your scheme; you shall talk at your ease, and I am going to listen as long and as attentively as you please!—Is that nice of me? There, I do not ask better than to be Mahomet's wife.'

She began to laugh, and Rabourdin could not help laughing too, for Célestine's mouth was white with soap, while there was a wealth of the truest and most perdurable affection in the tones of her voice.

'Go and dress, little one; and of all things, not a word of this to des Lupeaulx! Give me your promise. That is the only penance I require——'

'*Require?* Then I won't make any promise at all.'

'Come, Célestine, I spoke seriously though I was joking.'

'To-night your secretary-general will know the foes with whom we must fight; and I know whom to attack.'

'Whom?' asked Rabourdin.

'The Minister,' she said, growing two feet taller for her words.

But in spite of Célestine's winning charm, a few painful thoughts occurred to Rabourdin in spite of himself, and darkened his forehead.

'When will she learn to appreciate me?' he thought. 'She did not even understand that all this work was done for her sake. What waywardness! and how intelligent she is!—If I were not married, I should be very well off and in a high position by this time. I should have put by five thousand francs a year out of my salary; and by investing the money carefully, I should have an independent income of ten thousand francs at this day. I should be a bachelor; I should stand a

chance to become somebody; through a marriage——
Yes' (he interrupted himself), 'but I have Célestine
and the two children.'

He fell back upon his happiness. Even in the happiest
married life, there must always be some moments of
regret.

He went to the drawing-room and looked round.

'There are not two women in Paris who can manage
as she does. All this on twelve thousand livres a year!'
he thought, as he glanced at the jars full of flowers, and
thought of the coming pleasure of gratified vanity. 'She
was meant to be a Minister's wife. And when I think
that my Minister's wife is of no use to him—she
looks like a stout homely housewife—and when she goes
to the Tuileries, to other people's houses, she——'

He compressed his lips. A very busy man's ideas of
housekeeping are so vague, that it is easy to persuade
him to believe that a hundred thousand francs will do
everything or nothing.

But though des Lupeaulx was impatiently expected,
though the dinner had been designed to tickle the
palate of a professed epicure, he only came in at midnight, at which hour conversation is wont to grow more
personal and confidential. Andoche Finot, journalist,
was there likewise.

'I know all about it,' began des Lupeaulx, when he
was comfortably settled on the settee by the fireside,
with a cup of tea in his hand; and Mme. Rabourdin
stood before him holding out a plate full of sandwiches
and slices of the weighty substance not inappropriately
known as pound-cake.—'Finot, my dear and intelligent
friend, you may do our gracious queen a service by
letting loose some of your pack on some men whom
I am going to mention.'—Then turning to M. Rabourdin, and lowering his voice so that the words should not
travel beyond the three persons to whom they were
addressed, he continued—'You have the money-lenders

and the clergy, capital and the Church, against you. The paragraph in the Liberal paper was inserted at the instance of an old bill-discounter; the proprietors lay under some obligation to him, and the little fellow that actually did it did not think that it mattered very much. The whole staff of the paper is to be reconstituted in three days; we shall get over that. The Royalist Opposition (for, thanks to M. de Chateaubriand, we now have a Royalist Opposition, which is to say, that there are Royalists half-way over to the Liberals; but do not let us talk of mighty matters in politics),—the Royal Opposition, I say, hating Charles x. with a deadly hate, have promised their support to you, if we will pass one of their amendments. All my batteries are in the field. If they try to force Baudoyer upon us, we will say to the Grand Almonry, "Such and such newspapers and Messrs. So-and-So will attack this law that you want to pass, and you will have the whole press against you" (for the Ministerial papers under my control shall be deaf and dumb; and as they are pretty much deaf and dumb already—eh, Finot?—that will give them no difficulty). "Nominate Rabourdin, and you will have public opinion with you." To think of the poor simple provincials that intrench themselves in their armchairs by the fireside and rejoice over the independence of the organs of opinion! Ha! ha!'

'He! he! he!' chuckled Finot.

'So be quite easy,' continued des Lupeaulx. 'I arranged it all this evening. The Grand Almonry will give way.'

'I would rather have given up all hope and have had you here at dinner,' Célestine whispered, and the look of reproach in her eyes might easily have been taken for a love-distraught glance.

'Here is something that will obtain my pardon,' returned he, and he gave her the invitation for the party on Tuesday. Célestine's face lighted up with the reddest glow of pleasure, as she opened the envelope. No delight can be compared with the joy of vanity triumphant.

'Do you know what a Tuesday is?' continued des Lupeaulx, with an air of mystery; 'it is an inner circle; it is to our department as the Petit-Château is to the Court. You will be in the very centre. The Comtesse Féraud will be there (she is still in favour in spite of the death of Louis XVIII.); Delphine de Nucingen, Mme. de Listomère, and the Marquise d'Espard are invited, so is your dear de Camps; I sent the invitation myself, so that you might find a supporter in her in case the other women should "black-ball" you. I should like to see you among them.'

Célestine tossed her head; she looked like a norough-bred before the race. Again she read the card, as Baudoyer and Saillard had read their paragraphs in the paper; and, like them, she could not grasp the meaning of the words.

'This first, and some day the Tuileries!' she said, turning to des Lupeaulx with such ambition and confidence in her tone and manner that she struck dismay into him as he looked at her.

'How if I should only be a stepping-stone for her?' he asked himself.

He rose to his feet and went to her bedroom; she followed, for she understood by his sign that he wished to speak with her in private.

'Well, and the scheme?' he began.

'Pooh! an honest man's folly! He wants to put down fifteen thousand employés and keep a staff of five or six thousand. You could not imagine a more monstrous absurdity; I will give you his memoranda to read when they are copied out. He is quite in earnest. He made his analytical catalogue with the best of motives. The poor, dear man!'

Des Lupeaulx felt the more reassured because genuine

laughter accompanied the light contemptuous words ; a lie would not have deceived him, he was too old a hand, but Célestine was sincere while she thus spoke.

'But, after all, there is something at the bottom of it all,' he rejoined.

'Oh, well, he wants to do away with the land-tax and replace it by a tax upon articles of consumption.'

'Why, François Keller and Nucingen brought forward an almost identical plan a year ago ; and the Minister is thinking of removing the burden from the land.'

'There ! I told him that there was nothing new in the idea,' laughed Célestine.

'Yes ; but if he and the great financier of the age, the Napoleon of finance (I can say so between ourselves), if he and Nucingen have hit upon the same idea, he must at any rate have some notion of the way of carrying it out.'

'The whole thing is commonplace,' she said, pursing up her lips disdainfully. 'He wants to govern France (just think of it !) with five or six thousand employés ; when, on the contrary, it ought to be to the interest of every person in the country to maintain the present government.'

Des Lupeaulx seemed relieved to find that the chief clerk, whom he took for a man of extraordinary ability, was a mediocrity after all.

'Are you quite sure of the appointment ? Do you care to take a piece of woman's advice ? ' asked she.

'You women understand the art of polite treachery better than we do,' said des Lupeaulx, shaking his head.

'Very well ; say " Baudoyer " at Court and at the Grand Almonry, so as to lull suspicion ; but at the last moment write " Rabourdin." '

'Some women say " Yes " so long as they need a man, and " No " when he has served their turn,' remarked des Lupeaulx.

'I know them,' Célestine answered, laughing. 'But they are very silly, for in politics you must come across the same people again and again. It is all very well with fools, but you are a clever man. In my opinion, it is the greatest possible mistake in life to quarrel with a really clever man.'

'No,' said des Lupeaulx, 'for he will forgive. There is no danger except with petty rancorous minds that have nothing to do but plan revenge, and I spend my life on that.'

When every one had gone, Rabourdin stayed in his wife's room, begged her to listen to him for once, and took the opportunity of explaining his scheme. He made her understand that he had no intention of diminishing the estimates; on the contrary, he gave a list of public enterprises to be carried out with the public money; private enterprise or local improvements should be subsidised by a government grant of one-third or one-fourth of the total outlay, and these grants would set money in circulation. In short, he made it plain to his wife that his scheme was not so much a theory on paper as a practicable plan to be worked out in hundreds of ways. Célestine's enthusiasm grew; she sprang to her husband and put her arms about him, and sat on his knee beside the fire.

'And so, after all,' she said, 'I have found the husband of whom I dreamed. My ignorance of your worth saved you from des Lupeaulx's clutches. I slandered you to him amazingly, and in good earnest too.'

There were happy tears in Rabourdin's eyes. And so at last he had his day of triumph. He had undertaken it all to please his wife; he was a great man in the eyes of his public!

'And for any one who knows how good and kind and loving and equable you are, you are ten times greater! But a man of genius is always more or less of a child, and you are a child,' she said, 'a dearly-loved child.'

She drew out her invitation card from its hiding-place and showed it to him—

'This is what I wanted,' she continued. 'Des Lupeaulx has brought me in contact with His Excellency, and His Excellency shall be my servant for a while, even if he is made of bronze.'

Next day Célestine was absorbed in preparations for her introduction into the inner circle. It was to be her great day, her success. Never did courtesan take more pains with herself than this matron took. Never was dressmaker more tormented, more sensible how much depended upon her art. Mme. Rabourdin overlooked nothing, in short. She went herself to choose a brougham·for the occasion, so that her carriage should be neither old-fashioned, nor insolent, nor suggestive of the city madam. Her servant, as became the servant of a good house, was to look like a gentleman.

Then, about ten o'clock on the great Tuesday evening, Mme. Rabourdin emerged in an exquisite mourning toilet. In her hair she wore bunches of jet grapes, of the finest workmanship, part of a complete set of ornaments ordered at Fossin's by an Englishwoman who went away without taking them. The leaves were thin flakes of stamped iron, light as real vine-leaves, and the artist had not forgotten the little graceful tendrils that clung among her curls, as the vine-tendrils cling to every branch. The bracelets and earrings were of 'Berlin iron,' as it is called; but the delicate arabesques from Vienna might have been made by the hands of fairies for some task-mistress, some Carabosse with a passion for collecting ants' eyes, or for spinning pieces of stuff to pack into a hazel nut. Célestine's dress had been carefully cut to bring out all the grace of a slender figure, which looked slenderer still in black. The curves all stopped short at the line round the neck, for she wore no shoulder-straps; at every movement she seemed about to emerge like a butterfly from the sheath; yet, through the dressmaker's skill, the gown clung to the lines of her figure. The material was not yet known in Paris; it was a *mousseline de laine*, an 'adorable' stuff that afterwards became the rage. Indeed, the success outlasted the fashion in France; for the practical advantages of a thin woollen material, which saves the expense of washing, injured the cotton-spinning industry and revolutionised the Rouen trade. Célestine's feet were daintily shod in Turkey satin slippers (for bright satin could not be worn in mourning) and fine thin stockings.

Célestine looked very lovely thus dressed. Her complexion was brilliant and softly coloured, thanks to the reviving influence of a bran bath. Hope had flooded her eyes, her quick intelligence sparkled in them; she looked like the woman of a superior order, of whom des Lupeaulx spoke with such pride and pleasure. She knew how to enter a room; all women will appreciate the meaning of that phrase. She bowed gracefully to the Minister's wife, deference and dignity blended in the right proportion in her manner; and wore her air of majesty without giving offence, for every fair woman is a queen. With the Minister she used the pretty insolence that women are wont to assume with any male creature, were he a grand-duke. And as she took her seat, she reconnoitred the ground. She found herself in a small, carefully chosen circle in which women can measure each other and form accurate judgments; the lightest word reverberates in all ears, every glance makes an impression, and conversation becomes a duel before witnesses. Any remark pitched in the ordinary key sounds flat; and good talk is quietly accepted as a matter of course at that intellectual level. Rabourdin betook himself to an adjoining card-room, and there remained, planted on both feet, to watch the play, which proves that he was not wanting in sense.

'My dear,' said the Marquise d'Espard, turning to the Comtesse Féraud, Louis xviii.'s last mistress, 'Paris

s

is unique. Such women as this start up in it quite
unexpectedly from no one knows where, and seemingly
they have the will and the power to do anything——'

'And she has the will and the power to do anything,'
said des Lupeaulx, bridling as he spoke.

The crafty Célestine, meanwhile, was paying court to
the Minister's wife. Drilled by des Lupeaulx on the
previous day, she knew all the Countess's weaknesses and
flattered them, without seeming to touch upon them.
And she was silent too at the right moment; for des
Lupeaulx,in spite of his infatuation,had noticed Célestine's
shortcomings, and warned her against them. 'Of all
things, do not talk too much!' he had said the evening
before. 'Twas an extraordinary proof of attachment.
Bertrand Barrère left behind him the sublime maxim,
'Never interrupt a woman with advice while she is dancing;' which, with the supplementary apophthegm here
subjoined, 'Do not find fault with a woman for scattering
her pearls,' may be said to complete this article of the code
feminine. The conversation became general. From time
to time Mme. Rabourdin put in a word, much as a well-
trained cat touches her mistress's lace, with sheathed claws.
The Minister's heart was not very susceptible; in the
matter of gallantry, no statesman of the Restoration was
more accomplished; the Opposition *Miroir*, the *Pandore*,
and the *Figaro* could not reproach him with the faintest
acceleration of the pulse. His mistress was *L'Étoile*;
strange to say, she had been faithful in adversity, and
probably was reaping the benefit even at that moment.
This Mme. Rabourdin knew, but she knew also that
people change their minds in old châteaux, so she set
herself to make the Minister jealous of such good fortune
as des Lupeaulx appeared to enjoy. At that moment
des Lupeaulx was expatiating upon Célestine, for the
benefit of the Marquise d'Espard, Mme. de Nucingen,
and the Countess; he was trying to make them understand that Mme. Rabourdin must be admitted into

their coalition ; and Mme. de Camps, the fourth in the
quartette of listeners, was supporting him. At the end
of an hour the Minister had been well stroked down ;
he was pleased with Mme. Rabourdin's wit, and she
had charmed his wife ; indeed, the Countess was so
enchanted with this siren, that she had just asked her to
come whenever she pleased.

'For your husband will very soon be head of the
division, my dear,' she had said, 'and the Minister
intends to bring both the divisions under one head, and
then you will be one of us.'

His Excellency took Mme. Rabourdin to see one of
the rooms. His suite of apartments was famous in those
days, for Opposition journalism had made itself ridiculous
by denouncing the lavish display therein. He gave his
arm to the lady.

'Indeed, madame, you really ought to favour us, the
Countess and myself, by coming frequently——' and
His Excellency brought out his Ministerial pretty
speeches.

'But, monseigneur,' demurred Célestine, with one of
the glances that women keep for emergencies ; 'but,
monseigneur, that depends upon you, it seems to me.'

'How ?'

'Why, you can give me the right to do so.'

'Explain yourself.'

'No. When I came here, I said to myself that I
would not have the bad taste to solicit your interest.'

'Pray, speak ! *Placets* of this sort are never out of
place,' the Minister answered, laughing. And nothing
amuses your seriously-minded men so much as this kind
of nonsense.

'Very well ; it is rather absurd of a chief clerk's wife
to come here often, but a director's wife would not be
" out of place."'

'Never mind that,' said the Minister, 'we cannot do
without your husband ; he has been nominated.'

'Really and truly?'

'Will you come to my study and see his name for yourself? The thing is done.'

It seemed to her that there was something suspicious in the Minister's eagerness and alacrity.

'Well,' she said, as they stood apart in a corner, 'let me tell you that I can repay you——'

She was on the point of unfolding her husband's scheme, when des Lupeaulx came forward on tiptoe with an angry little cough, which, being interpreted, meant that he had been listening to their conversation, and did not wish to be found out. The Minister looked in no pleasant humour at the elderly coxcomb thus caught in a trap. Des Lupeaulx had hurried on the work of the staff beyond all reason, in his impatience for his conquest; he had put it in the Minister's hands, and next day he intended to bring the nomination to her who passed for his mistress.

Just at that moment the Minister's footman came, and with a mysterious air informed des Lupeaulx that his own man had brought a letter to be delivered to him immediately, adding that it was of great importance.

The Secretary-General went to a lamp and read a missive thus conceived:—

'Contrary to my habit, I am waiting in an ante-chamber; there is not a moment to lose if you mean to arrange with your servant

Gobseck

The Secretary-General shuddered at the sight of that signature. It would be a pity not to give a facsimile of it, for it is rare on the market, and should be valuable to those persons who discover character in handwriting. If ever hieroglyph represented an animal, surely this

name, with its initial and final letter, suggests the
voracious insatiable jaws of a shark, jaws that are always
agape, always catching hold of the strong and the weak
alike, and gobbling them down. It has been found impossible to reproduce the whole note in facsimile, for the
handwriting, though clear, is too small and close and
fine; the whole sentence, indeed, only fills one line.
The spirit of bill-discounting alone could inspire so
insolently imperative, so cruelly irreproachable a sentence; an explicit yet non-committal statement, which
told all yet revealed nothing. If you had never heard
of Gobseck before, you might have guessed what
manner of man it was that wrote that line; and seen
the implacable money-lender of the Rue des Grès, who
could summons you into his presence without sending
an order. Accordingly, des Lupeaulx straightway disappeared, like a dog when the sportsman calls him off
the scent; and went to his own abode, pondering by the
way. His whole position seemed to be compromised.
Picture to yourself the sensations of a general-in-chief
when his aide-de-camp announces that 'the enemy with
thirty thousand men, all fresh troops, is taking us in
flank'! A word will explain the arrival of Messieurs
Gigonnet and Gobseck upon the field; for both those
worthies were waiting upon des Lupeaulx.

At eight o'clock that evening, Martin Falleix had
arrived on the wings of the wind (thanks to three francs
per stage and a postillion sent on ahead). He had
brought the contracts, which all bore yesterday's date.
Mitral took the documents at once to the Café Thémis;
they were duly handed over, and the two money-lenders
hurried off to des Lupeaulx. They went on foot,
however. The clock struck eleven.

Des Lupeaulx shuddered as he watched the two
sinister-looking faces light up with a gleeful expression,
and saw a look that shot out straight as a bullet, and
blazed like the flash of powder.

'Well, my masters, what is the matter?'

The two money-lenders sat motionless and impassive. Gigonnet glanced from his bundle of papers to the man-servant.

'Let us go into my study,' said des Lupeaulx, dismissing the man with a sign.

'You understand French admirably,' remarked Gigonnet.

'Have you come to torment a man that put you in the way of making two hundred thousand francs apiece?' asked des Lupeaulx, and in spite of himself his gesture was disdainful.

'And will put us in the way of making more, I hope,' said Gigonnet.

'Is it a bit of business? If you want me, I have a memory.'

'And we have memoranda of yours,' riposted Gigonnet.

'My debts will be paid,' des Lupeaulx returned loftily. He did not wish to be led into a discussion on the subject.

'Truly?' asked Gobseck.

'Let us go to the point, my son,' said Gigonnet. 'Don't you draw yourself up in your stock like that; it won't do with us. Take these contracts and read them through.'

Des Lupeaulx read with surprise and amazement; angels might have flung those contracts down from the clouds for him; and meanwhile the pair took stock of his room.

'You have a couple of intelligent men of business in us, haven't you?' asked Gigonnet.

'But to what do I owe such ingenious co-operation?' des Lupeaulx inquired uneasily.

'We knew, a week ago, what you will not know till to-morrow unless we tell you: the President of the Commercial Court finds that he is obliged to resign his seat in the Chamber.

Des Lupeaulx's eyes dilated till they grew as large as meadow daisies.

'Your Minister was playing this trick upon you,' added Gobseck, the curt-spoken.

'You are my masters,' said des Lupeaulx, saluting the pair with a profound respect in which there was a certain tinge of irony.

'Precisely,' said Gobseck.

'But are you about to strangle me?'

'That is possible.'

'Very well, then; set about it, you executioners!' returned the Secretary-General with a smile.

'Your debts,' began Gigonnet, 'are inscribed along with the loan of the purchase-money, you see.'

'Here are the deeds,' added Gobseck, as he drew a bundle of documents from the pocket of his faded greatcoat.

'And you have three years to pay the lot,' said Gigonnet.

'But what do you want?' asked des Lupeaulx, much alarmed by so much readiness to oblige, and such a fancy settlement.

'La Billardière's place for Baudoyer,' Gigonnet answered quickly.

'It is a very small thing,' returned des Lupeaulx, 'though I should have to do the impossible. I myself have tied my hands.'

'You are going to gnaw the cords with your teeth,' said Gigonnet.

'They are sharp enough!' added Gobseck.

'Is that all?'

'We shall keep the contracts until these claims are admitted,' said Gigonnet, laying a statement under the Secretary-General's eyes as he spoke; 'if these are not recognised within six days by the committee, my name will be filled in instead of yours on the deeds.'

'You are clever,' exclaimed des Lupeaulx.

'Precisely,' said Gobseck.

'And that is all?'

'True,' replied Gobseck.

'Is it a bargain?' demanded Gigonnet.

Des Lupeaulx nodded.

'Very well, then, sign this power of attorney,' said Gigonnet. 'Baudoyer's nomination in two days; the admission of the claims in six; and——'

'And what?'

'We guarantee you——'

'What?' cried des Lupeaulx, more and more astonished.

'*Your* nomination,' replied Gigonnet, swelling with pride. 'We are secure of a majority; fifty-two tenant-farmers and tradesmen are ready to vote at the election as the lender of the money may direct.'

Des Lupeaulx grasped Gobseck's hand.

'We are the only people among whom misapprehensions are impossible. This is what you may call business. So I will throw in a make-weight.'

'Precisely' (from Gobseck).

'What is it to be?' asked Gigonnet.

'The cross for your oaf of a nephew.'

'Good!' said Gigonnet. 'You know him.'

With that the pair took their leave. Des Lupeaulx went with them to the stairs.

'Those are secret envoys from some foreign power!' said the footmen among themselves.

Out in the street the money-lenders looked in each other's faces by the light of a lamp and laughed.

'He will have to pay us nine thousand francs per annum in the shape of interest, and the land scarcely brings in five thousand nett,' cried Gigonnet.

'He will be in our hands for a long while to come,' said Gobseck.

'He will begin to build; he will do foolish things,' returned Gigonnet. 'Falleix will buy the land.'

'He wants to be a deputy; the wolf' (*le loup*) 'laughs at the rest.'

'Eh! eh!'

'Eh! eh!'

The dry chirping exclamations did duty for laughter. The usurers returned on foot to the Café Thémis.

Des Lupeaulx went back to the drawing-room and found Mme. Rabourdin in all her glory. She was charming. The Minister's countenance, usually so melancholy, had relaxed and grown gracious.

'She is working miracles,' des Lupeaulx said to himself. 'What an invaluable woman! One must probe to the bottom of her heart.'

'Your little lady will decidedly do very well indeed,' said the Marquise; 'she wants nothing but your name.'

'Yes, she is an auctioneer's daughter, it is the one thing against her; her want of birth will be the ruin of her.' Des Lupeaulx's air of cool indifference contrasted strangely with his warmth of a few minutes ago.

The Marquise d'Espard looked steadily back at him.

'The glance you gave them just now was not lost upon me,' she said, indicating the Minister and Mme. Rabourdin; 'it pierced through the mist of your eyeglasses. You are amusing, you two, to quarrel over that bone.'

As the Marquise made her way past the door, the Minister hurried across the room to her.

'Well,' said des Lupeaulx, addressing Mme. Rabourdin, 'what do you think of our Minister?'

'He is charming. Really,' she added, raising her voice for the benefit of His Excellency's wife, 'really, the poor ministers must be known to be appreciated. The minor newspapers and the slanders of the Opposition give one such distorted ideas of politicians, and in the end one is influenced. But the prejudice turns in their favour when you meet them.'

'He is very pleasant.'

'Well, I can assure you that one could be very fond of him,' she returned good-humouredly.

'Dear child,' said des Lupeaulx, assuming a good-natured and ingratiating air, 'you have achieved the impossible.'

'What?' asked she.

'You have raised the dead to life, I did not think that he had a heart; ask his wife! He has just enough to defray a passing fancy, but take advantage of it. Come this way; do not be surprised.'

He led the way to the boudoir and sat down beside her on a sofa.

'You are crafty,' he said, 'and I like you the better for it. Between ourselves, you are no ordinary woman. Des Lupeaulx introduced you here, and there is an end of him; is it not so? And besides, when we decide to love for interest, a minister of seventy is to be preferred to a secretary-general of forty; it pays better, and is less irksome. I wear eyeglasses, and my hair is powdered, and I am the worse for a life of pleasure; a romantic love affair it would be! Oh! I have told myself all this. If one absolutely must, one makes some concession to the useful, but I shall never be the agreeable, shall I? A man in my position would be mad if he did not look at it from all sides. You can confess the truth, and show me the bottom of your heart. We are two partners, not two lovers; are we not? If there is some fancy on my side, you rise superior to such trifles; you will pass it over in me; you are not a little boarding-school miss, nor a tradesman's wife from the Rue Saint-Denis. Pooh! we are above that, you and I. There is the Marquise d'Espard, now leaving the room, do you suppose that she thinks otherwise? We came to an understanding two years ago' (the coxcomb!), 'and now she has only to write me a line, and not a very long one—"My dear des Lupeaulx, you will oblige me by doing so-and-so"—and the thing is done forthwith.

We are thinking of bringing a petition for a commission in lunacy on her husband. You women can have anything that you will at the cost of pleasure. Well, then, dear child, take His Excellency with your wiles; I will help you, it is to my interest to do so. Yes, I should like to have him under a woman's influence; he would never slip through my fingers then, as he sometimes does, and naturally, for I only keep a hold on his common-sense, but with a pretty woman to help me, I should have him on his weak side, and that is the surest. So let us be good friends as before, and divide the credit that you will gain.' Mme. Rabourdin heard this singular profession of rascality with the utmost astonishment. The barefaced simplicity of the political business transaction put any idea of expressing surprise quite out of the question. She fell into the snare.

'Do you think that I have made any impression upon him?' she asked.

'I know you have, I am sure of it.'

'Is it true that Rabourdin's appointment is signed?'

'I put the report before him this morning. But it is nothing to be the head of the division; he must be Master of Requests.'

'Yes.'

'Very well, go in again and flirt with His Excellency.'

'Indeed,' she said, 'I never really knew you till to-night. There is nothing commonplace about you.'

'And so, we are two old friends, and there is an end of tender airs and tiresome love-making; we understand things as they used to do under the Regency; they had plenty of sense in those days.'

'You are in truth a great man, I admire you,' she said, smiling at him as she held out her hand. 'You shall know that a woman does more for her friend than for her——'

She left the sentence unfinished and went.

'Dear little thing! Des Lupeaulx need feel no

remorse over turning against you,' said her companion, as he watched her cross the room to the Minister. 'To-morrow evening when you hand me a cup of tea, you will offer me something else which I shall not care to take.—There is no more to be said. Ah! when you come to your fortieth year, women take you in; it is too late to be loved.'

Des Lupeaulx also went back to the drawing-room, scanned himself in a mirror, and knew that he was a very fine fellow for political purposes, but unmistakably superannuated for the court of Cytherea. Mme. Rabourdin meanwhile was working up her climax; she meditated taking her departure, and did her best to leave a last pleasing impression upon every one present. She succeeded. An unwonted exclamation of 'Charming woman!' broke from every one as soon as she had gone, and the Minister went with her to the farthest door.

'I am quite sure that you will think of me to-morrow,' he said, alluding to the nomination.—'I am quite satisfied with our acquisition, not many high officials have such charming wives,' he added, as he came back to the room.

'Do you not think that she is inclined to encroach a little?' des Lupeaulx began. He seemed rather put out.

The women exchanged meaning glances; the rivalry between the Secretary-General and the Minister amused them. And forthwith they began one of those charming mystifications in which the Parisienne excels. They all began to talk about Mme. Rabourdin; they stirred up the Minister and des Lupeaulx. One lady thought Mme. Rabourdin too studied, she aimed too much at wit; another began to compare the graces of the bourgeoisie with the manners of persons of fashion, criticising Célestine by implication; and des Lupeaulx defended the mistress attributed to him, but his defence was of a kind reserved exclusively in polite society for absent enemies.

'Pray be fair to her, mesdames! Is it not an extra-ordinary thing that an auctioneer's daughter should be so charming? You see where she comes from, and where she is; and she will go to the Tuileries, she is aiming at that, she told me so.'

'And if she is an auctioneer's daughter,' said Mme. d'Espard, smiling over her words, 'how should that injure her husband's prospects?'

'As times are, you mean?' asked the Minister's wife, pursing up her lips.

'Madame,' the Minister said sternly, turning on the Marquise, 'such language brings on revolutions, and, unfortunately, the Court spares no one. You would not believe how much the heedlessness of the upper classes displeases certain clear-sighted persons at the Château. If I were a great lord, instead of a little provincial of good family, set here, as it would seem, to do your business for you, the Monarchy should rest on a firmer basis than it does at present. What will be the end if the throne cannot shed its lustre upon its representatives? We are far indeed from the times when the King's will ennobled a Louvois, a Colbert, a Richelieu, a Jeannin, a Villeroy, or a Sully. Yes, Sully in the beginning was nothing more than I. I speak in this way because we are among ourselves, and I should be small indeed if I took offence at such trifles. It rests with us, and not with others, to make a great name for ourselves.'

'You have the appointment, dear,' said Célestine, squeezing her husband's hand. 'If it had not been for des Lupeaulx, I would have explained your project to the Minister; but that must be left till next Tuesday now, and you will be Master of Requests all the sooner.'

There is one day in every woman's life in which she shines in all her glory—a day that she remembers, and loves to remember, as long as she lives. As Mme. Rabourdin undid her artfully adjusted ornaments one by one, she went over that evening again, and reckoned it among the glorious days of her life. All her beauty had been jealously noted; the Minister's wife had paid her compliments (she was not ill-pleased to praise the newcomer at the expense of her friends); and more than all, satisfied vanity had redounded to her husband's advantage. Xavier's appointment had been made!

'Did I not look well to-night?' she asked her husband, as though there were any need to kindle his admiration.

At that very moment Mitral at the Café Thémis saw the two usurers come in. Their impassive faces gave no sign.

'How are we getting on?' he asked, when they sat down to the table.

'Oh, well, as usual,' said Gigonnet, rubbing his hands; 'victory is on the side of the francs.'

'That is so,' remarked Gobseck.

Mitral lost no time. He took a cab and drove away with the news. The game of boston had been long drawn out that night at the Saillards, but every one had left except the Abbé Gaudron. Falleix had gone to bed; he was tired out.

'You will get the appointment, nephew, and there is a surprise in store for you.'

'What?' asked Saillard.

'The Cross!' cried Mitral.

'God is with those that care for His altars!' commented Gaudron.

And thus was the *Te Deum* chanted with equal joy in either camp.

Next day was Friday. M. Rabourdin was to go to

the Minister, for he had done the work of the head of the division ever since the late La Billardière fell ill. On these occasions the clerks were remarkably punctual, the office-messengers zealous and attentive, for on signature days the offices are all in a flurry. Why and wherefore? Nobody knows. The three messengers accordingly were all at their posts; they flattered themselves that fees of some sort would come their way, for rumours of M. Rabourdin's appointment had been spread abroad on the previous day by des Lupeaulx. So Uncle Antoine and Laurent were in full dress at a quarter to eight when the Secretary's messenger came over with a note, asking Antoine to give it, in private, to M. Dutocq. The Secretary-General had bidden him take it round to the first clerk's house at seven o'clock. 'And I don't know how it happened, old man, but I slept on and on, and I am only just awake now. He would give me an infernal blowing up if he knew that the note had not gone to the private address; 'stead of which I shall tell him as how I took it to M. Dutocq's. It is a great secret, Daddy Antoine. Don't say anything to the clerks; or, my word, he would turn me away. I should lose my place if I said a word about it, he said.'

'Why, what is there inside it?'

'Nothing; for I looked into it, like this—there!'

He pressed open the folded sheet, but they could only see white paper inside.

'To-day is a great day for you, Laurent,' continued the Secretary's messenger. 'You are going to have a new director. They will retrench beyond a doubt, and put both divisions under one director; messengers may look out!'

'Yes! nine clerks pensioned off,' said Dutocq, coming up at the moment. 'How came you fellows to know that?'

Antoine handed over the letter, Dutocq opened it,

and rushed headlong down the staircase to the Secretary's rooms.

Since the day of M. de la Billardière's death, the Rabourdins and Baudoyers had settled down by degrees into their wonted ways and the *dolce-far-niente* habits of administrative routine. There had been plenty of gossip at first; but an access of industry usually sets in among the clerks towards the end of the year, and the doorkeepers and messengers become more unctuously obsequious about the same time. Everybody was punctual of a morning, and more faces might be seen in the office after four o'clock; for the bonus at the New Year is apt to depend upon the final impression left on the mind of your chief. Then rumour said that the La Billardière and Clergeot divisions were to be brought under one head. The news had caused a flutter in the department on the previous day. The number of clerks to be dismissed was known, but no one knew their names as yet. It was pretty certain that Poiret would not be replaced—they would effect an economy over his salary. Young La Billardière had gone. Two new supernumeraries were coming, and both were sons of deputies—an appalling circumstance. This tidings had arrived just as they were going away. It struck terror into every conscience. And so for the first half-hour, as the clerks were dropping in, there was talk round about the stoves.

Des Lupeaulx was shaving when Dutocq appeared; he did not put down his razor as he gave the clerk a glance with the air of a general that issues an order.

'Are we by ourselves?'

'Yes, sir.'

'Very well. Go for Rabourdin; walk ahead, and hold on. You must have kept a copy of that list.'

'Yes.'

'*Inde iræ*—you understand. We must have a general hue and cry. Try to invent something to raise a clamour.'

'I can have a caricature drawn, but I have not five hundred francs to pay for it.'

'Who will draw it?'

'Bixiou.'

'He shall have a thousand francs and the assistant's place under Colleville. Colleville will come to an understanding with him.'

'But he will not believe me.'

'You want to mix me up in it perhaps? It is that or nothing—do you understand?'

'If M. Baudoyer is director, he might possibly lend the money——'

'Yes, he is going to be director. Leave me, and be quick about it. Don't seem as if you had been to see me, Go down by the back stairs.'

Dutocq went back to the office, his heart throbbing with joy. He was wondering how to raise an outcry against his chief without committing himself, when Bixiou looked in just to wish his friends the Rabourdins good-day. Having given up his wager for lost, it pleased that practical joker to pose as though he had won.

BIXIOU (*mimicking Phellion's voice*). 'Gentlemen, I present my compliments to you, and wish you collectively a good day. I appoint the coming Sunday for the dinner at the *Rocher de Cancale*. But a serious dilemma presents itself: are the retiring clerks to come or not?'

POIRET. 'Yes; even those that are pensioned off.'

BIXIOU. 'It is all one to me; I shall not have to pay for it' (*general amazement*). 'Baudoyer has been appointed. I should love to hear him calling Laurent at this moment.' (*Mimics Baudoyer.*) '"Laurent, lock up my hair-shirt, and my scourge along with it!"' (*peals of laughter from the clerks.*) '*Ris d'aboyeur d'oie!* There is sense in

T

Colleville's anagrams, for Xavier Rabourdin's name makes *D'abord rêva bureaux e u fin riche,* you know. If 'my name happened to be "Charles x., by the grace of God King of France and Navarre," I should quake for fear lest my anagram might come true likewise.'

THUILLIER. 'Oh, come now, you want to make fun of it ! '

BIXIOU (*laughing in his face*). '*Ris-au-laid !* (*riz-au-lait*). That is neat, Daddy Thuillier, for you are not good-looking. Rabourdin is sending in his resignation in a fury because Baudoyer is director.'

VIMEUX (*coming in*). 'What stuff ! I have just been repaying Antoine thirty or forty francs, and he tells me that M. and Mme. Rabourdin were at the Minister's private party last night, and stopped till a quarter to twelve. His Excellency came as far as the stairs with Mme. Rabourdin. She was divinely dressed, it seems. He is director in fact, and no mistake. Riffé, the confidential copying-clerk, stopped late to finish the report sooner. There is no mystery about it now. M. Clergeot is retiring. After thirty years of service, it is no disgrace. M. Cochin, who is well-to-do——'

BIXIOU. 'He makes cochineal (*cochenille*), according to Colleville.'

VIMEUX. 'Why, he is in the cochineal trade ; he is a partner in Matifat's business in the Rue des Lombards. Well, he is to go, and Poiret is to go. Nobody else is coming on instead. That much is positive, no more is known. M. Rabourdin's appointment came this morning. They are afraid of intrigues.'

BIXIOU. 'What sort of intrigues ? '

FLEURY. 'Baudoyer, begad ! The clericals are backing him up. There is something new here in the Liberal paper ; it is only a couple of lines, but it is funny '—(*reads*)—' "In the *foyer* of the Italiens yesterday there was some talk of M. de Chateaubriand's return to office. This belief was founded upon the appointment of M. Rabourdin to fill the post originally intended for M. Baudoyer—M. Rabourdin being a protégé of the Vicomte's friends. The clerical party would never have withdrawn except to make a compromise with the great man of letters." Scum of the earth !'

DUTOCQ (*comes in after listening outside*). 'Scum! Who ? Rabourdin. Then you have heard the news ?'

FLEURY (*rolling his eyes fiercely*). 'Rabourdin !— scum! Have you taken leave of your wits, Dutocq ? And do you want a bullet for ballast in your brains ?'

DUTOCQ. 'I did not say a word against M. Rabourdin; only just now, out in the courtyard, it was told me as a secret that he had been informing against a good many of the staff, and had given notes; in short, I was told that he had sent in a report of the departments, and we are all done for; that is why he is in favour——'

PHELLION (*shouts*). ' M. Rabourdin is incapable——'

BIXIOU. 'Here is a nice state of things! I say, Dutocq ?' (*They exchange a word or two, and go out into the corridor.*)

BIXIOU. ' What ever can have happened ?'

DUTOCQ. ' Do you remember the caricature ?'

BIXIOU. ' Yes ; what about it ?'

DUTOCQ. 'Draw it, and you will be chief clerk's assistant, and you will get something handsome besides. You see, my dear fellow, dissension has been sown in the upper regions. The Minister is pledged to Rabourdin ; but if he does not appoint Baudoyer, he will get into trouble with the clergy. Don't you know ? The King, the Dauphin, the Dauphiness, the Grand Almonry, the whole Court, in fact, are for Baudoyer ; the Minister wants Rabourdin.'

BIXIOU. ' Good !——'

DUTOCQ. ' The Minister has begun to see that he must give way, but he must get quit of the difficulty before he can go over. He wants a reason for ridding himself of Rabourdin. So somebody has unearthed an old report that he made with a view to reforming the service, and some of it is getting about. That is how I try to explain the thing to myself, at least. Do the drawing; you come on in a match played among great folk; you will do a service to the Minister, the Court, and all concerned, and you get your step. Do you understand?'

BIXIOU. 'I do not understand how you can know all this, or whether you are just making it up.'

DUTOCQ. 'Would you like me to show you your paragraph?'

BIXIOU. 'Yes.'

DUTOCQ. 'Very well, come round to my place, for I want to put the report in sure hands.'

BIXIOU. 'Go by yourself' (*goes back to the Rabourdins*). 'People are talking of nothing but this news that Dutocq has brought; upon my honour. M. Rabourdin's notes on the men that he meant to reform out of the service can't have been very complimentary. That is the secret of his promotion. Nothing astonishes us in these days' (*strikes an attitude, after Talma*).

> '"Illustrious heads have fallen before your eyes,
>   And yet, oh senseless men! ye show surprise"—

—if somebody points out a reason of this sort when a man gets into favour! Our Baudoyer is too stupid to make his way by such methods. Accept my congratulations, gentlemen, you are under an illustrious chief' (*goes*).

POIRET. 'I shall retire from the service without understanding a single thing that that gentleman has said since he came here. What does he mean with his falling heads?'

FLEURY. 'The four sergeants of La Rochelle, egad! Berton, Ney, Caron, the brothers Faucher, and all the massacres.'

PHELLION. 'He says risky things in a flippant manner.'

FLEURY. 'Why don't you say at once that he lies;

that he humbugs you ; that truth turns to *verdegris* in his throat ? '

PHELLION. ' Your remarks transgress the limits of politeness and the consideration due to a colleague.'

VIMEUX. ' It seems to me that if what he says is false, such remarks are called slander and defamation of character, and the man who utters them deserves a horsewhipping.'

FLEURY (*waxing wrathful*). ' And if a government office were a public place, it would be an indictable offence, and go straight to a court of law.'

PHELLION (*anxious to avoid a quarrel, endeavours to change the subject*). ' Calm yourselves, gentlemen. I am at work upon a little treatise on morality, and have just come to the soul——'

FLEURY (*interrupting*). ' What do you say to it, M. Phellion ? '

PHELLION (*reading aloud*). ' " *Question.*—What is the soul of man ?

' " *Answer.*—A spiritual substance which thinks and reasons." '

THUILLIER. ' A spiritual substance ! You might as well say an ethereal block of stone.'

POIRET. ' Just let him go on——'

PHELLION (*continues*). ' " *Q.*—' Whence comes the soul ?

' " *A.*—It comes from God, by whom it was created ; God made it simple and indivisible, consequently its destructibility is inconceivable, and He has said——" ' '

POIRET (*bewildered*). ' God ? '

PHELLION. ' Yes, môsieur, tradition says so.'

FLEURY (*to Poiret*). ' Don't you interrupt ! '

PHELLION (*resumes*). ' " —has said that He created it immortal, which means that it will never die.

' " *Q.*—To what end does the soul exist ?

' " *A.*—To comprehend, to will, and to remember ; it comprises the understanding, the will, and the memory.

'"*Q.*—To what end have we understanding?
'"*A.*—That we may know.   The understanding is
the eye of the soul."'

FLEURY. 'And the soul is the eye of what?'

PHELLION (*continuing*). '"*Q.*—What is the understanding bound to know?

'"*A.*—The truth.

'"*Q.*—Why has man a will?

'"*A.*—In order that he may love good and eschew evil.

'"*Q.*—What is good?

'"*A.*—The source of man's happiness."'

VIMEUX. 'And are you writing this for young ladies?'

PHELLION. 'Yes' (*continues*). '"*Q.*—How many kinds
of good are there?"'

FLEURY. 'This is prodigiously improper!'

PHELLION (*indignantly*). 'Oh! môsieur' (*cooling
down*). 'Here is the answer, anyhow.   I have come
to it'—(*reads*)—'"*A.*—There are two kinds of good—
temporal good and eternal good."'

POIRET (*with a contemptuous countenance*). 'And will
there be a great sale for *that*?'

PHELLION. 'I venture to hope so.   It takes a lot of
mental exercise to keep up a system of questions and
answers; that was why I asked you to allow me to think,
for the answers——'

THUILLIER. 'The answers might be sold separately
though.'

POIRET. 'Is it a pun?'

THUILLIER. 'Yes.   They will sell the gammon without spinach.'

PHELLION. 'It was very wrong, indeed, of me to
interrupt you.' (*Dives in among his pasteboard cases.—To
himself.*) 'But they have forgotten M. Rabourdin.'

Meanwhile a scene that took place between the
Minister and des Lupeaulx decided Rabourdin's fate.
The Secretary-General went to find his chief in his
study before breakfast.

'Your Excellency is not playing aboveboard with me,' he began, when he had made sure that La Brière could hear nothing.

'Here, he is going to quarrel with me,' thought the Minister, 'because his mistress flirted with me yesterday.' Aloud he said, 'I did not think that you were such a boy, my dear friend.'

'Friend,' repeated the Secretary-General; 'I shall soon know about that.'

The Minister looked haughtily at des Lupeaulx.

'We are by ourselves, so we can have an explanation. The deputy for the district in which my estate of des Lupeaulx is situated——'

'Then it really is an estate?' laughed the Minister, to hide his surprise.

'Enlarged by purchases to the extent of two hundred thousand francs,' des Lupeaulx added carelessly. 'You knew ten days ago that the deputy was going to resign his seat, and you said nothing to me—you were not bound to do so; still, you knew very well that it is my wish to sit on the Centre benches. Did you not think that I might throw in my lot with the doctrinaires, the party that will eat you up, Monarchy and all, if they are allowed to recruit all the able men that you slight? Do you not know that there are not more than fifty or sixty dangerous heads at a time in a nation, and that in those fifty or sixty the intellect is on a level with the ambition? The whole art of government consists in finding out those heads, so that you may buy them or cut them off. I do not know whether I have talent, but I have ambition; and you make a blunder when you do not come to an understanding with a man who means nothing but good to you. The coronation dazzled you for a minute, but what follows? The war of words and arguments will begin again and grow more acrimonious. Well, so far as you are concerned, you don't find me in the Left Centre, believe me!

Your prefect has had confidential instructions no doubt,
but, in spite of his manœuvres, I am sure of a majority.
It is time that we came to a thorough understanding.
Sometimes people are better friends after a little *coup de
Jarnac.* I shall be a Count, and the Grand Cross of
the Legion will not be refused after my services; but I
insist not so much on these two points as upon a third
which your influence can decide. You have not yet
appointed Rabourdin; I have had news this morning;
you will give general satisfaction by nominating
Baudoyer——'

'*Baudoyer!*' exclaimed the Minister; 'you know him!'

'Yes,' said des Lupeaulx; 'but when he gives proof
of his incompetence, you can get rid of him by asking
his patrons to take him into their employ. Then you
will have an important post in your gift, and that may
facilitate a compromise with some ambitious man.'

'I have given my word to Rabourdin !'

'Yes, but I do not ask you to change your mind at
once. I know that it is dangerous to say "Yes" and
"No" on the same day. Wait, and you can sign the
day after to-morrow. Well, in two days' time you will
see that it is impossible to keep Rabourdin; and besides,
he will have sent in his resignation, plump and plain.'

'Resignation ?'

'Yes.'

'Why ?'

'He has been at work for some power unknown,
playing the spy on a large scale all through the departments. This was found out by accident; it has got
about, and the clerks are furious. For mercy's sake, do
not work with him to-day; let me find an excuse. Go to
the King, I am sure you will find that certain persons will
be pleased by your concession as to Baudoyer, and you will
get something in exchange. Then you will strengthen
your position later on by getting rid of the fool, seeing that he has been forced upon you, as one may say.'

'What made you change your mind about Rabourdin in this way?'

'Would you assist M. de Chateaubriand to write an article against the Government? Well, this is how Rabourdin treats me in his report,' said des Lupeaulx, handing his note to the Minister. 'He is reorganising the whole system, no doubt, for the benefit of a confederation which we do not know. I shall keep on friendly terms with him, so as to watch over him. I think I will do some great service to the Government, so as to reach the peerage; a peerage is the one thing that I care about. I do not want office, nor anything else that can cross your path. I am aiming at the peerage; then I shall be in a position to marry some banker's daughter with two hundred thousand livres a year. So let me do you some great service, so that the King can say that I have saved the throne. This long time past I have said, "Liberalism no longer meets us in the field; Liberalism has given up conspiracy, the Carbonari, and violent methods;" it is undermining us and preparing to say once for all, "Get thee hence that I may take thy place!" Do you think that I pay court to a Rabourdin's wife for my pleasure? No; I had information! So for to-day there are two things—the adjournment of the nominations and your *sincere* support at my election. At the end of the session you shall see whether I have not paid my debt with interest.'

For all answer the Minister handed over the report.

'And I will tell Rabourdin that you postpone him till Saturday.'

The Minister nodded. In a few minutes the messenger had crossed the building and informed Rabourdin that he must go to the Minister on Saturday; for that then the Chamber would be engaged with petitions, and the Minister would have the whole day at liberty.

Meanwhile Saillard went on his errand to the Minister's wife and slipped in his speech, to which the lady replied, with dignity, that she never meddled in State affairs, and besides, she had heard that Rabourdin was appointed. Saillard in alarm went up to Baudoyer's office, and there found Dutocq, Godard, and Bixiou in a state of exasperation which words fail to describe; for they were reading the rough draft of Rabourdin's terrible report.

BIXIOU (*pointing to a passage*). 'Here you are, Saillard: "SAILLARD.—Cashiers to be suppressed throughout. The departments should keep accounts current with the Treasury. Saillard is well-to-do, and does not need a pension." Would you like to see your son-in-law?' (*turns over the leaf.*) 'Here he is: "BAUDOYER.— Utterly incompetent. Dismiss without pension; he is well-to-do." And our friend Godard' (*turns over another leaf*). '"GODARD.—Dismiss. Pension one-third of present salary." In short, we are all here. Here am I—"An artist to be employed at the Opéra, the Menus-Plaisirs, or the Muséum, with a salary from the Civil List. Plenty of ability, not very steady, incapable of application, a restless disposition." Oh! I will give you enough of the artist.'

SAILLARD. 'Cashiers to be suppressed? . . . Why, the man is a monster!'

BIXIOU. 'What has he to say about our mysterious Desroys?' (*Turns the leaf and reads.*) '"DESROYS.— A dangerous man, in that he holds subversive principles that cannot be shaken. As a son of a member of the Convention he admires that institution; he may become a pernicious publicist."'

BAUDOYER. 'A detective is not so clever.'

GODARD. 'I shall go at once to the Secretary-General and lodge a complaint in form. If that man is nominated, we ought all to resign in a body.'

DUTOCQ. 'Listen, gentlemen; let us be prudent. If you revolt at once, we should be accused of personal motives and a desire for revenge. No, let the rumour spread; and when the whole service rises in protest, your proceedings will meet with general support.'

BIXIOU. 'Dutocq works on the principles of the sublime Rossini's great *aria* in *Basilio*, which proves that the mighty composer is a politic man. This seems to me to be fair and reasonable. I think of leaving my card on M. Rabourdin to-morrow morning; I shall have the name engraved upon it, and the titles underneath: "BIXIOU.— Not very steady, incapable of application, restless disposition."'

GODARD. 'A good idea, gentlemen. Let us all have our cards printed, and Rabourdin shall have them to-morrow morning.'

BAUDOYER. 'M. Bixiou, will you undertake these little details, and see that the plates are destroyed after a single card has been printed from each?'

DUTOCQ (*taking Bixiou aside*). 'Well, will you draw that caricature now?'

BIXIOU. 'I see, my dear fellow, that you have been in the secret for ten days.' (*Looks him full in the face.*) 'Am I going to be chief clerk's assistant?'

DUTOCQ. 'Yes, upon my word of honour, and a thousand francs besides, as I told you. You do not know what a service you are doing to powerful personages.'

BIXIOU. 'Do you know them?'

DUTOCQ. 'Yes.'

BIXIOU. 'Very well, then, I want to speak with them.'

DUTOCQ (*drily*). 'Do the caricature or let it alone; you will be chief clerk's assistant, or you will not.'

BIXIOU. 'Well, then, let us see those thousand francs.'

DUTOCQ. 'You shall have them against the drawing.'

BIXIOU. 'Go ahead! The caricature shall go the round of the offices to-morrow. So let us make fools of

.the Rabourdins!' (*To Saillard, Godard, and Baudoyer, who are conferring in whispers.*) 'We are going to set our neighbours in a ferment.' (*Goes out with Dutocq, and crosses over to Rabourdin's office. At sight of him, Fleury and Thuillier show signs of excitement.*) 'Well, gentlemen, what is the matter? All that I told you just now is so true that you may have ocular demonstration at this moment of the most shameful delation. Go to the office of the virtuous, honest, estimable, upright, and pious Baudoyer; he is "incompetent," at any rate, in such a business as this! Your chief has invented a sort of guillotine for clerks, that is certain. Go and look at it, follow the crowd, there is nothing to pay if you are not satisfied, you shall have the full benefit of your misfortune *gratis*. What is more, the appointments have been postponed. The offices are in an uproar; and Rabourdin has just heard that he is not to work with the Minister to-day.—Just go!'

Phellion and Poiret stayed behind. Phellion was too much attached to Rabourdin to go in search of proof that might injure a man whom he had no wish to judge, and Poiret was to retire in five days' time. Just at that moment Sébastien came downstairs to collect some papers to be included with the documents for signature. He was sufficiently astonished to find the office empty, but he showed no sign of surprise.

PHELLION (*rising to his feet, a rare event*). 'My young friend, do you know what is going on? what rumours are current with respect to Môsieur Rabourdin, to whom you are attached; for whom' (*lowering his voice for Sébastien's ear*), 'for whom my affection is as great as my esteem? It is said that he has been so imprudent as to leave a report of the clerks lying about somewhere——'. (*stops suddenly short, for Sébastien turns as pale as a white rose, and sinks into a chair. Phellion is obliged to hold him in his muscular arms.*) 'Put a key down his back; Môsieur Poiret! have you a key?'

POIRET. 'I always carry my door-key.' (*Old Poiret, junior, pushes his key down Sébastien's collar; Phellion brings a glass of cold water. The poor boy opens his eyes, only to shed a torrent of tears; he lays his head on Phellion's desk, flings himself down in a heap as if stricken by lightning, and sobs in such a heartrendiug fashion, with such a genuine outpouring of grief, that Poiret, for the first time in his life, is touched by the sorrow of a fellow-creature.*)

PHELLION (*raising his voice*). 'Come, come, my young friend! bear up! One must have courage in a great crisis! You are a man. What is the matter? What is there to upset you so in this affair? it is out of all reason.'

SÉBASTIEN (*through his sobs*). '*I* have ruined M. Rabourdin! I left the paper about; I had been copying it; I have ruined my benefactor. This will kill me! Such a great man! A man that might have been a Minister!'

POIRET (*blowing his nose*). 'Then he really made the report?'

SÉBASTIEN (*through his sobs*). 'But it was for—— There! I am telling his secrets now!... Oh! that miserable Dutocq, *he* took it——'

At that the tears and sobs began afresh, and grew so violent, that Rabourdin came out of his office, recognised the voice, and went upstairs. He found Sébastien, half swooning, like a figure of Christ, in the arms of Phellion and Poiret; and the two clerks, with countenances distorted by compassion, grotesquely playing the parts of the Maries in the composition.

RABOURDIN. 'What is the matter, gentlemen?'

SÉBASTIEN (*starting up, falls on his knees before Rabourdin*). 'Oh, sir, I have ruined you! That list! Dutocq is showing it about. He found it out, no doubt!'

RABOURDIN (*composedly*). 'I knew it.' (*Raises Sébastien and draws him away.*) 'My friend, you are a child!' (*To Phellion.*) 'Where are they all?'

PHELLION. 'They have gone to M. Baudoyer's study, sir, to look at a list which is said——'

RABOURDIN. 'That will do' (*goes out with Sébastien. Poiret and Phellion, overcome with astonishment, look at one another, completely at a loss*).

POIRET (*to Phellion*). 'M. Rabourdin! ...'

PHELLION (*to Poiret*). 'M. Rabourdin! ...'

POIRET. 'Well, if ever! M. Rabourdin! ...'

PHELLION. 'Did you see how he looked—quite calm and dignified in spite of everything?——'

POIRET (*with a grimace intended for a knowing air*). 'I should not be at all surprised if there were something at the bottom of all this.'

PHELLION. 'A man of honour, blameless and stainless——'

POIRET. 'And how about Dutocq?'

PHELLION. 'Môsieur Poiret, you think as I think about Dutocq; do you not understand me?'

POIRET (*with two or three little knowing nods*). 'Yes.' *The others come back.*

FLEURY. 'This is coming it strong! I have seen it with my own eyes, and yet I can't believe it! M. Rabourdin, the best of men! Upon my word, if such as he can play the sneak, it is enough to sicken you with virtue. I used to put Rabourdin among Plutarch's heroes.'

VIMEUX. 'Oh! it is true.'

POIRET (*bethinking himself that he has but five days to stay*). 'But, gentlemen, what do you say about the man that lay in wait for M. Rabourdin and stole the papers?'

Dutocq slips out of the room.

FLEURY. 'A Judas Iscariot! Who is he?'

PHELLION (*adroitly*). 'He is not among us, that is certain.'

VIMEUX (*an idea beginning to dawn upon him*). 'It is Dutocq!'

PHELLION. 'I have seen no proof whatever, môsieur. While you were out of the room, that young fellow, M. de la Roche, came in and was nearly heartbroken over it. Look, you see his tears on my desk.'

POIRET. 'He swooned in our arms—— Oh! my door-key; dear, dear! it is still down his back!' (*goes out.*)

VIMEUX. 'The Minister would not work to-day with M. Rabourdin; the head of the staff came to say a word or two to M. Saillard; M. Baudoyer was advised to make application for the Cross of the Legion of Honour; one will be granted to the division at New Year, and it is to go to M. Baudoyer. Is that clear? M. Rabourdin is sacrificed by the very people for whom he worked. That is what Bixiou says. We were all dismissed except Phellion and Sébastien.'

DU BRUEL (*comes in*). 'Well, gentlemen, is it true?'

THUILLIER. 'Strictly true.'

DU BRUEL. 'Good-day, gentlemen' (*puts on his hat aud goes out*).

THUILLIER. 'That vaudevilliste does not waste time on file-firing; he is off to the Duc de Rhétoré and the Duc de Maufrigneuse, but he may run! Colleville is to be our chief, they say.'

PHELLION. 'Yet he seemed to be attached to M. Rabourdin.'

POIRET (*returns*). 'I had all the trouble in the world to get back my door-key. The youngster is crying, and M. Rabourdin has completely disappeared. (*Dutocq and Bixiou come in together.*)

BIXIOU. 'Well, gentlemen, queer things are happening in your office!' Du Bruel!—(*looks into du Bruel's cabinet.*) 'Gone?'

THUILLIER. 'Out.'

BIXIOU. 'And Rabourdin?'

FLEURY. 'Melted away, evaporated, vanished in smoke! To think that such a man, the best of men!——'

POIRET (*to Dutocq*). 'That youngster Sébastien, in his grief, accused you of taking the work, M. Dutocq, ten days ago——'

BIXIOU (*looking at Dutocq*). 'My dear fellow, you must clear yourself' (*all the clerks stare at Dutocq*).

DUTOCQ. 'Where is the little viper that was copying it?'

BIXIOU. 'How do you know that he was copying it? Nothing but a diamond can cut a diamond, my dear fellow!' (*Dutocq goes out.*)

POIRET. 'Look here, M. Bixiou; I have only five days and a half to stay in the office, and I should like for once—just for once—to have the pleasure of understanding you. Do me the honour to explain where the diamond comes in under the circumstances.'

BIXIOU. 'It means, old man (for I am quite willing to descend to your level for once), it means that as the diamond alone can polish the diamond, so none but a pry is a match for his like.'

FLEURY. '"Pry" in this case being put for "spy."'

POIRET. 'I do not understand——'

BIXIOU. 'Oh, well, another time you will.'

M. Rabourdin had hurried away to the Minister. His Excellency was at the Chamber. Thither, accordingly, Rabourdin went and wrote a few lines, but the Minister was on his legs in the midst of a hot discussion. Rabourdin waited, not in the Salle des Conférences, but outside in the courtyard; he decided in spite of the cold to take up his post by His Excellency's carriage, and to speak with him as he came out. The sergeant-at-arms told him that a storm had been brewed by the nineteen members of the Extreme Left, and there had been a scene in the House. Rabourdin meanwhile, in feverish excitement, paced up and down in the courtyard. He waited for five mortal hours. At half-past

six the House rose, and the Minister's chasseur came
out with a message for the coachman.'

'Hey, Jean! His Excellency has gone to the Palace
with the Minister of War; they will dine together
afterwards. We are to fetch them at ten o'clock.
There is to be a meeting of the council.'

Slowly Rabourdin walked home again in a state of
exhaustion easy to imagine. It was seven o'clock. He
had barely time to dress.

'Well!' his wife cried joyously, as he came into
the drawing-room. 'You have the appointment now.'

Rabourdin raised his head in melancholy anguish.
'I am very much afraid that I shall never set foot in the
office again.'

'What!' cried his wife, trembling with cruel anxiety.

'That memorandum of mine on the staff has been
the round of the department; I tried to speak with the
Minister, and could not.'

A vision flashed before Célestine's eyes; some demon
flung a sudden lurid light upon her last conversation
with des Lupeaulx.

'If I had behaved like a vulgar woman,' she thought,
'we should have had the place.'

She gazed at Rabourdin with something like anguish.
There was a dreary silence, and at dinner both were
absorbed in musings.

'And it is our Wednesday!' she exclaimed.

'All is not lost, dear Célestine,' he answered, putting
a kiss upon her forehead; 'I may perhaps see the
Minister to-morrow morning, and all will be cleared up.
Sébastien sat up late last night, all the fair copies are
made and in order. I will put the whole thing on the
Minister's desk, and beg him to go through it with me.
La Brière will help me. A man is never condemned
without a hearing.'

'I am curious to see whether M. des Lupeaulx will
come to us to-day.'

'He!—Of course he will come, he will not fail. There is something of the tiger in him—he loves to lick the blood after he has given the wound.'

'My poor love, I do not know how a man that could think of so grand a reform should not see, at the same time, that no one must hear of it. Some ideas a man must keep within himself, because he, and he alone, can carry them out. You, in your sphere, should have done as Napoleon did in his; he bent and twisted and crawled —yes, crawled !—for Bonaparte married Barras's mistress to gain a command. You should have waited; you should have been elected as a deputy; you should have watched the political changes, now in the trough of the sea, now on the crest of a wave; you should have adopted M. de Villèle's Italian motto *Col tempo*, otherwise rendered, 'All things come round to him that will but wait.' For seven years it has been M. de Villèle's aim to be in office; he took the first step in 1814, when he was just your present age, with a protest against the Charter. That is your mistake; you have been ready to act under orders; you were made to issue them.'

The arrival of Schinner the painter put an end to this talk, but Rabourdin grew thoughtful over his wife's words.

Schinner grasped his hand. 'An artist's devotion is of very little use, my dear fellow; but at such times as these we are staunch, we artists. I got an evening paper. Baudoyer is to be director I see, and he is to have the Cross of the Legion of Honour.'

'I am first in order of seniority, and I have been twenty-four years in the service,' smiled Rabourdin.

'I know M. le Comte de Sérizy, the Minister of State, pretty well; if you like to make use of him, I can see him,' said Schinner.

The rooms were filled with persons who knew nothing of the movements of the administration. Du Bruel did not appear. Mme. Rabourdin was more charming, and in higher spirits than usual; the horse, wounded on the battlefield, will summon up all its strength to carry its master.

The women behaved charmingly to her, now that she was defeated.

'She is very brave,' said some.

'And yet she was very attentive to des Lupeaulx,' the Baronne du Châtelet remarked to the Vicomtesse de Fontaine.

'Then do you think——?'

'If so, M. Rabourdin would at least have had the Cross,' said Mme. de Camps, defending her friend.

Towards ten o'clock des Lupeaulx appeared. To give an idea of his appearance, it can only be said that his spectacles looked melancholy, while there was laughter in his eyes; the glass veiled their expression so completely, that no one but a physiognomist could have seen the diabolical gleam in them. He grasped Rabourdin's hand, and Rabourdin could only submit to the pressure.

'We must have some talk together by and by,' he said, as he seated himself beside the fair Rabourdin, who behaved to admiration.—'Ah! you are great,' he said, with a side glance at her; 'I find you as I imagined you —sublime in defeat. Do you know how very seldom people respond to our expectations of them! And so you are not overwhelmed by defeat. You are right, we shall triumph,' he continued, lowering his voice. 'Your fate will always be in your own hands so long as you have an ally in a man who worships you. We will hold a council.'

'But Baudoyer is appointed, is he not?'

'Yes.'

'And the Cross?'

'Not yet, but he is going to have it.'

'Well?'

'You do not understand policy.'

To Mme. Rabourdin it seemed as if that evening

would never come to an end. Meanwhile, in the
Place Royale a comedy was being played, a comedy
that is always repeated in seven different salons after
every change of government. The Saillards' sitting-
room was full. M. and Mme. Transon came at eight
o'clock. Mme. Transon kissed Mme. Baudoyer *née*
Saillard. M. Bataille, the captain in the National
Guard, came with his wife and the curé of Saint-Paul's.

'M. Baudoyer, I want to be the first to congratulate
you,' said Mme. Transon; 'your talents have met with
their deserts. Well, you have fairly earned your
advancement.'

. 'So now you are a director,' added M. Transon, rubbing his hands; 'it is a great honour for the Quarter.'

'And without scheming for it, one may say indeed,'
cried old Saillard. '*We* are not intriguers; *we* do not
go to the Minister's parties.'

Uncle Mitral rubbed his nose, and smiled and looked
at his niece; Elizabeth was talking with Gigonnet.
Falleix did not know what to think of the blindness of
Saillard and Baudoyer. Dutocq, Bixiou, du Bruel, and
Godard came in, followed by Colleville, now chief
clerk.

'What chumps!' said Bixiou, in an undertone for
du Bruel's benefit. 'What a fine caricature one might
make of them—a lot of flat fish, stock-fish, and winkles
all dancing a saraband.'

'M. le Directeur,' began Colleville, 'I have come to
congratulate you, or rather we all congratulate ourselves
upon your appointment, and we have come to assure
you of our zealous co-operation.'

M. and Mme. Baudoyer, Isidore's father and mother,
were there, to enjoy the triumph of their son and his
wife. Uncle Bidault had dined at home; his little
twinkling eyes dismayed Bixiou.

'There is a character that would do for a vaudeville,'
he said, pointing him out to du Bruel. 'What does

that fellow sell? Such an odd fish ought to be hung out for a sign at the door of an old curiosity shop. What a greatcoat! I thought that no one but Poiret could keep such a thing on exhibition after ten years of exposure to the inclemencies of the seasons.'

'Baudoyer is magnificent,' said du Bruel.

'Stunning!' returned Bixiou.

'Gentlemen,' said Baudoyer, 'this is my own uncle, M. Mitral; and this is my wife's great-uncle, M. Bidault!'

Gigonnet and Mitral looked keenly at the clerks; the metallic gleam of gold seemed to glitter in the old men's eyes; it impressed the two scoffers.

'Did you take a good look at that pair of uncles, eh?' asked Bixiou, as they walked under the arcades of the Palais Royal. 'Two specimens of the genus Shylock. They go the Market, I will be bound, and lend money at a hundred per cent. per week. They lend on pledges, traffic in clothes, gold lace, cheese, women and children; they be Arabs, they be Greeks, they be Genoese-Genevese-Lombard Jews; brought forth by a Tartar and suckled by a she-wolf.'

'Uncle Mitral was a bailiff once, I am certain,' said Godard.

'There, you see!' said du Bruel.

'I must just go and see the sheets pulled off,' continued Bixiou; 'but I should dearly like to make a careful study of M. Rabourdin's salon; you are very lucky, du Bruel, you can go there.'

'I?' said du Bruel; 'what should I do there? My face does not lend itself to the expression of condolence. And besides, it is very vulgar nowadays to dance attendance on persons out of office.'

At midnight Mme. Rabourdin's drawing-room was empty; three persons only remained—des Lupeaulx and the master and mistress of the house. When Schinner went, and M. and Mme. Octave de Camps had taken their leave, des Lupeaulx rose with a mysterious air, stood with his back to the clock, and looked at the husband and wife in turn.

'Nothing is lost, my friends,' he said, 'for we remain to you—the Minister and I. Dutocq, put between two powers, chose the stronger, as it seemed to him. He served the Grand Almonry and the Court and played me false; it is all in the day's work, a man in politics never complains of treachery. Still, Baudoyer is sure to be cashiered in a few months' time and transferred to the Prefecture of Police, for the Grand Almonry will not desert him.'

With that, des Lupeaulx broke out into a long tirade over the Grand Almonry, and expatiated on the risks run by a Government that looked to the Church and the Jesuits for support. Still, it is worth while to point out that, though the Liberal papers laid such stress upon the influence of Court patronage and the Grand Almonry, neither of these counted for much in Baudoyer's promotion. Petty intrigue died away in the higher spheres because greater questions were at stake. Perhaps M. Gaudron's importunities extorted a few words in Baudoyer's favour, but at the Minister's first remark the matter was allowed to drop. Passion in itself did the work of a very efficient spy among the members of the Congrégation; they used to denounce each other. And surely it was permissible to oppose that society to the brazen-fronted fraternity of the doctrine summed up by the formula, 'Heaven helps him who helps himself.' As for the occult power exercised by the Congrégation, it was for the most part wielded by subordinates who used the name of that body to conjure with for their private ends. Liberal rancour, in fact, delighted to represent the Grand Almonry as a giant; in politics, in the administration, in the army or the civil service. Fear always makes idols for itself. At this moment Baudoyer believed in the Grand Almonry, and all the while the only almonry that befriended him held its sessions at the Café Thémis. There are times in the history of the world when everything that happens amiss is set down to the account of some one institution, or man in power; nobody will give them credit for their abilities, they serve as synonyms and equivalent terms for crass stupidity. As M. de Talleyrand was supposed to hail every political event with an epigram, so in the same manner the Grand Almonry· did and undid everything at this period. Unluckily, it did and undid nothing whatever. Its influence was not in the hands of a Cardinal Richelieu or a Cardinal Mazarin; it fell, on the contrary, to a sort of Cardinal Fleury, the kind of man that is timid for five years and rash for a day. At Saint-Merri, at a later day, the doctrine above-mentioned did with impunity what Charles x. only attempted to do in July 1830. If the proviso as to the censorship had not been so stupidly inserted in the new Charter, journalism also would have seen its Saint-Merri. The Orleans Branch would have carried out the scheme of Charles x., with the law at its back.

'Stop on under Baudoyer, summon up courage for that,' continued des Lupeaulx, 'be a true politician, put generous thoughts and impulses aside, confine yourself to your duty, say not a word to your director, never give him advice, and act only upon his orders. In three months' time Baudoyer will leave the department; they will either dismiss him or transfer him to some other sphere of activity. Perhaps he may go to the Household. Twice in my life I have been buried under an avalanche of folly in this way; I let it go by.'

'Yes,' said Rabourdin, 'but you were not slandered, your honour was not involved, you were not compromised——'

Des Lupeaulx interrupted him with a peal of Homeric laughter. 'Why, that is the daily bread of every man of mark in the whole fair realm of France! There are two ways of taking it; you can go under, which means you pack yourself off and plant cabbages somewhere or other; or you rise above it, and walk fearlessly on without so much as turning your head.'

'In my own case,' said Rabourdin, 'there is but one way of untying the slip-knot which espionage and treachery have tightened about my neck; it is this—I must have an explanation with the Minister at once; and if you are as sincerely attached to me as you say, it is in your power to bring me face to face with him to-morrow.'

'Do you wish to lay your plan of administrative reform before him?'

Rabourdin bowed.

'Very well then, intrust your projects and memoranda to me, and he shall spend the night over them, I will engage.'

'Then let us go together,' Rabourdin answered quickly; 'for after six years of work, at least I may expect the gratification of explaining it for an hour or two to a member of His Majesty's Government, for the Minister cannot choose but commend my perseverance.'

Des Lupeaulx hesitated for a moment; Rabourdin's tenacity of purpose had put him on a road in which there was no cover for duplicity, so he looked at Mme. Rabourdin. 'Which shall turn the scale?' he asked himself—'my hatred of him, my liking for her?'

'If you cannot trust me,' he returned after a pause, 'I can see that, as far as I am concerned, you will always be the writer of that "secret note."—Good-bye, madame.'

Mme. Rabourdin bowed coldly. Célestine and Xavier went to their own rooms without a word, so heavily their misfortune lay upon them. The wife thought of her own unpleasant position. The chief clerk was making up his mind never to set foot in the office again; he was lost in far-reaching thoughts. This step was to change the course of his life; he must strike out a new path. He sat all night before his fire; Célestine, in her night-dress, stole in on tiptoe now and again, but he did not see her.

'Since I must go back for the last time to take away my papers and to put Baudoyer in possession, let us try the effect of my resignation.'

He drafted his resignation, meditated over his expressions, and wrote the following letter :—

'MONSEIGNEUR,—I have the honour to enclose my resignation in the same cover; but I venture to believe that your Excellency will recollect that I said that I had placed my honour in your hands, and that an immediate explanation was necessary. The explanation which I implored in vain would probably now be useless, for a fragment of my work has been surreptitiously taken and distorted and misinterpreted by malevolence, and I am compelled to withdraw before the tacit censure of those in authority. Your Excellency may have thought, when I tried to obtain an interview that morning, that I wished to speak of my own advancement, whereas I was thinking only of the honour of your Excellency's department and the public good; it is of some consequence to me that your Excellency should lie under no misapprehension on this head,' and the letter ended with the usual formulas.

By half-past seven o'clock the sacrifice had been made, the whole manuscript had been burnt. Tired out with thought and overcome by moral suffering, Rabourdin fell into a doze, with his head resting on the back of the armchair. A strange sensation awakened him; he felt hot tears falling on his hands, and saw his wife kneeling beside him. Célestine had come in and read the letter. She understood the full extent of their ruin. They were reduced to live upon four thousand livres; and reckoning up her debts, she found that they amounted to thirty-two thousand francs. It was the most sordid poverty of all. And the noble man that had put such trust in her had no suspicion of the way in which she had abused his confidence. Célestine, fair as the Magdalen, was sobbing at his feet.

'The misfortune is complete,' Xavier exclaimed in his dismay; 'dishonoured in the department, dishonoured——'

A gleam of stainless honour flashed from Célestine's eyes; she sprang up like a frightened horse, her eyes flashed lightnings.

'I, *I?*' she cried in sublime tones. 'Am I too an ordinary wife? If I had faltered, would you not have had your appointment? But it is easier to believe *that* than to believe the truth.'

'What is it?' asked Rabourdin.

'You shall have it all in a few words,' said she; 'we owe thirty thousand francs.'

Rabourdin caught her to him in a frenzy of joy, and made her sit on his knee.

'Never mind, darling,' he said, and a great kindness that slid into the tones of his voice changed the bitterness of her tears into something vaguely and strangely sweet. 'I too have made mistakes. I worked for my country to very little purpose; when I thought, at any rate, I might have done something worth the doing. . . . Now I will start out on a new path. If I had sold spices all this while, we should be millionaires by now. Very well, let us sell spices. You are only twenty-eight years old, my darling. In ten years' time, hard work will give you back the luxury that you love, though we must give it up now for a little while. I too, darling, am not an ordinary husband. We will sell the farm; the value of the land has been going up for seven years; the surplus and the furniture will pay *my* debts.'

In Célestine's kiss there was love given back a thousandfold for that generous word.

'And then we shall have a hundred thousand francs to put into some business or other. In a month's time I shall find an investment. If Saillard happened upon a Martin Falleix, chance cannot fail us. Wait breakfast for me. I will come back from the Minister with my neck free of that miserable yoke.'

Célestine held her husband in a tight clasp, with superhuman force; for the might of love gives a woman more than a man's strength, more power than the utmost transports of rage give to the strong. She was laughing and crying, talking and sobbing all at once.

When Rabourdin went out at eight o'clock, the porter handed him the burlesque visiting-cards sent in by Baudoyer, Bixiou, Godard, and the rest. Nevertheless, he went to the office, and found Sébastien waiting for him at the door; the lad begged him not to attempt to enter the place, a scurrilous caricature was being handed about.

'If you wish to alleviate the bitterness of my fall, bring me that drawing; for I am just taking my resignation myself to Ernest de la Brière, so that it may not be twisted out of all knowledge on its way to headquarters. I have my reasons for asking to see the caricature.'

Rabourdin waited till he was sure that his letter was in the Minister's hands; then he went down to the courtyard. Sébastien gave him the lithographed drawing, of which a sketch is given here. There were tears in the boy's eyes.

'It is very clever,' said Rabourdin, and the face that he turned upon the supernumerary was as serene as the Saviour's brow beneath the crown of thorns.

He walked in quietly as usual, and went straight to Baudoyer's general office to give the necessary explana-

tions before that slave of red-tape entered upon his new duties as director.

'Tell M. Baudoyer there is no time to lose,' he added before Godard and the clerks. 'My resignation is now in the Minister's hands, and I do not choose to stay in the office five minutes longer than I can help.'

Then catching sight of Bixiou, Rabourdin walked up to him, held out the drawing, and said, to the astonishment of the clerks—

'Was I not right when I said that you were an artist? Only it is a pity that you used your pencil against a man whom it was impossible to judge in such a manner, or in the offices. But people ridicule everything in France—even God Himself.'

With that he drew Baudoyer into the late La Billardière's rooms. At the door he met Phellion and Sébastien. They alone dared to show that they were faithful to the accused, even in this great shipwreck. Rabourdin saw the tears in Phellion's eyes, and in spite of himself he wrung the clerk's hand.

'Môsieur,' the good fellow said, 'if we can be of any use whatever, command us——'

'Come in, my friends,' Rabourdin said with a gracious dignity.—'Sébastien, my boy, send in your resignation by Laurent; you are sure to be implicated in the slander that has driven me from my place, but I will take care of your future. We will go together.'

Sébastien burst into tears.

M. Rabourdin closeted himself with M. Baudoyer in the late La Billardière's room, and Phellion assisted him to explain the difficulties of the position to the new head of the division. With each new file of papers displayed by Rabourdin, with the opening of every pasteboard case, Baudoyer's little eyes grew large as saucers.

'Good-day, monsieur,' concluded Rabourdin, with ironical gravity.

Sébastien meantime made up a packet of papers

belonging to the chief clerk, and took them away in a cab. Rabourdin crossed the great courtyard to wait on the Minister. All the clerks in the building were at the windows. Rabourdin waited for a few minutes, but the Minister made no sign. Then, accompanied by Phellion and Sébastien, he went out. Phellion bravely went as far as the Rue Duphot with the fallen official, by way of expressing his admiration and respect ; then he returned to his desk, quite satisfied with himself. He had paid funeral honours to a great unappreciated talent for administration.

BIXIOU (*as Phellion comes in*). '*Victrix causa diis placuit, sed victa Catoni.*'

PHELLION. 'Yes, monsieur.'

POIRET. 'What does that mean ?'

FLEURY. 'It means that the clericals rejoice, and that M. Rabourdin goes out with the esteem of all men of honour.'

DUTOCQ (*nettled*). 'You talked very differently yesterday.'

FLEURY. 'Say another word to me, and you shall feel my fist in your face. You sneaked M. Rabourdin's work, that is certain !' (*Dutocq goes out.*) 'Now, go and complain to your M. des Lupeaulx, you spy !'

BIXIOU (*grinning and grimacing like a monkey*). 'I am curious to see how the division will get on. M. Rabourdin was such a remarkable man, that he must have had something in view when he made that list. The department is losing an uncommonly clever head ' (*rubbing his hands*).

LAURENT. 'M. Fleury is wanted in the secretary's office.'

OMNES. 'Sacked !'

FLEURY (*from the door*). 'It is all one to me ; I have got a berth as a responsible editor. I can lounge about all day, or find something amusing to do in the newspaper office.'

BIXIOU. 'Dutocq has had poor old Desroys dismissed already; he was accused of wanting to cut off people's heads——'

THUILLIER. '*Les têtes des rois ?*' (*Desroys.*)

BIXIOU. 'Accept my congratulations. That is neat.'

Enter COLLEVILLE (*exultant*). 'Gentlemen, I am your chief clerk!'

THUILLIER (*embracing him*). 'Oh, my friend, if I were chief myself, I should not be so pleased!'

BIXIOU. 'His wife did that stroke of business, but it is not a master-stroke.'

POIRET. 'I should like to know the meaning of all this.'

BIXIOU. 'You want to know?—There it is. The Chamber is, and always will be, the ante-chamber of the Administration, the Court is the boudoir, the ordinary way is the cellar, the bed is made now more than ever in the little by-ways thereof.'

POIRET. 'M. Bixiou, explain yourself, I beg.'

BIXIOU. 'I will give you a paraphrase of my opinion. If you mean to be anything at last, you must be everything at first. Obviously, administrative reforms must be made; for, upon my word and honour, if the employés rob the Government of the time they ought to give to it, the Government robs them in return to make matters even. We do little because we get next to nothing; there are far too many of us for the work to be done, and *La Vertueuse Rabourdin* saw all that! That great man among the scribes foresaw the inevitable result, gentlemen, the "working" (as simpletons are pleased to call it) of our admirable Liberal institutions. The Chamber will soon want to meddle with the Administration, and officials will want to be legislators. The Government will try to administer the laws, and the Administration will try to govern the country. Laws, accordingly, will be transformed into rules and regulations, and regulations will be treated as laws. God made

this epoch for those that can enjoy a joke. I am looking on in admiration at the spectacle set forth for us
by Louis xviii., the greatest wag of modern times
(*general amazement*). And if France, gentlemen, the
best administered country in Europe, is in such a way,
think what a state the others must be in. Poor countries!
I wonder how they get on at all without the two
Chambers, the Liberty of the Press, the Report, the
Memorial, and the Circular, and a whole army of
clerks!—Think, now, how do they contrive to have
an army or a navy? How can they exist when there is
no one to weigh the pros and cons of every breath they
draw and every mouthful that they eat?—Can that
sort of thing be called a government or a country?
These funny fellows that travel about have stood me
out that foreigners pretend to have a policy of their
own, and that they enjoy a certain influence; but,
there—I pity them! They know nothing of "the
spread of enlightenment"; they cannot "set ideas in
circulation"; they have no free and independent tri-
bunes; they are sunk in barbarism. There is no nation
like the French for intelligence! Do you grasp that,
M. Poiret? (*Poiret looks as if he had received a sudden
shock.*) Can you understand how a country can do
without heads of divisions, directors-general, and dispense with a great staff of officials that is, and has been,
the pride of France and of the Emperor Napoleon, who
had his very sufficient reasons for creating places to fill?
But, there—since these countries have the impudence to
exist; since the War Office at Vienna employs scarcely
a hundred clerks all told (whereas with us, little as they
expected it before the Revolution, salaries and pensions
now eat up one-third of the revenue), I will sum up by
suggesting that as the Académie des Inscriptions et
Belles Lettres has very little to do, it might as well
offer a prize for the solution of the following problem:
"Which is the better constituted—the State that does a

great deal with a few officials, or the State that does little and keeps plenty of officials to do it?"'

POIRET. 'Is that your last word?'

BIXIOU. '*Ja, mein Herr!—Oui, monsieur!—Si, signor!—Da!* I spare you the other languages.'

POIRET (*raising his hands to heaven*). 'Good Lord! and they tell me that you are clever!'

BIXIOU. 'Then did you not understand after all?'

PHELLION. 'Anyhow, there is plenty of sense in that last remark——'

BIXIOU. 'It is like the budget, as complicated as it seems to be simple; and thus I set it for you, like an illumination lamp upon the edge of that break-neck precipice, that hole, that abyss, volcano, or what not, which the *Constitutionnel* calls "the political horizon."'

POIRET. 'I would rather have an explanation that I can understand.'

BIXIOU. 'Long live Rabourdin!—that is my opinion. Are you satisfied?'

COLLEVILLE (*gravely*). 'There is only one thing to be said against M. Rabourdin.'

POIRET. 'What is it?'

COLLEVILLE. 'He was not a chief clerk; he was a statesman.'

PHELLION (*planting himself in front of Bixiou*). 'Môsieur, if you appreciated M. Rabourdin so well, what made you draw that disgus—that inf—that shocking caricature?'

BIXIOU. 'How about that wager? Do you forget that I was playing the devil's game, and that your office owes me a dinner at the *Rocher de Cancale*?'

POIRET (*much ruffled*). 'It seems to be written that I am to leave this place without comprehending a single idea in anything that M. Bixiou says.'

BIXIOU. 'It is your own fault. Ask these gentlemen!—Gentlemen, did you understand the gist of my

x

observations? Were they just? Were they luminous?'

OMNES. 'Yes, alas!'

MINARD. 'Here is proof of it: I have just sent in my resignation. Good-day, gentlemen; I am going into business——'

BIXIOU. 'Have you invented a mechanical corset or a feeding-bottle, a fire-pump or pattens, a stove that gives heat without fuel, or cooks a cutlet with three sheets of paper?'

MINARD (*going*). 'I shall keep my secret to myself.'

BIXIOU. 'Ah, well, young Poiret, junior, these gentlemen all understand me, you see!'

POIRET (*mortified*). 'M. Bixiou, will you do me the honour to descend to my level just for once——'

BIXIOU (*winking at the others*). 'By all means. Before you go, you may perhaps be glad to know what you are——'

POIRET (*quickly*). 'An honest man, sir.'

BIXIOU (*shrugging his shoulders*). 'To define, explain, explore, and analyse the employé. Do you know how?'

POIRET. 'I think so.'

BIXIOU (*twisting one of Poiret's buttons*). 'I doubt it.'

POIRET. 'An employé is a man paid to work for the Government.'

BIXIOU. 'Obviously. Then a soldier is an employé?'

POIRET (*perplexed*). 'Why, no.'

BIXIOU. 'At any rate, he is paid by the Government to go on guard and to be passed in review. You will tell me that he is too anxious to leave his post, that he is not long enough at his post, that he works too hard, and touches metal too seldom (the barrel of his gun always excepted).'

POIRET (*opening wide eyes*). 'Well, then, sir, an employé, more strictly speaking, is a man who must draw his salary if he is to live; he is not free to leave his post, and he can do nothing but copy and dispatch documents.'

BIXIOU. 'Ah, now we are arriving at a solution! So the government office is the employé's shell? You cannot have the one without the other. Now, what are we to say about the tide-waiter? (*Poiret tries to stamp in vexation, and escapes; but Bixiou, having pulled off one button, holds him by another.*) 'Bah! in the bureaucratic world he probably is a neuter. The customs-house official is a semi-employé; he is on the frontier just as he is on the borderland between the civil service and the army; he is not exactly a soldier, and not precisely an employé either. But look here, Daddy, where are we going?' (*twists the button.*) 'Where does the employé end? It is an important question. Is a prefect an employé?'

POIRET (*nervously*). 'He is a functionary.'

BIXIOU. 'Oh! you are coming to a contradiction in terms! So a functionary is not an employé!'

POIRET (*looks round exhausted*). 'M. Godard looks as though he had something to say.'

GODARD. 'The employé represents the order, the functionary the genus.'

BIXIOU. 'Clever *sub*-ordinate! I should not have thought you capable of so ingenious a distinction.'

POIRET. 'Where are we going?'

BIXIOU. 'There, Daddy, let us not trip ourselves up with words. Listen, and we shall come to an understanding in the end. Look here, we will establish an axiom, which I bequeath to the office—The functionary begins where the employé ends, and the functionary leaves off where the statesman begins. There are very few statesmen, however, among prefects. So the prefect would seem to be a kind of neuter among superior orders of being; he is halfway between the statesman and the employé, much as the tide-waiter is not exactly a soldier or a civilian, but something of both. Let us continue to unravel these lofty questions.' (*Poiret grows red in the face*). 'Can we not state the matter in a theorem worthy of La Rochefoucauld? When salaries reach the limit line of twenty thousand francs, the employé ceases. Hence we may logically deduce the first corollary—The statesman reveals himself in the sphere of high salaries. Likewise this second and no less important corollary—It is possible for a director-general to be a statesman. Perhaps deputies mean something of this kind when they think within themselves that "it is a fine thing to be a director-general." Still, in the interests of the French language and the Academy——'

POIRET (*completely fascinated by Bixiou's fixity of gaze*). 'The French language!—the Academy!——'

BIXIOU (*twisting off a second button, and seizing upon the one above it*). 'Yes, in the interests of our noble language, your attention must be called to the fact that if a chief clerk, strictly speaking, may still be an employé, a head of the division is of necessity a bureaucrat. These gentlemen'—(*turning to the clerks, and holding up Poiret's third button for their inspection*)—'these gentlemen will appreciate all the delicacy of that subtle shade of distinction.—And so, Papa Poiret, the employé ends absolutely at the head of a division. So here is the question settled once for all—there is no more doubt about it; the employé, who might seem to be indefinable, is defined.'

POIRET. 'Beyond a doubt, as it seems to me.'

BIXIOU. 'And yet, be so far my friend as to solve me this problem: A judge is permanently appointed, consequently, according to your subtle distinction, he cannot be a functionary; and as his salary and the amount of work do not correspond, ought he to be included among employés?'

POIRET (*gazing at the ceiling*). 'Monsieur, I cannot follow you now——'

BIXIOU (*nipping off a fourth button*). 'I wanted to show you, monsieur, in the first place, that nothing is simple;

but more particularly—and what I am about to remark
is meant for the benefit of philosophists (if you will
permit me to twist a saying attributed to Louis XVIII.)
—I wish to point out that, side by side with the need of
a definition, lies the peril of getting mixed.'

POIRET (*wiping his forehead*). 'I beg your pardon,
monsieur, I feel queasy' (*tries to button his overcoat*).
'Oh! you have cut off all my buttons!'

BIXIOU. 'Well, *now* do you understand?'

POIRET (*vexed*). 'Yes, sir. Yes. I understand that
you meant to play me a very nasty trick by cutting off
my buttons while I was not looking.'

BIXIOU (*solemnly*). 'Old man, you err. I was trying
to engrave upon your mind as lively an image of the
Government as is possible' (*all eyes are turned on Bixiou.
Poiret, in his amazement, looks round at the others with
vague uneasiness*). 'That is how I kept my word. I
took the parabolic method known to savages. (Now
listen!) While the Ministers are at the Chambers,
starting discussions just about as profitable and con-
clusive as ours, the Administration is cutting off the
taxpayers' buttons.'

OMNES. 'Bravo, Bixiou!'

POIRET (*as he begins to comprehend*). 'I do not grudge
my buttons now.'

BIXIOU. 'And I shall do as Minard does. I do not
care to sign receipts for such trifling sums any longer;
I deprive the department of my co-operation' (*goes
out amid general laughter*).

Meanwhile another and more instructive scene was
taking place in the Minister's reception-room; more
instructive, be it said, because it may give some idea of
the way in which great ideas come to nothing in lofty
regions, and how the inhabitants thereof find consolation
in misfortune. At this particular moment des Lupeaulx
was introducing M. Baudoyer, the new director. Two

or three Ministerialist deputies were present besides M. Clergeot, to whom His Excellency gave assurance of an honourable retiring pension.   After various commonplace remarks, the event of the day came up in conversation.

A Deputy. 'So Rabourdin has gone for good.'

Des Lupeaulx. 'He has sent in his resignation.'

Clergeot. 'He wanted to reform the service, they said.'

The Minister (*looking at the deputies*). 'Perhaps the salaries are not proportionate to the services required.'

De la Brière. 'According to M. Rabourdin, a hundred men, with salaries of twelve thousand francs a-piece, will do the same work better and more expeditiously than a thousand at twelve hundred francs.'

Clergeot. 'Perhaps he is right.'

The Minister. 'There is no help for it! The machine is made that way; the whole thing would have to be taken to pieces and reconstructed; and who would have the courage to do that in front of the tribune and under the fire of stupid declamation from the Opposition or terrific articles in the press?   Still, some day or other there will be a disastrous hitch somewhere between the Government and the Administration.'

The Deputy. 'What will happen?'

The Minister. 'Some Minister will see a good thing to be done, and will be unable to do it.   You will have created interminable delays between legislation and carrying the law into effect.   You may make it impossible to steal a five-franc piece, but you cannot prevent collusion to gain private ends.   Some things will never be done until clandestine stipulations have been made; and it is very difficult to detect such things. And, then, every man on the staff, from the chief down to the lowest clerk, will soon have his own opinion on this matter and that; they will no longer be hands directed by a brain, they will not carry out the intentions of the Government. The Opposition is gradually giving them a right to speak and vote against the Government, and to condemn it.'

BAUDOYER (*in a low voice, but not so low as to be inaudible*). 'His Excellency is sublime!'

DES LUPEAULX. 'Bureaucracy certainly has its bad side; it is slow and insolent, I think; it hampers the action of the department overmuch; it snuffs out many a project; it stops progress; but, still, the French administration is wonderfully useful——'

BAUDOYER. 'Certainly.'

DES LUPEAULX. '—— if only as a support to the trade in stationery and stamps. And if, like many excellent housewives, the civil service is apt to be a little bit fussy, she can give an account of her expenditure at any moment. Where is the clever man in business that would not be only too glad to drop five per cent. on his turnover if some insurance agent would undertake to guarantee him against "leakage."'

THE DEPUTY (*a manufacturer*). 'Manufacturers on both sides of the Atlantic would be delighted to make a bargain with the imp known as "leakage" on such terms as those.'

DES LUPEAULX. 'Well, statistics may be the weakness of the modern statesman; he is apt to take figures for calculation, but we must use figures to make calculations; therefore, let us calculate. If a society is based on money and self-interest, it takes its stand on figures, and society has been thus based since the Charter was drawn up; so I think, at least. And, then, there is nothing like a column of figures for carrying conviction to the "intelligent masses." Everything, in fact, so say our statesmen of the Left, can be resolved into figures. So to figures let us betake ourselves' (*the Minister takes one of the deputies aside and begins to talk in a low voice.*) 'Here, in France, there are about forty thousand men in the employ of the Government; not counting road-menders, crossing-sweepers, and cigarette-makers. Fifteen hundred francs is the average amount of a salary. Multiply fifteen hundred francs by forty thousand, and you get sixty millions.— And before we go any farther, a publicist might call the attention of China, Austria, Russia (where civil servants rob the government), and diverse American republics to the fact that for this sum France obtains the fussiest, most fidgety, interfering, inquisitive, meddlesome, painstaking, categorical set of scribblers and hoarders of wastepaper, the veriest old wife among all known administrations. Not one farthing can be paid or received in France but a written order must be made out, checked off by a counterfoil, produced again and again at every stage of the business, and duly receipted at the end. And afterwards the demand and the receipt must be filed, entered, posted, and checked by a set of men in spectacles. The official understrapper takes fright at the least sign of an informality, for he lives by such *minutiæ*. Well, plenty of countries would be satisfied with that; but Napoleon went further. He, great organiser as he was, re-established supreme magistrates in one court, a unique court in the world. These functionaries spent their days in checking off all the bills, pay-sheets, muster-rolls, deposit certificates, receipts, and statements of expenditure, and all the files and bundles of wastepaper which the staff first covered with writing. Those austere judges possessed a talent for *minutiæ*, a genius for investigation, and a lynx-eyed perspicacity in book-keeping, which reached such an extreme, that they went through every column of additions in their quest of frauds. They were sublime martyrs of arithmetic; they would send back a statement of accounts to a superintendent of army stores because they had detected an error of two farthings made two years previously. So the French administration is the most incorruptible service that ever accumulated wastepaper on the surface of the globe; theft, as His

Excellency observed just now, is all but impossible in France, and malversation a figment of the imagination.

'Well, where is the objection? France draws an annual revenue of twelve hundred millions, and she spends it; that is all. Twelve hundred millions come into her cash-box, and twelve hundred millions go out. She actually handles two milliards four hundred millions, and only pays two and a half per cent. to guarantee herself against leakage. Our political kitchen account only amounts to sixty millions; the gendarmerie, the law-courts, the prisons, and detectives cost us more and do nothing in return. And we find employment for a class of men who are fit for nothing else, you may be very sure. The waste, if waste there is, could not be better regulated; the Chambers are art and part in it; the public money is squandered in strictly legal fashion. The real leakage consists in ordering public works that are not needed, or not immediately needed; in altering soldiers' uniforms; in ordering men-of-war without ascertaining whether timber is dear or no at the time; in unnecessary preparations for war; in paying the debts of a state without demanding repayment or security, and so forth, and so forth.'

BAUDOYER. 'But the employé has nothing to do with leakage in high quarters. Mismanagement of national affairs concerns the statesman at the helm.'

THE MINISTER (*his conversation being concluded*). 'There is truth in what des Lupeaulx was saying just now; but' (*turning to Baudoyer*) 'you must bear in mind that no one is looking at the matter from a statesman's point of view. It does not follow that because such and such a piece of expenditure was unwise or even useless that it was a case of maladministration. In any case, it sets money circulating; and in France, of all countries, stagnation in trade is fatal, because the profoundly illogical habit of hoarding coin is so prevalent in the provinces, and so much gold is kept out of circulation as it is——'

THE DEPUTY (*who has been listening to des Lupeaulx*). 'But it seems to me that if Your Excellency is right, and if our witty friend here' (*taking des Lupeaulx by the arm*), 'if our friend is not wrong, what are we to think?'

DES LUPEAULX (*after exchanging a glance with the Minister*). 'Something must be done, no doubt.'

DE LA BRIÈRE (*diffidently*). 'Then M. Rabourdin is right?'

THE MINISTER. 'I am going to see Rabourdin.'

DES LUPEAULX. 'The poor man was so misguided as to constitute himself supreme judge of the administration and the staff; he wants to have no more than three departments.'

THE MINISTER (*interrupting*). 'Why, the man is mad!'

THE DEPUTY. 'How is he going to represent the different parties in the Chamber?'

BAUDOYER (*with an air that is meant to be knowing*). 'Perhaps, at the same time, M. Rabourdin is changing the Constitution which we owe to the King-Legislator.'

THE MINISTER (*growing thoughtful, takes de la Brière by the arm and steps aside*). 'I should like to look at Rabourdin's scheme; and since you know about it——'

DE LA BRIÈRE (*in the cabinet*). 'He has burnt it all. You allowed him to be dishonoured; he has resigned. You must not suppose, my lord, that he entertained the preposterous idea, attributed to him by des Lupeaulx, of making any change in the admirable centralisation of authority.'

THE MINISTER (*to himself*). 'I have made a mistake.' (*A moment's pause*). 'Bah! there will never be any scarcity of schemes of reform——'

DE LA BRIÈRE. 'We have ideas in plenty; we lack the men that can carry them out.'

Just then Lupeaulx, insinuating advocate of abuses, entered the cabinet.

'I am going down to my constituents, Your Excellency.'

'Wait!' returned His Excellency, and turning from his private secretary, he drew des Lupeaulx to a window. 'Give up that arrondissement to me, my dear fellow; you shall have the title of Count, and I will pay your debts. . . . And—and if I am still in office after next election, I will find a way of putting you in with a batch to be made a peer of France.'

'You are a man of honour; I accept.'

And so it came to pass that Clément Chardin des Lupeaulx, whose father was ennobled by Louis xv., and bore *quarterly; of the first, argent, a wolf sable, ravissant, carrying a lamb, gules; of the second, purpur, three buckles argent, two and one; of the third, barry of six, gules and argent; of the fourth, gules, a caduceus winged and wreathed with serpents, vert;* with four griffins' claws for supporters; and EN LUPUS IN HISTORIA for a motto, managed to surmount his half-burlesque escutcheon with a Count's coronet.

Towards the end of December 1830, business brought Rabourdin back to his old office. The whole department had been shaken by changes from top to bottom; and the revolution affected the messengers more than anybody else—they are never very fond of new faces. Knowing all the people in the place, Rabourdin had come early in the morning, and so chanced to overhear a conversation between Laurent's nephews, for Antoine had been pensioned.

'Well, how is your chief?'

'Don't speak of him; I can make nothing of him. He rings to ask whether I have seen his pocket-handkerchief or his snuff-box. He does not keep people waiting, but has them shown in at once; he has not the least dignity, in fact. I myself am obliged to say, " Why, sir, the Count, your predecessor, in the interests of authority, used to whittle his armchair with a penknife to make people believe that he worked." In short, he makes a regular muddle of it; the place does not know itself, to my thinking; he is a very poor creature. How is yours?'

'Mine? Oh, I have trained him at last; he knows where his paper and envelopes are kept, and where the firewood is, and all his things. My other used to swear; this one is good-tempered. But he is not the big style of thing; he has no order at his buttonhole. I like a chief to have an order; if he hasn't, they may take him for one of us, and that is so mortifying. He takes home office stationery, and asked me if I could go to his house to wait at evening parties.'

'Ah! what a Government, my dear fellow!'

'Yes, a set of swindlers.'

'I wish they may not nibble at our poor salaries.'

'I am afraid they will. The Chambers keep a sharp lookout on you. They haggle over the firewood.'

'Oh well, if that is the style of them, it will not last long.'

'We are in for it! Somebody is listening.'

'Oh! it is M. Rabourdin that used to be. . . . Ah, sir, I knew you by your way of coming in. . . . If you want anything here, there is nobody that will know the respect that is owing to you; there is nobody of your time left now but us. M. Colleville and M. Baudoyer did not wear out the leather on their chairs after you went. Lord! six months afterwards they got appointments as receivers of taxes at Paris.'

Paris, *July* 1836.

Printed by T. and A. Constable, Printers to Her Majesty
at the Edinburgh University Press